My Indiana

101 Places to See

My Indiana

101 Places to See

Text and Photos by Earl L. Conn

INDIANA HISTORICAL SOCIETY PRESS
INDIANAPOLIS 2006

Printed in China

This book is a publication of the
Indiana Historical Society Press
450 West Ohio Street
Indianapolis, Indiana 46202-3269 USA
www.indianahistory.org

Telephone orders 1–800–447–1830
Fax orders 317–234–0562
Online orders @ shop.indianahistory.org

The paper in this publication meets the minimum requirements of American National Standard for Information Sciences—Permanence of Paper for Printed Library Materials, ANSI Z39.48-1984. ∞

ISBN–13: 978–0–87195–195–3
ISBN–10: 0–87195–195–9

To the 100,000 Hoosiers
in the tourism and recreation business and especially
to those of you who have helped me
over the years with my travel column writing.

Table of Contents

CENTRAL

WESTERN

SOUTH CENTRAL

SOUTHERN

Preface

I started my weekly newspaper column, "Traveling Indiana," on June 21, 1998. During the years since then, readers frequently have asked me, "Why don't you publish a book of your columns?" As a person long associated with the publishing industry, I know that is easier said than done.

That doesn't mean I didn't like the idea. I thought for a long time about how such a book might be organized, what columns might be selected for publication, and who might be interested in publishing such a book if it were to be attempted.

Finally, all of the above came together. I decided that the organization of the book would follow the format provided by the Indiana Department of Commerce in dividing the state into six areas. These divisions are used in its annual *Indiana Travel Guide*, which I have utilized extensively over the years: Northern, Eastern, Central, Western, South Central, and Southern. Column selection would incorporate as many different locations in each area as possible. The publication question was answered when I proposed the idea to the Indiana Historical Society Press and, to my pleasure, its editors quickly agreed.

Using the six-area format for the state and spreading the columns out over each as much as possible—seventeen in five areas and the sixth with sixteen—provided the book's title: *My Indiana—101 Places to See*. That meant, of course, some equally delightful sites had to be omitted. Maybe next time. In most cases, the numbers used for identification on the maps in each area move from west to east, except in some places where a grouping of two or more numbers in the same general region seemed a more logical choice.

I wanted to include columns noting some obvious locations, such as the Indiana Dunes, Fort Wayne's Lincoln Museum, White River State Park, and West Baden Springs Hotel, while also noting some lesser-known ones, such as the site of the Reno gang's first train robbery at Seymour, the Topeka Draft Horse Auction, the Lawrence D. Bell Aircraft Museum at Mentone, and the Marion National Cemetery for veterans.

In most cases my reporting style was to simply show up at a site so that I would see what any visitor would see. In a few visits I was assisted by some excellent Indiana tourism people.

Also, I didn't want the book to be all about museums, or all about state parks, or all about historic sites, or all about recreation. So, it is a mixture of a little bit of this and a little bit of that. Hopefully, every reader will be especially attracted to certain locations if not all of them.

I have written these columns in a conversational style. Most of the time, I have tried to engage the reader in as close to a dialogue as writing allows.

All of the photographs in this book are mine, taken when I visited each location.

A lifetime in journalism has taught me how easily mistakes can be made. I have made every effort to determine that the information is current and accurate. Preparing the book also included asking that each column be checked by a knowledgeable individual at every location. Still, I accept the responsibility for whatever errors exist. In addition, I have edited some columns for specific date references, language, and length. Remember, too, that things do change, so it is always a good idea if you plan to visit any of these places to call or go to the Web site to make certain when a location is open and that its hours still are correct.

A number of excellent Indiana travel books already have been published. This one is different in that no scheduled itineraries are outlined, it is not meant to be inclusive, it deals with an eclectic variety of subjects, and it has a "personal" style.

I very much hope you like it.

Earl L. Conn
Muncie, Indiana
January 2006

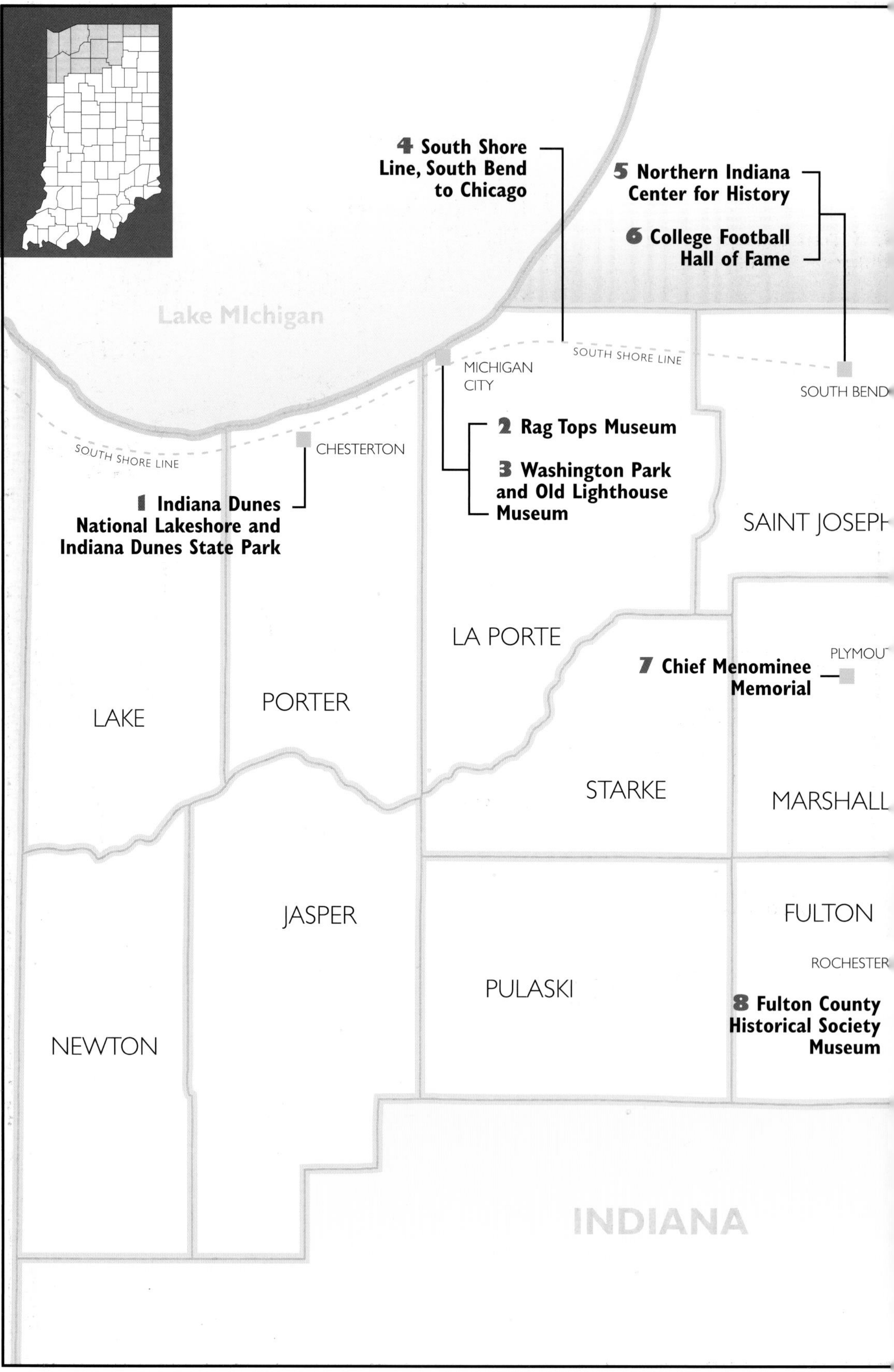

4 South Shore Line, South Bend to Chicago

5 Northern Indiana Center for History

6 College Football Hall of Fame

Lake MIchigan

SOUTH SHORE LINE

MICHIGAN CITY

SOUTH BEND

2 Rag Tops Museum

3 Washington Park and Old Lighthouse Museum

SOUTH SHORE LINE

CHESTERTON

1 Indiana Dunes National Lakeshore and Indiana Dunes State Park

SAINT JOSEPH

LA PORTE

PLYMOUTH

7 Chief Menominee Memorial

LAKE

PORTER

STARKE

MARSHALL

JASPER

FULTON

ROCHESTER

PULASKI

8 Fulton County Historical Society Museum

NEWTON

INDIANA

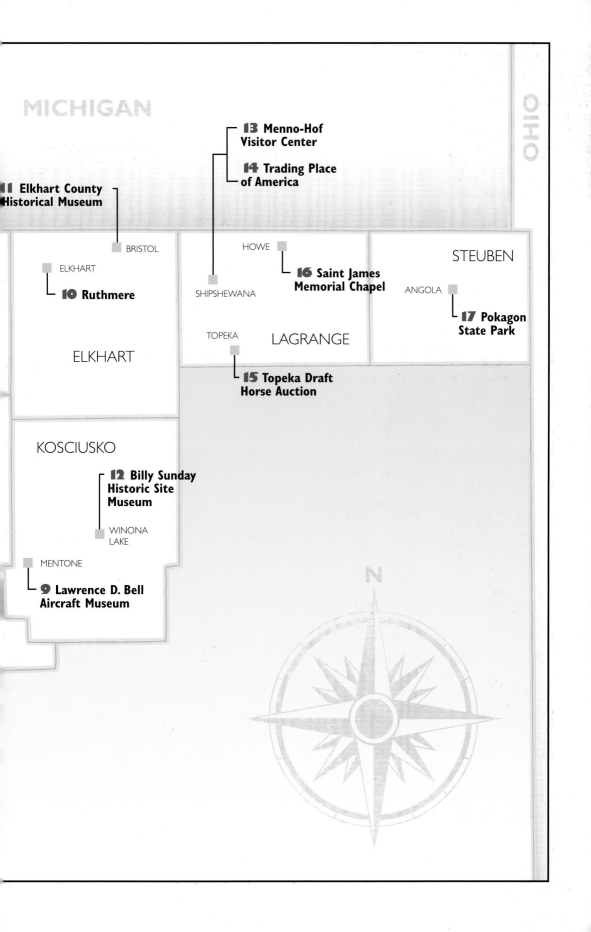

MICHIGAN

OHIO

13 Menno-Hof
Visitor Center

14 Trading Place
of America

11 Elkhart County
Historical Museum

BRISTOL

HOWE

STEUBEN

ELKHART

16 Saint James
Memorial Chapel

ANGOLA

10 Ruthmere

SHIPSHEWANA

17 Pokagon
State Park

TOPEKA

LAGRANGE

ELKHART

15 Topeka Draft
Horse Auction

KOSCIUSKO

12 Billy Sunday
Historic Site
Museum

WINONA
LAKE

MENTONE

9 Lawrence D. Bell
Aircraft Museum

N

MOUNT BALDY. It requires some strenuous walking up through this dune in northern Indiana—or you can go around to the side of the dune to follow an easier route to the top. Its elevation is 126 feet.

DEVIL'S SLIDE. One of the dunes' features in the Indiana Dunes State Park, which makes up more than two thousand acres of the fifteen thousand acres of dunes country along Lake Michigan.

BUELL VISITOR CENTER. Starting point for the Indiana Dunes National Lakeshore, located toward the eastern end of the more than twenty miles of dunes stretching along the south end of Lake Michigan.

Indiana Dunes National Lakeshore and Indiana Dunes State Park

CHESTERTON—You can pick your own best time—or times—to visit the Indiana Dunes, stretching along the southern shore of Lake Michigan from the Gary area almost to Michigan City.

It might be in the autumn months when, with a warm jacket and cap as part of your gear, you walk along the beach or back into the dunes as the chill of winter is but a short time away. It might be the opposite time in the spring with the warmth of summer approaching as the sun and breezes seem to be warming. The beaches along the dunes likely are somewhat lonely places in both seasons.

Of course, it might also be during those lazy, hot summer days when the swimmers take over—that is, on the days you can get in the water when the bacteria count isn't too high. Swimmers also are warned to be cautious because the lake bottom has holes, drop-offs, and dangerous currents. Your favorite time may less likely be during the winter months, when a bonfire may be needed to ward off those icy blasts that can rip across the lake. However, hiking, cross-country skiing, and snowshoeing are popular.

Whatever the season, the dunes identify northwestern Indiana. It might not have been so.

The mills, power plants, and commercialization of sand along with urbanization were spreading eastward rapidly from the Chicago area in the twentieth century before ecologists and other environmentalists convinced both the federal and state governments to preserve the area through their "Save the Dunes Council." The state park was created in 1925, followed by the Indiana Dunes National Lakeshore in 1966.

Today, these efforts to save this natural habitat have paid off.

The Indiana Dunes State Park includes 2,182 acres along nearly three miles of lakeshore from its western end where Indiana 49 dead-ends into the park to the eastern end just north of the Dorothy Buell Memorial Visitor Center of the Indiana Dunes National Lakeshore on U.S. 12. Like most other state parks, it offers a campground, youth tent camping, shelters, picnic sites, hiking trails, nature center, and a free public beach open Memorial Day to Labor Day.

The national dunes area of 15,084 acres surrounds the state park, beginning at the west where U.S. 12 intersects with Indiana 53 to the east at Mount Baldy, more than twenty miles away.

The National Lakeshore is broken up by a number of parcels of land still in private hands, including the huge U.S. Steel operations at Gary; the communities of Ogden Dunes, Dune Acres, and Beverly

BUT IT ISN'T. It looks like a Florida beach, but it's part of the extensive Indiana Dunes beach. Lake Michigan is in the background as a few bathers test the water.

Shores; Midwest Steel; Bethlehem Steel; the Port of Indiana north of Portage; and Northern Indiana Public Service Company's plant.

So, unless you know the territory, you really need to pick up a map, probably at the Buell Visitor Center or at the gatehouse for the Indiana Dunes State Park. The parks are not a place to spend an hour. Rather, you want to commit a larger block of time, first to merely familiarize yourself and, then, to poke around to see what you might most enjoy.

Also, the battle to save the dunes is far from over. Visitors are reminded to stay on marked trails to prevent further erosion. Both the national lakeshore and state park maps identify marked trails. In addition, efforts continue to buy back private lands to incorporate within the national lakeshore.

Plus, the dunes themselves play an ever-changing role. Several are termed "living" or "moving" as, over time, they are continually blown inland, burying whatever may be in their path.

RAG TOPS. The museum is housed in this former men's pants manufacturing building in Michigan City. It is located at the north edge of downtown on U.S. 12.

COST $3,890 NEW. The Japanese Imperial Palace owned this 1957 DeSoto Fireflight. It has 385 horsepower.

TOPPED 331 MPH. A 6,000-horsepower motor is the power plant for this 2001 dragster. The racing vehicle was sponsored by the New York Yankees.

Rag Tops Museum, Michigan City

MICHIGAN CITY—It's definitely a work in progress.

"Every day we add more and more," says Harry Anderson of Rag Tops Museum of Michigan City. The name says it all about the new museum—more than 90 percent of the cars on display are convertibles.

As we walked through the museum, he would point to a display—"I finished that yesterday"—to a piece of automobile memorabilia—"that came over last week"—and to a replica of a gasoline station from yesteryear—"I built that. I tried to make it like an old-time gas station." Nearby, there was also an old diner with a jukebox and soda fountain.

We walked into a large room at the back of the museum, housed in a building where Jamar men's slacks were once produced. At the moment, the room was being used for storage. Not for long, however. The plan is to have about thirty-five more cars back there, plus a Lionel model train display the museum recently purchased.

"It was one of those Lionels hauled around in the '50's in a semi. It's humongous. We've got a second floor, too, but we haven't decided exactly what to do with it yet," Anderson adds.

"We" are Anderson; Dennis Moran, the museum's founder; and a not-for-profit board of directors that pours ticket receipts and any other income back into the museum.

"Moran started collecting cars years ago and this is kind of a dream of his to put this together. He actually came by my house to buy a car just about a year ago and that's how we got started," says Anderson.

Moran started as a mechanic and began specializing in transmissions. He opened his own franchise business, and today "his family is the franchisor of eight automobile trademarks with franchise locations throughout the country," says Anderson.

When the museum's board acquired the building and started work, it found the building to be in good condition. "We painted, removed a lot of pipes, built a few things like around the electrical boxes and over the old radiator heaters, but that was about it," says Anderson.

Anderson is proud that few of the displays and none of the cars have ropes around them to keep museum visitors from touching them. "We've had almost no problems since we opened May 3, 2003," he says. "We're about a year ahead of where we expected to be at this time. Attendance has been real good, even during the week."

Anderson is using as many local historical artifacts as possible. These include a box office from a Gary theater; "George's barbershop," with chairs and equipment that were used in a Michigan City business for

OLD-TIME GAS STATION. It was constructed inside Rag Tops by Harry Anderson as one of the displays in the Michigan City museum, largely made up of collectors' convertibles.

seventy-three years until the owner's death; neon signs from car dealerships; and license plates. If it's associated with automobiles, it's probably here or will be.

"Almost all the memorabilia are original," says Anderson. "Not all the neon signs are functioning yet, but we keep working on them."

At last count the museum had about fifty vehicles. Again, though, Anderson talks about this one "purchased last week" and a 1956 Packard Caribbean convertible found two blocks from Moran's home.

How Anderson keeps track of everything must be a challenge. Nevertheless, visit the museum and then go back a month later. It probably won't look the same, but he will know where everything is on display—or soon will be.

GETTING THERE: The museum is at the corner of U.S. 12 and Washington Street in Michigan City, one block north of the Lighthouse Place Premium Outlets mall.

INFORMATION: Open daily from 10 a.m. to 7 p.m. The telephone number is (219) 878–1514 and the Web site is http://www .ragtopsmuseum.com/. The mailing address is 209 W. Highway 12, Michigan City, Indiana 46360.

FEES: Admission charged.

LAKE MICHIGAN SHIPWRECKS. Those around the lake's southern shore are identified on this Old Lighthouse Museum map.

MILLENNIUM PARK. When Michigan City constructed Millennium Park in 2000, it added a decorative area to the land adjacent to the lighthouse museum.

MICHIGAN CITY'S LIGHTHOUSE. An addition to the right in 1904 made room for an assistant lighthouse keeper and family.

Washington Park and Old Lighthouse Museum, Michigan City

MICHIGAN CITY—When the summer season begins winding down and the kids head back to school, you might be looking for one last weekend at the beach. Why not at "the big lake," as they call it up in northern Indiana—Lake Michigan? You can go earlier in the summer, too, but wait for the water to warm up first.

While many lake swimming and relaxing choices exist, one possibility would be the beach at Michigan City's Washington Park. Plus, you can couple your trip with a visit to the Old Lighthouse Museum only a few blocks away.

Washington Park's ninety acres has shoreline, bathhouses, refreshments, picnicking sites, shelters, a fishing pier, and even a close-at-hand zoo—the Zoological Garden, although a separate admission is required for the zoo. Parking is available adjacent to the beach. On a recent warm summer early afternoon, swimmers played in the water while others dozed or just relaxed on the beach in what seemed to be about equal numbers.

Only a short distance to the west is the Old Lighthouse Museum. That lighthouse's sperm oil-fed light with its Fresnel lens is said to have been seen for up to fifteen miles and was the guiding light for many a Great Lakes ship over the decades. The original Fresnel lens is on display in the museum.

Land for the lighthouse was deeded to the U.S. government by Isaac C. Elston, founder of Michigan City. Michigan City turned out to be a busy commercial port, handling lumber from northern Michigan, grain from Indiana farmers, and sand from the dunes.

(It's estimated by *Indiana: A New Historical Guide* that 13.5 million tons of sand from the nearby so-called Hoosier Slide were shipped between 1890 and 1920, quite a bit of it to Ball Brothers Glass Company in Muncie. Before that started, it's said the two hundred-foot-high mountain of sand could be seen from Chicago.)

The lighthouse building was closed by the government in 1939 when the care of the lanterns was turned over to the Coast Guard and the old lighthouse no longer had use. It was rented for about four years and then left empty. Extensive vandalism followed, and by 1965 it appeared the building would be demolished.

At the last moment, the Michigan City Historical Society volunteered to raise the necessary funds to restore the building. It took eight years and more than $80,000 but the Society's members did it. The building opened as a museum in June 1973, shortly after a lantern reproduction was delivered and hoisted into place.

OLD LIGHTHOUSE MUSEUM. The Michigan City museum stands some distance from the Lake Michigan shoreline today. A replica of the lantern was added before the museum opened in 1973.

The lighthouse, constructed in 1858, had four rooms on the first floor and four rooms on the second floor plus a ground-level area, making up the southern two-thirds of the present building. It replaced an earlier forty-foot tower, built in 1837 at the corner of the lot, which at that time was the Lake Michigan shoreline. That lighthouse, sitting on sand and not firmly anchored, simply fell over.

Rooms were added in 1904 to the north end of the present building when an assistant lightkeeper was named. The keeper and his family used the rooms to the east and the assistant those to the west.

The government also moved the lantern out to the end of the east pier, so lightkeepers needed to make daily treks to service it. It's still there today, with a more modern beacon light, as the lighthouse for the Port of Michigan City.

Next to the museum is Millennium Park, built by the city to commemorate the year 2000. According to the museum's tour guide, the park spruced up the area considerably in addition to new fencing and a paint job for the museum.

IF YOU GO

GETTING THERE: From U.S. 12, turn right on Pine Street at the Chamber of Commerce building. Turn right on Franklin Street and cross the drawbridge. After crossing the bridge, the museum will be seen on the left. Turn right after crossing the bridge as if you were going into Washington Park. Make the first left turn and circle back to the museum parking lot. Watch for signs.

INFORMATION: The Lighthouse Museum is open Tuesday through Sunday, 1 p.m. to 4 p.m., central daylight time. Last tour is 3:30 p.m. Closed on Mondays and in January and February. Web site is http://www.michigancity.com/MCHistorical/ and the telephone number is (219) 872–6133. The Zoological Gardens are closed November through March. In September and October, it is open from 10:30 a.m. to 4 p.m. with the gates closing at 3 p.m.

FEES: Admission charged for the museum. Washington Park, admission per vehicle.

COMPLETES THE CIRCUIT. This is the electrical connection that completes the circuit for the South Shore train running between South Bend and Chicago. It's believed to be the last interurban making regular intercity runs in the United States.

UNIVERSITY OF CHICAGO. One of the more imposing views seen through the windows of the South Shore are buildings of the University of Chicago.

EVERYBODY'S OUT. An emptied South Shore passenger car stands at the Randolph Street terminal in downtown Chicago. Moments before, nearly every seat was occupied. A little while later, it starts its return route to the terminal at the South Bend Regional Airport.

South Shore Line, South Bend to Chicago

SOUTH BEND—You probably need to have a little of the adventurous spirit to try this "Traveling Indiana" trip.

First, you drive to South Bend, where you park your car at the South Bend Regional Airport, west of town. There you catch the South Shore electric train into Chicago.

The whole trip—east central Indiana to Chicago—is going to take roughly the same amount of time as if you drove to Chicago, give or take work stoppages and the time of day. It's also assuming that the South Shore leaves the station just minutes after you park at the airport. (It usually runs on two-hour intervals from South Bend. During the week, other trains originate in Michigan City and Gary, running about every hour.)

Plus, the scenery isn't anything to get excited about. There's some countryside to be sure, but there's also narrow streets, backyards, and factories—reflecting the history of the interurban route—as the train passes through towns between South Bend and Chicago.

So why do it?

The biggest reason is to ride the last interurban left in the United States—electric trains that travel between cities. In the 1920s, according to historian William Middleton, these electric trains reached almost every city of any consequence in Indiana. In fact, the state was considered to have one of the finest interurban systems in the nation. By the early 1940s, however, most of them were gone, replaced by family cars, buses, trucks, and freight trains.

For the folks in northwestern Indiana, however, the South Shore remains a major way in and out of Chicago for work, entertainment, and shopping.

My ninety-mile South Shore trip was on a late Saturday morning. When our 10 a.m. train left the airport, I doubt if more than twenty-five to thirty people were on board in the five cars. By the time we reached the end of the line at the Randolph Street station in downtown Chicago, however, the train was full.

And it was close to on time. Somewhere between the airport and Dune Park (Chesterton), we lost five minutes, which we never made up. Still, for a two-hour and twenty-minute trip, five minutes off "the advertised" schedule didn't seem too bad.

The South Shore travels along the "southern shore" of Lake Michigan—through Michigan City, Gary, East Chicago, Hammond, and into Illinois—before swinging north into Chicago.

At one point we waited briefly while an eastbound South Shore passed us. On another nearby track, an Amtrak passenger train roared past.

When we reached Hammond, almost two hours into our trip, I saw the

ALL ABOARD! Last passengers board the South Shore at the South Bend Regional Airport terminal before starting the two-hour, twenty-five-minute trip into downtown Chicago.

first passengers get off the train. So far as I could tell, about everyone else rode to the end of the line at Chicago's Randolph Street station.

Arriving there, it was obvious that, had Dorothy from *The Wizard of Oz* been with us, I could have said, "Dorothy, I don't think we're in Indiana any more." Downtown sidewalks were crowded with tens, if not hundreds, of thousands of people, a fleet of motorcycles roared down Ontario Street (apparently in some sort of parade); and young people marched down Michigan Avenue calling for the legalization of marijuana.

It was an absolutely beautiful Saturday afternoon. Every third couple, so it seemed, was pushing a baby stroller. It even appeared that pedestrians and drivers were on the same page about intersections and traffic control. How often do you suppose that happens? It was Chicago at its best and a grand time to be out among the people.

On the trip back to South Bend, we started right on time and stayed on schedule until we approached the airport. Somehow, we lost the same five minutes by the time we arrived.

When we left Chicago, the train was full of passengers. After all, the South Shore carries 3.6 million passengers annually. Rush-hour trains are standing room only. By East Chicago, on our trip, about half of the passengers were gone.

Do it again? Probably not just to be traveling, but it's America's last interurban making scheduled intercity runs, and it's history.

ENTRANCE. The front entrance to Copshaholm with a veranda spreading in both directions. The floor of the veranda uses marble, limestone, and granite to form a mosaic.

SOUTH BEND GIFT. This Tiffany-made, solid-gold loving cup was presented by "the people of South Bend" to James Oliver on the occasion of his thirty-fourth wedding anniversary. It was in appreciation for Oliver's contributions to the city.

Northern Indiana Center for History, South Bend

SOUTH BEND—Imagine taking common fieldstones and turning them into an absolutely beautiful mansion. That's exactly what J. D. Oliver, president of the Oliver Chilled Plow Works, did when construction got under way on his thirty-eight-room residence, Copshaholm, in 1895.

Like many another Hoosier entrepreneur during the 1800s, Oliver wasn't born in the place he prospered, but rather in nearby Mishawaka. Later he made his fortune with a "chilled" plow blade, invented by his father, James. James's patent for the cast-iron blade made it smooth and durable as it cooled or "chilled"—perhaps as good as steel and less expensive. By the early twentieth century, the Olivers' South Bend factory was producing more than 800,000 plows a year.

Quite naturally, there's more to the story of J. D.'s home, Copshaholm.

According to his diary, it was James who handpicked most of the stones from Saint Joseph and surrounding counties for his son's Washington Street house.

It wasn't merely any fieldstone, of course, that was used on the exterior. It was granite with its subtle, speckled coloring—quite different from the usual plain limestone so widely used throughout Indiana in construction. Once the stones were brought to the building site, European stonemasons did the cutting. Four years later, J. D. named his home Copshaholm, after the town in Scotland that was his father's birthplace.

The house did not want for embellishments. For example, it had leaded-glass windows and clay tile and pressed copper in the roof. Inside the house, oak, mahogany, and cherry wood were used. The American oak in the main hall was stained dark. (Catherine, J. D.'s unmarried daughter, changed that in the 1930s when she had it stripped, bleached, and varnished to give it the blond color it has today. Actually, all four children owned the home, and major redecorating decisions had the approval of all.)

And the furnishings! They date from the late eighteenth to the mid-twentieth centuries. So many furnishing treasures exist, they can't all be displayed in the mansion at any one time. That's why special exhibitions frequently are mounted at the Northern Indiana Center for History, often including paintings, sculpture, furniture, porcelain, and textiles.

The mansion's furnishings reflect what the home looked like during the seventy-five years that members of the Oliver family lived there. Its three floors include fourteen fireplaces, ten bedrooms, and nine bathrooms.

The rest of the story is the rest of the Center for History.

WORKER'S HOUSE. Nearby Copshaholm is this modest "Worker's Home," or "Dom Robotnika" in Polish. It illustrates the community's ethnic and lifestyle diversity in the 1930s.

IF YOU GO

As interesting as the mansion may be, it's only part of this extensive historical enterprise. Adjacent are the "Worker's Home," a cottage that reflects the lifestyle typical of a factory worker in the 1930s; the Oliver Gardens, two and a half acres of landscaped grounds including a teahouse, formal Italianate garden, rose garden, pergola, tennis lawn, and fountain; and, not least of all, the Center for History building.

The complex really didn't exist as such until the museum was built in 1994. Its two levels include:

the renovated Kidsfirst Children's Museum, a hands-on exhibit, and play space;

the Voyages Gallery of local history, telling the story of this Saint Joseph River area from its early exploration into twentieth-century industry;

the attached Carriage House, built at the same time as Copshaholm;

the 125-seat Wiekamp Auditorium;

the Carroll, Leighton, and other changing galleries;

in addition to the gift shop, restrooms, archives, outdoor amphitheater, and information lobby.

The Center for History also is the national repository for the All-American Girls Professional Baseball League. (Remember the film, *A League of Their Own?*) Showcases display photographs, bats, gloves, uniforms, trophies, and other artifacts. South Bend was home for the South Bend Blue Sox from 1943 to 1954.

GETTING THERE: Turn west on Washington Street in downtown South Bend to the center at 808 W. Washington Street. Parking is in the front lot off Thomas Street.

INFORMATION: Call (574) 235–9664. The Web site is http://www.centerforhistory.org/, and the fax is (574) 235–9059. The museum is open Tuesday through Saturday from 10 a.m. to 5 p.m. and Sunday noon to 5 p.m. The last Copshaholm tour begins at 2 p.m.

FEES: Admission charged.

PURSUIT OF A DREAM. The circular ramp leading to the hall's lower level leads the visitor past a forty-three-foot tall sculpture that is part of the display depicting how a young man's experiences can lead him to become a college football player.

EQUIPMENT EVOLUTION. This display shows how football equipment has changed from the 1920s through the late 1990s. Leather and fiber helmets of the 1920s and 1930s, for example, gave way to more durable plastic in the outer shell after 1945. Head protection was not mandatory until 1939.

College Football Hall of Fame, South Bend

SOUTH BEND—If you're a college football junkie, what do you do when the bowl games are over and you have eight months to go before the next season begins? While it won't fill every moment, you could get a quick fix by visiting the College Football Hall of Fame in downtown South Bend.

It's one of five sports halls of fame in Indiana. (Can you name the other four? The answer is at the end of this article.)

The hall prides itself on offering "Every day is Saturday at the College Football Hall of Fame," and it may do just that. Like similar museums, its combination of hands-on activities, memorabilia, plaques, videos, music, and literature offers something for everyone. Among these choices, each fan will find a favorite.

For me, it was the plaques of those inducted into the Hall of Fame, especially those from the 1940s and 1950s when I first began to follow college football. I found plaques in the Hall of Champions devoted to many of my heroes of that day—Doc Blanchard and Glenn Davis from the U.S. Military Academy, John Lujack from the University of Notre Dame, and Charlie Trippi from the University of Georgia among them.

The plaques also confirmed—almost—the story I've told about watching George "Barney" Poole play his eighth year of college football in 1948 while I was a University of Kentucky sportswriter.

Actually, I was off by one year. His plaque notes he played seven years—at Mississippi in 1942, then North Carolina in 1943, three years at the U.S. Military Academy during World War II from 1944 to 1946, and, finally, two more years at Mississippi in 1947 and 1948. The army years apparently did not count toward his years of eligibility.

The College Football Hall of Fame consists of four areas.

The nineteen-thousand-square-foot outdoor plaza is used to host large events. It's marked off from the thirty-yard line to the end zone, complete with a goalpost.

Inside the museum, the press box is on the upper level. It, too, is used for special events. It has an art gallery of mixed media paintings of all the Heisman Trophy winners.

(Second trivia question: Who won the first Heisman Award in 1935?)

The main level, which descends on a circular ramp to the lower level, is built around the theme, Pursuit of a Dream. It depicts the experiences of a young player on his way toward a career in college football.

The lower level is where most of the action is. The recommendation is to go to the stadium auditorium first to see a ten-minute pre-

COLLEGE FOOTBALL HALL OF FAME. Looking at the Hall of Fame from the west with the thirty-yard outdoor plaza in the foreground.

IF YOU GO

game and a fourteen-minute feature showing the hoopla and thrills of a college football game.

One clear favorite on this level are the kiosks with videos that capture some of the sport's great moments. You can watch memorable plays, legendary games, great upsets, and bloopers.

Along with the plaques honoring the College Football Hall of Fame inductees, the lower level includes areas titled: Locker Room, Strategy Clinic, Fitness Room, Training and Sports Science, Evolution of Equipment, Pigskin Pageantry, Bowl Games, National Championships, Pantheon (where recipients of ten major awards are honored), and Practice Field (where you can test your skills in passing, blocking, and kicking).

The immortals get special displays—Jim Thorpe, Amos Alonzo Stagg, Knute Rockne, and John Heisman among them.

How much time do you need for your visit? It all depends. You could do it in an hour or spend all day. For the all-day viewers, there's a restaurant in the building.

Naturally, there's a gift shop, too.

The annual inductions into the hall now take place across the street at Century Center. It's connected to the hall by an underground tunnel.

Oh, yes, those other four sports halls of fame located in Indiana. Most sports fans will know two or three immediately: automobile racing at the Indianapolis Motor Speedway, high school basketball at New Castle, and Indiana football at Richmond. Probably less known is the Indiana baseball hall of fame at Jasper. And the first Heisman winner? Jay Berwanger, halfback at the University of Chicago.

GETTING THERE: In South Bend, stay on Business U. S. 31, Michigan Street, until Saint Joseph Street, one-way north. In downtown South Bend, the Hall of Fame is on your left just after you reach Jefferson Avenue. (The Century Center is on your right.) Turn left into the parking lot.

INFORMATION: Open year-round, 10 a.m. to 5 p.m. Closed Thanksgiving, Christmas Day, and New Year's Day. For information, call (800) 440–3263. The Web site is http://www.collegefootball .org/.

FEES: Admission charged.

CHIEF MENOMINEE. The date and cause of his death are unknown. He may have died in Kansas of typhoid fever in 1841 after surviving the 1838 "Trail of Death."

Chief Menominee Memorial, Plymouth

PLYMOUTH—It's one of the saddest stories in Indiana history. Historian James Madison in his *The Indiana Way* sketches the background: More and more settlers in the 1830s were moving into the "western" states, including Indiana, which had been opened as the Native Americans who lived there gave away ever-increasing amounts of land in treaty after treaty.

The War of 1812 had been fought not many years earlier when frontiersmen battled the British and their Native American allies. The Black Hawk War was just barely over. Now, with the force of the Indian Removal Act of 1830, the United States had the legal means to push the remaining Native Americans even farther west.

It was all done with the best of motives. The Native Americans would be better off, it was argued, if they were not around the influences of frequently corrupt federal agents and the "degrading effects of white culture."

When the Potawatomi and the Miami ceded lands for the building of the Michigan Road and the Wabash and Erie Canal, the stage was set for their removal from Indiana.

There was only one problem. They didn't want to go.

So they were forced. For the Potawatomi, it was "the Trail of Death."

The story of what happened is best told by another Hoosier historian, Ross Lockridge, in *The Story of Indiana*, which was used for many years in Indiana history classes in junior high school.

The key person in the Potawatomi removal was General John Tipton, veteran of the Battle of Tippecanoe, a federal agent, and then a U.S. senator. Tipton, accompanied by trader George Ewing and a company of militia, entered a Potawatomi village in late 1838, disarmed the men while they were gathered for a tribal council, and rounded up everyone in the vicinity. Chief Menominee resisted but finally was roped and "tied down like a dog." It isn't known exactly what happened to him, but the best evidence is that he later died in Kansas in 1841.

Eventually, 859 Potawatomi in the Twin Lakes region, south of Plymouth, were brought together into a camp. On September 4, 1838, the militia started them on a nine-hundred-mile trip to Kansas.

When the Native Americans were some distance from their village, they could see smoke rising behind them from the fires that had been set to their homes. It was better, the opinion was, for them to know they couldn't return because everything had been destroyed.

LAND CLEARED FOR MONUMENT. The statue of Chief Menominee stands in the midst of a cleared area on Peach Road in southern Marshall County. The land was donated in 1909 by John A. McFarlin.

The trip west was a disaster. Too few wagons were available to carry those who had difficulty walking long distances. According to Lockridge, "the suffering . . . became worse . . . some infants and old people were dying at every camp." When they finally arrived on the Osage River in Kansas two months after they left Indiana, their number was 150 less—some dead and some simply left on the way because they could go no farther.

Seventy-one years later, a Marshall County resident, John A. McFarlin, donated land to build a monument where the Potawatomi reservation had been. A granite statue of Chief Menominee was erected. The inscription reads:

"In memory of Chief Menominee and his band of 859 Pottawattomie Indians removed from this reservation September 4, 1838, by a company of soldiers under the command of General John Tipton authorized by Governor David Wallace. Site donated by John A. McFarlin. 1909."

That's it. The monument stands in the middle of a small clearing south of Plymouth, the Marshall County seat. It's a lonely spot. It's never going to attract large numbers of visitors. More likely, almost none. Maybe that's okay, though. That way Chief Menominee has the land to himself.

IF YOU GO

GETTING THERE: U.S. 31 runs north/south in Marshall County. At Thirteenth Road in Marshall County, turn west. (The turn is marked by a highway sign.) Go four and a half miles to Peach Road and turn right about one-half mile.

INFORMATION: To learn about events in Marshall County, contact the Convention and Visitors Bureau at its Web site, http://www.blueberrycountry .org/, or call (800) 626–5353.

PIONEER WOMEN'S LOG CABIN. Constructed from logs used in two 1860s cabins, this cabin, part of the Living History Village, now is furnished as it would have been by nineteenth-century Indiana pioneers. It was a bicentennial project in 1976.

Fulton County Historical Society Museum, Rochester

ROCHESTER—The young, athletic Hoosier didn't have a marquee name, but, even in those days, Hollywood took care of such things. Rochester's Otto Elmo Linkenhelt became Elmo Lincoln. That seemed a fit name for the first Tarzan of the movies when, in 1918, the twenty-nine-year-old Fulton County native appeared in a silent black-and-white motion picture as "Tarzan, king of the jungle." Later he was "Elmo the mighty."

Fulton County residents take justifiable pride in his worldwide fame with his films still shown, they say, around the globe. They also like to point out that another native of the county is Doctor Otis Bowen, former Indiana governor and secretary of health and human services in President Ronald Reagan's cabinet. Bowen has called Bremen his home for many years, but he was born here and attended Fulton High School, where his father was a teacher and coach.

Both Lincoln and Bowen are prominently featured in the Fulton County Museum, part of the rich, historical series of buildings along U.S. 31, four miles north of Rochester. They include, in addition to the extensive museum, the Round Barn Museum and the Village of Loyal.

Let's take them one at a time.

Frequently, county museums are in buildings that have been converted to that use—an old library, a former school. That's no longer true in Fulton County. After several years in rented rooms at the old downtown high school, a new building for the museum was constructed in 1988.

Not only that, but a 2,400-square-foot addition has been added that includes a large meeting room. The museum was able to sell some property that had been donated and use the proceeds for the new construction.

Museum staff have finished installing shelving for old newspapers and artifacts, plus working on cataloging information. Also, they've completed compiling data about the county's former 120 one-room school buildings.

When you visit the museum, you'll find that it just goes on and on. It features seventeen different display areas on subjects including military, schools, scouts, toys, churches, old-fashioned kitchens, dining rooms, the circus, health, and transportation. The circus was especially important, as the Cole Brothers Circus had its winter quarters in Rochester from 1935 to 1940. The circus moved away following a major fire.

Now about those round barns. Of Indiana's more than two hundred, less than one hundred still exist. Eight are in Fulton County, including one built on the Bert Leedy farm in 1924—the last round barn built in the county. In 1989 a tornado took off the roof, and

TARZAN OF THE APES. Rochester's Otto Elmo Linkenhelt—known professionally as Elmo Lincoln—was the movies' first Tarzan in a 1918 silent film.

ROUND BARN MUSEUM. This round barn lost its roof in 1989. It was given to the Fulton County Historical Society, moved, and restored during 1990–91 at a cost of $65,000. Today it holds the Fulton County Round Barn Museum.

IF YOU GO

its owner donated it to the Fulton County Historical Society. With a $40,000 loan from Historic Landmarks Foundation of Indiana and $25,000 in other funds raised, the barn was moved and restored at its present site to become the Fulton County Round Barn Museum. It's fifty-five feet to the top of the cupola.

Inside you'll find antique farm machinery and tools, a 1910 buggy, and a 1912 Lincoln truck. The hayloft has circular pews, donated by a church, so that two hundred people, most often schoolchildren, can be seated during tours.

Finally, the Village of Loyal.

The small community of Germany, west of the museum, changed its name to Loyal when World War I started with Germany as an enemy. Later its name was changed to Pershing, in honor of the American commander, General John J. Pershing.

Today, that village no longer exists. But a re-created Loyal, a living history village representing the period of 1900 to 1925, stands next to the county museum and the Round Barn Museum. It includes a windmill, bridge, eleven historic buildings, 160 feet of railroad track, a caboose, and a boxcar.

The historical society sponsors three annual historic festivals: the Redbud Trail Rendezvous, held on the last weekend in April; the Historical Power Show, held on the third weekend in June; and the Trail of Courage Living History Festival, held on the third weekend in September.

GETTING THERE: Located four miles north of Rochester at the intersection of U.S. 31 and County Road 375N in Fulton County.

INFORMATION: Open all year, 9 a.m. to 5 p.m.; closed on holidays and Sunday, but open on Sunday during festivals. Call (574) 223–4436 or go to the Web site at http://dilbert.htctech.net/~fchs/.

FEES: Free, but donations accepted.

FRIEND OF PRESIDENTS. Bell's career brought him in contact with the world's leaders, including President Harry S Truman, left. This photo is in Mentone's Bell Museum.

Lawrence D. Bell Aircraft Museum, Mentone

MENTONE—How did Lawrence D. Bell, an Indiana boy from a small rural community, become a twentieth-century leader in aviation, even building the world's first faster-than-sound airplane?

The answer lies at least partly in when he was born (1894, so he was a young boy at the birth of aviation), watching the first major U.S. air show in 1910 (he and his brother went home and built their own model airplane that flew), joining a stunt pilot's troupe (where his brother soon died in a crash), and then going to work for another early plane manufacturer (Glenn L. Martin).

Ultimately, Bell's company established twenty aviation firsts, including:

First U.S. jet-propelled fighter aircraft

First commercial helicopter

First supersonic airplane, the X-1

First airplane able to vary its degree of wing sweepback during flight

First turbine-powered aircraft

First jet-propelled vertical takeoff and landing plane

First automatic carrier landing system

First airplane able to fly at two and a half times the speed of sound and at an altitude of ninety thousand feet

It was breaking the sound barrier for which Bell may be best known. That was the famous flight of Charles "Chuck" Yeager in 1947. He was the pilot of Bell's X-1 that soared to a record of more than seven hundred miles per hour—at the time, an unheard-of speed.

Bell lived in Mentone for the first thirteen years of his life before the family moved to California. His formal education ended a month before his high school graduation when he teamed with his brother, Grover, as ground crew for Lincoln Beachey, a stunt flyer of the day.

Bell came back a number of times to his Indiana hometown. His foundation funded the Mentone library, named in honor of Bell's parents, Isaac and Harriet Bell. The twenty-eight thousand items in the library serve this town of less than one thousand residents.

Bell died of a heart attack in 1956, and he willed his memorabilia to Mentone. It took awhile to build the museum, which explores the early history of American aviation. Materials first were stored and displayed at the town library.

The present museum building, considered phase one of a two-phase plan, is staffed by volunteers and is only open on summer and autumn Sunday afternoons. Phase two—building a hangar and acquiring, restoring, and displaying each model of Bell aircraft—obviously is going to require considerable funding. Even phase one was a stretch

BELL'S INVENTION. A medical rescue aircraft in front of the Lawrence D. Bell Aircraft Museum at Mentone.

IF YOU GO

for this small northern Indiana town's citizens. It was only possible, Mentone volunteer Linda Cochran notes, with the assistance of interested persons from throughout the nation.

While phase two is in the works, one example of Bell's work has been on display on the museum grounds. That's the IUH-IH Bell helicopter, called the "Huey." This Medvac troop transport was the beginning of the air-mobile units used in Vietnam. The museum also has a 47G helicopter, such as those used by M*A*S*H units in Korea, and is acquiring a Cobra helicopter.

A ten-minute video presentation about Bell's life and career shows the museum visitor the extent to which the Indiana native helped shape the future of American aviation. The video tells how Bell stayed with Martin's aircraft firm, becoming shop foreman and then general manager before leaving in 1928 to join Consolidated Aircraft in Buffalo, New York. When Consolidated moved to California in 1935, Bell formed his own firm, Bell Aircraft Corporation.

Today, Mentone probably is best known as the "Egg Basket of the Midwest" because of its production of poultry and eggs. The museum's volunteer staff, however, does its best to keep alive the memory of a hometown boy who became one of aviation's giants.

GETTING THERE: The museum is two blocks west of Indiana 19 on Oak Street.

INFORMATION: Call (574) 353–7113 or the Kosciusko County Convention and Visitors Bureau at (800) 800–6090 or visit the bureau's Web site at http://www.koscvb.org/. Open June 1 through September on Sunday, 1 p.m. to 5 p.m., or Monday through Saturday by appointment.

FEES: None, but donations accepted. The museum also offers contributing memberships.

SIX FOR DINNER. The formal dining room of Ruthmere is set for a party of six. A. R. and Elizabeth Beardsley had lived in another home, given to them by her father, for thirty-eight years before moving into their new home, Ruthmere, in 1910.

DECORATED FOR CHRISTMAS. A Christmas tree and other festive holiday decorations are part of the Ruthmere experience during the holidays.

Ruthmere, Elkhart

ELKHART—It's not unusual to see a greenhouse conservatory near a mansion. They're somewhat common to grand homes built near the turn of the last century. But the one at Ruthmere has a special feature about it.

A. R. Beardsley had married Elizabeth Baldwin in 1872 in a quiet wedding—something else a bit unusual, given that they already were an important couple in Elkhart society. He was a twenty-five-year-old rising businessman who later became prominent in Republican state politics and in developing Miles Laboratories into one of America's largest over-the-counter medical products companies.

Their only daughter, Ruth, born in December 1880, died the following summer. For the next quarter of a century, the Beardsleys threw themselves into their work, their community enterprises, and their special interests.

Then in 1908 they commissioned Chicago-trained architect E. Hill Turnock to design and build a new home that would overlook the Saint Joseph River with a view toward downtown Elkhart. They named their new home Ruthmere for their daughter, Ruth, and mere, which can mean "near the water." What Turnock designed was a three-story Beaux Arts structure that was completed in 1910 and for the next fourteen years served as a center of Elkhart social life until both Beardsleys died in 1924 within five months of each other.

After the Beardsleys' deaths, their nephew, Arthur L. Beardsley, acquired the property, and his family lived there until 1944. The S. S. Deputy family then lived in Ruthmere until 1969, when the Beardsley Foundation purchased the mansion. It was opened to the public in 1973.

Turnock had arrived in Elkhart as a young man the same year the Beardsleys were married. He returned to Elkhart in 1907 from Chicago for health reasons after a successful architectural career there. He designed a number of Elkhart buildings, but Ruthmere is his best known.

The facing of the structure is Belden brick from Ohio and native Indiana limestone from Bedford. The covered entrance is supported by square brick pillars. A marble piazza or veranda goes across the south side of the home, wrapping around to the east where a porte cochere (covered porch) protected visitors arriving by carriage or automobile.

As impressive as the exterior is, it is the interior of the building that is especially compelling. O'Hara Decorating Services in Chicago was

RUTHMERE. This side of Ruthmere faces the Saint Joseph River and downtown. The mansion is listed on the National Register of Historic Places. The greenhouse conservatory is to the right.

a lead contractor in restoring the mansion. It handled painting, gilding, gold leafing, sewing and hanging of wall fabrics, refinishing wood trim, and handwork in re-creating ornate ceilings.

The firm's greatest challenge was the master bedroom ceiling involving flower garlands, ribbons, and wild roses that had been smeared and faded through repeated washings over the decades. In addition, the frieze or border around the room just below the ceiling was badly faded and covered with coats of white latex. Laborious analysis, newly painted canvasses, and varnishings re-created the originals.

Ruthmere's carved mahogany woodwork and paneling, furnishings, silk wall coverings, walnut flooring, murals, fine arts collections, central vacuum system, service call buzzers, elevator, and other features all are worthy of examination.

In the below-ground-level game room is an eighteen-rank Choralcelo pipe organ/player piano, installed in 1916. Nearby in the room is a 1955 Steinway grand concert piano. Up to seventy can be seated for performances.

In the game room the special conservatory feature is found. It's an underground tunnel that connects the game room with the conservatory, where today more than 150 plants can be viewed. Elizabeth Beardsley never had to brave the cold Elkhart winters to tend her flowers and plants.

IF YOU GO

GETTING THERE: On Main Street in downtown Elkhart, turn east on Beardsley Avenue, just north of the Saint Joseph River.

INFORMATION: Open Tuesday through Saturday in April through mid-December. Guided tours are at 10 and 11 a.m., 1, 2, and 3 p.m. Open Sunday for 2 and 3 p.m. tours in July and August. Closed January through March, Memorial Day, Labor Day, Thanksgiving Day, and Christmas Day. Its Web site is http://www.ruthmere.org/, telephone (219) 264–0330, or toll-free (888) 287–7696, or fax (219) 266–0474.

FEES: Admission charged.

PRESENT LIBRARY. This main floor former classroom now is the library for the museum. The museum hopes to construct an annex to the building, with part of the new space combining the present library and archives rooms.

LOOKING INTO THE WORLD'S LARGEST. This fifty-pound sousaphone is on display at the Elkhart County Historical Museum. Manufactured in Elkhart, the sousaphone is part of the Greenleaf Collection of Musical Instruments.

Elkhart County Historical Museum, Bristol

BRISTOL—"We've got permission from the City of Bristol to fire muzzle-loaders that day," Gary Richards tells me as he discusses plans for a Revolutionary War encampment as part of an open house sponsored by the Elkhart County Historical Museum.

Richards, interpretation coordinator for the museum, is showing me around the former Washington Township schoolhouse, now converted into the county museum. It was the county's first consolidated school. We are in the auditorium looking at photos of the two best-known members of the county sports hall of fame. Know who they are?

The museum originally was in the county courthouse at Goshen. That space was needed, so the next move was to a vacant building near the Carnegie Library. Soon that space, too, was needed and the museum's collection went into storage. Enter into the picture the museum's major benefactor, Howard Rush, a county grocer. He bought the old school building and made arrangements for the park department to operate the museum in what now is called the Rush Memorial Center.

Rush wasn't the only person who has helped the museum, however. The Elkhart County Historical Society was organized in 1896, so it's been around for a while. It immediately started collecting artifacts. "We have about 22,000 items in the museum and they've all been donated," Richards says.

Former schoolrooms now house the collection, arranged by themes and time periods. For example, there's a Victorian period room; a children's room, including a one-room school and toys; a general store; a train depot; and a barn room.

"Our Amish residents like to come in the barn room and spend time looking at the old equipment," says Richards.

The archives are on the ground floor with a library on the main floor. Within a few months in one recent year, 283 researchers from twenty-six states used the facility. They were part of the four thousand visitors during the year from thirty-one states and five countries.

It's a busy place. The museum staff in another recent year offered eighty-three tours, programs, and workshops. Plus, necessary repairs of the old building have been under way. An $11,000 grant provided half the cost of replacing the building's roof.

A second grant of $5,000 could lead to a major expansion. It was to pay architectural fees for a hoped-for three-story annex to the north of the present structure. The present building has had its own

COUNTY MUSEUM. The former Washington Township school building at Bristol now serves as the Elkhart County Historical Museum. The original building was constructed in 1903.

additions. The first in 1923 added more rooms, indoor plumbing, and water to the 1903 building. The gymnasium/auditorium was constructed in 1925.

"We'd like to do something about the band business in the new annex, if we can," Richards notes. "More band instruments were manufactured here in Elkhart County than any place else in the world, making it the 'band instrument capital of the world.'"

Presently, the museum has twelve instruments from the Greenleaf Collection of Musical Instruments on loan from Interlochen Center for the Arts. It includes the world's largest playable sousaphone, weighing in at fifty pounds, and one of the first sousaphones developed for John Phillip Sousa himself.

The two best-known members in the sports hall of fame? You're right if you guessed basketball player Shawn Kemp from Concord High School, a former National Basketball Association player, and Rick Mirer, quarterback at Goshen High School, who played at the University of Notre Dame and in the National Football League.

GETTING THERE: In Bristol the museum is located on Indiana 120 (Vistula Street).

INFORMATION: Call the museum at (574) 848–4322 or the park office at (574) 535–6458 to schedule a tour. The Web site is http://www.elkhartcountyparks .org/, and the fax number is (574) 848–5703. The museum is open Tuesday through Friday from 10 a.m. to 4 p.m. and Sunday from 1 p.m. to 5 p.m.

FEES: None, but donations are accepted.

THE EVANGELIST. A museum display depicts Billy Sunday as evangelist. According to one estimate, he preached to more than one hundred million people—long before modern-day telecommunications.

Billy Sunday Historic Site Museum, Winona Lake

THE OUTFIELDER. Although Billy Sunday only hit .248 in eight seasons of professional baseball, his base stealing and acrobatic outfield catches made him a valued player. This image of Billy as a baseball player is in the visitor center at Winona Lake.

WINONA LAKE—Baseball players of the day often were saloon-brawling, tobacco-spitting, foul-mouthed athletes, frequently only a few dollars removed from poverty. Still, it was the goal of many a young man to play professional baseball.

Young William Ashley Sunday was one. When his father died in the Civil War, Billy grew up in the Iowa Soldier's Orphan Home. Later at Marshalltown, Iowa, he began to make a name for himself as a fleet-footed base runner with the local semipro team. When the famed Cap Anson of the Chicago White Stockings came calling, Billy joined his team. During his eight seasons of professional baseball, he was known as a base stealer whose speed also helped him make dazzling plays in the outfield.

Then one day, after carousing at a saloon with his teammates, Billy was sitting on a Chicago street curb. From there, he heard a troupe from a mission singing hymns his mother sang to him as a child. As the story goes, Billy turned to his teammates and said, "Boys, I bid the old life good-bye."

Supposedly both Philadelphia and Cincinnati were offering him $400-a-month contracts or more for the next season. Instead, Billy went to work at the Chicago YMCA for $83.33 a month. In 1893 he joined evangelist Wilbur Chapman, who traveled the country conducting revivals, with Billy working as an advance man in putting up revival tents and selling books. When the evangelist retired two years later, Billy, who sometimes had preached before Chapman would arrive in town, replaced him.

Over the decades he spent on the revival circuit, the now world-famous Billy Sunday perfected his preaching style. In his fiery sermons, he would slide across the stage as if he were sliding into second base. He ran up and down the aisles. He would leap from the pulpit to the piano. He would smash sin by swinging a baseball bat to demolish a chair. He especially denounced liquor and became a leader in the prohibition movement. It is estimated that, without the aid of radio, television, or speaker systems, he preached to more than one hundred million people.

In 1911 Billy and his wife, Helen, or Nell as she was known, moved their base of operations from Chicago to a home they built at Winona Lake. It was here, a few miles from Warsaw, that their annual Bible conferences and chautauqua meetings drew big crowds. Now a museum, the house, together with a nearby newly constructed visitor center, comprise the Billy Sunday Historic Site Museum.

VISITOR CENTER. This new visitor center near the Billy Sunday Historic Site Museum contains memorabilia about the evangelist, including a partial re-creation of a revival tabernacle.

The Sundays lived in their home, calling it Mount Hood, until Nell's death in 1955. Nell started conducting tours of their bungalow for interested visitors shortly after Billy's death in 1935. Nell has been termed "the first and best tour guide the house has ever had," says Bill Firstenberger, the home's curator.

Nell had an advantage as a tour guide. Not only had she lived in the house for more than forty years, but she also had designed the structure. A gifted artist in her own right, her paintings and needlework are on display throughout the house.

She also served as Billy's business manager. Part of her job was to assist in erecting the tabernacles they hastily put up at revival sites, rather than using tents. Raising the wooden tabernacles caught the public's attention long before Billy arrived for his revivals. The biggest would seat up to eighteen thousand persons.

After her death, the Sunday home was given first to the Winona Christian Assembly and later to Grace College. For twenty-five years, the second floor was used as a women's dormitory. The Winona Restoration Company has worked at restoring the house, using a Build Indiana Grant and local cost-sharing funds.

The new visitor center is filled with artifacts, photographs, scrapbooks, and displays depicting Billy Sunday's career. An eight-minute orientation film is shown to visitors before they tour the house.

GETTING THERE: Take U.S. 30 into Winona Lake. Turn west at the Center Street exit to the second traffic signal. Turn left on Argonne Road. After you pass under a railroad viaduct, you come to another traffic signal. Continue straight, with Argonne now named Park Avenue. The museum is about half a mile on the left-hand side.

INFORMATION: The Web site is http://www.villageatwinona .com/ or call (574) 268–0660. The street address is 1101 Park Avenue. Open from 10 a.m. to 5 p.m. Tuesday through Saturday. Last tour of the home begins at 4 p.m.

FEES: Billy Sunday accepted donations at his revival meetings. So does the visitor center. Admission charged for tours of the Sunday home.

Menno-Hof Visitor Center, Shipshewana

SHIPSHEWANA—Mention the Shipshewana Flea Market and just about everyone has heard about it, probably even been there.

Mention Menno-Hof Visitor Center just across Indiana 5 from the flea market and mostly you get blank stares or, at best, "Oh, yes, I think I noticed it." While the flea market easily has more than a million people visiting it annually, the Amish-Mennonite center has between 30,000 and 35,000.

That's too bad.

The center, which displays the history of the Mennonite and Amish movements, gets its name from Menno Simons, who, according to Mennonite literature, "brought stability to the early Anabaptists" and the word "hof," German for farmstead. "Anabaptist" means to rebaptize—its adherents believing voluntary, adult baptism should be an option at a time when only infant baptism was allowed.

You are greeted at the entrance of the center—almost literally across the road from the flea market—by a volunteer. The guide quietly leads you to the first of a series of small rooms, explains what will happen, and then leaves you to absorb the experience. You are met once again as you exit the room and go on to the next.

First is a helpful introduction to the history of the Anabaptist movement, which includes the Mennonites, Amish, and the Hutterites. The exhibit traces how church history moved from the time of Christ to the sixteenth-century Reformation period. The fourth stop on the tour is a dungeon. Anabaptists were imprisoned, tortured, and executed because of their efforts to establish church practices free from state control. As you leave the room, you are invited to look down into what a dungeon pit might have looked like at the time. You wouldn't want to be there.

The tour progressively takes the visitor through Europe as the Anabaptists tried to find refuge and, finally, their migration to the New World. William Penn, the Quaker who established Pennsylvania, invited the Anabaptists to join him and gave them access to wooded lands in America.

The Amish first arrived in Indiana in 1841, and their experience here is recounted. Next, Mennonite and Amish religious beliefs and common experiences in today's world are featured. An important part of those beliefs is a commitment to simplicity and stewardship of resources, explained as you move through the exhibit.

The tour makes extensive use of multimedia presentations. One highlight is the tornado room, where the destructive power of a tor-

VISITOR CENTER. The attractive grounds and buildings of the Menno-Hof Visitor Center at Shipshewana, where the history and practices of Mennonites, Amish, and Hutterites are explained through multimedia and demonstrations.

nado is demonstrated along with the role of Mennonite and Amish work teams to clean up areas ravaged by storms, fires, and floods. The Anabaptist peace testimony and commitment to the principle of nonviolence are demonstrated. There's even a play stop along the way where children can try out toys produced by the Hutterites.

Finally, at the end, a lounge is provided for relaxing, examining books for sale, and talking. Computers can help you find ways to learn more about these Anabaptist groups.

If you are of a religious persuasion other than Anabaptist, one thought you probably have is that you wish your religious affiliation could do as good a job explaining itself in such a careful and interesting way as these Mennonites, Amish, and Hutterites have.

IF YOU GO

GETTING THERE: The Menno-Hof Visitor Center is on Indiana 5 in Shipshewana.

INFORMATION: Hours are from 10 a.m. to 5 p.m. Monday through Saturday. Closed Thanksgiving Day, Christmas Day, and New Year's Day. The Web site is http://mennohof.org/. Off-hour tours for bus groups can be arranged. Call (260) 768–4117.

FEES: Donations are requested.

WHAT DO YOU BID? Equipped with an attached microphone, much like a musical performer, an auctioneer seeks bids at the Shipshewana Wednesday auction.

IF IT'S BEEN MADE. Chances are good that, if it's been made, it's probably on sale at Shipshewana's Trading Place. Here, it's mostly furniture.

Trading Place of America, Shipshewana

SHIPSHEWANA—They call it "the Crystal Valley"—named because of the clear water springs that run through the area. It stretches from Lagrange in northeastern Indiana to the west at Elkhart. It includes Bristol, Goshen, Howe, Middlebury, Nappanee, Topeka, Wakarusa, and Wolcottville as well as some of Indiana's best farmland. It's the home of many of the state's Amish. The centerpiece, at least for shoppers and flea market aficionados, is Shipshewana.

Now *that's* a flea market.

Located just north of U.S. 20 on Indiana 5, it's billed as the "Midwest's largest outdoor flea market"—more than a thousand vendors. Open from the first of May through September, the market takes place on Tuesday and Wednesday. In the parking lot, you can see cars from as far west as Chicago and from all over Indiana, southern Michigan, and Ohio.

As a matter of fact, cars are the problem.

Shipshewana's Web site warns to "expect large crowds" while the outdoor flea market is in session. That's no exaggeration. Traffic backs up outside the market, going both ways on Indiana 5. Patience is a virtue, both as you wait your turn to get into parking areas and, later, as you try to leave. It is not difficult to believe that as many as fifty thousand people show up each week at Shipshewana, a town of not many more than five hundred residents.

Inside the large auction house, a number of auctioneers are going full speed in different parts of the building. When you first enter, you wonder how any order can ever come from this apparent chaos. Very quickly, you learn to tune out the other auctioneers' calls and concentrate on the one you're interested in. Like other auctions, the callers move from item to item. You either need to have signed for a number to bid or pay cash on the floor.

Auctions on Wednesday starting at 8 a.m. are when antiques and miscellaneous goods are sold. This part of the operation goes on year-round, in contrast to the flea market. Additionally, there's a hay auction, which begins at 10 a.m., and a livestock auction of small animals, pigs, sheep, and cattle at 11 a.m. Every Friday, again year-round, a horse, pony, and tack auction begins at 9 a.m.

There's also the Trading Place Antique Gallery—thirty-one thousand square feet of antiques, which is open all year.

Just to the north in the small town's business district and in the immediate surrounding areas are more than fifty shops, plus restaurants and lodging facilities, ranging from campgrounds through motels

AT LEAST THERE'S ROOM TO MOVE. Although thousands of people attend the Tuesday and Wednesday flea markets at Shipshewana, the one-thousand-plus vendors cover so much space that patrons have room to see all they wish.

IF YOU GO

and hotels to bed-and-breakfasts. Most of the shops are open year-round with about everything closed on Sunday. (The tourist association recommends nearby museums and recreational activities on Sunday.)

The largest concentration of shops is just west and north of where Middlebury Street crosses Indiana 5, also called locally Van Buren Street. In the heart of this area is where you "awaken to yesterday's main street era, horse and buggy style."

You're probably not going to want to try both—flea market/auction and shops—in one day unless you're prepared for an especially long one. Remember, things move a little slower here—literally, too. Amish buggies are everywhere, and drivers are cautioned to reduce their speed.

GETTING THERE: Indiana 5 passes through Shipshewana and the flea market.

INFORMATION: The flea market and auction telephone number is (260) 768–4129. Its Web site is http://www.tradingplaceamerica.com/. The visitor bureau number is (800) 254–8090.

FEES: None to enter the flea market or auction, but there's a parking fee Memorial Day to Labor Day.

FOR NEXT DAY'S AUCTION. An eight-year-old is held by its owner, Roy Rosenberger of Brookville, Indiana. Rosenberger had just arrived at the auction and was unloading his horses for sale the following morning.

ONE PARKING LOT. Amish carriages and horses are parked across the road from the Topeka Draft Horse Auction grounds.

BOOTS FOR SALE. Among vendors at the Topeka Draft Horse Auction was one selling boots of all descriptions.

Topeka Draft Horse Auction, Topeka

TOPEKA—I'm hesitant about writing this column.

First, I'm a city boy, and I really don't know all that much about horses. Second, the last thing I would want to do would be to inadvertently offend the people I spent several hours with at the Topeka Draft Horse Auction.

I had heard about the auction a number of times in the past years. Then at a high school football game, I ran into a friend who asked if I had thought of writing about the Topeka auction. "It's next week," he told me. So I went.

Topeka is just across the Noble County line into Lagrange County, north of Ligonier. When I got there about nine on a Thursday morning, the auction's parking lots had long since been filled since the auction began an hour earlier.

The parking lots had the mix that might be expected—automobiles, pickup trucks, and horse trailers. The lot across the road from the auction was reserved for Amish carriages and horses. I was directed to an auxiliary parking lot about a quarter mile away.

Once on the grounds, I made my way to where the auction was taking place in a low building connected to stalls. The procedure is to bring the horses, by number, from the stalls into the sales ring. The horses are trotted up and down the ring to be looked over by prospective buyers—always with a two-person crew, one leading the horse and one following with a switch "to keep it lined up straight," my friend later told me.

The size of the crowd, mostly seated on two sides of the ring, was difficult to estimate but was well into the hundreds. They were predominantly Amish.

The sale itself was fascinating. It was almost as if I were on a motion-picture set—a fast-talking auctioneer, cries of "yes" from ring men when someone would bid, and the careful scrutiny by the audience of each horse offered for sale. While there was considerable background noise, most in the crowd were quiet and intent.

Rather quickly I realized I was at a disadvantage if I didn't have the sale catalog in hand. An inquiry led me to the sales office. "That door says 'exit,' but just go in there and pick up one," a man standing nearby told me.

Now, with catalog in hand, I could follow the sale. As each horse, all of them Belgians this day, came into the ring, the auctioneer would tell his audience something about the horse. Its vaccinations were important, and any slight imperfections were certain to be pointed out—a scratch on the rump, a lump behind a leg, for example.

A HORSE FOR SALE. The Topeka Draft Horse Auction is under way. The lunch stand is under the grandstand in the background.

Of course, its advantages were also noted. Many of the mares were "in foal." In some cases, the name of the owner who had broke the horse and trained it seemed well known to the audience and was worthy of mention. The ability of the Belgian to immediately go into the field to work obviously was important.

While I was there, the horses seemed to be selling between $500 and $2,000. My friend, who was there all day, told me one mare sold later for more than $9,000, and several sold for more than $4,000.

For some time, I stood near the place where the horses were led away from the ring after the bidding ended. I noticed especially two things. One, some of these horses were really big—standing much taller than I do. Second, not every bid was accepted. With some frequency, as the horse was led away, the auctioneer would say, "no sale." The owner's bottom-line price hadn't been met.

Under the stands on one side of the auction house was a lunch stand that was doing a good business. However, I had been told by another friend of a Topeka landmark restaurant, Tiffany's, just across the road from the sale. I stopped there.

The menu was abbreviated, the waitress told me, because they were so busy during auction week. Nevertheless, my lunch of chicken and noodles, mashed potatoes and gravy, and mixed vegetables was excellent. And the size—and taste—of the blackberry pie and ice cream, well, I've never had a bigger—or better—pie a la mode.

IF YOU GO

GETTING THERE: In Topeka, the auction house is on the north side of the street just after the four-way stoplight.

INFORMATION: Go to the Web site at http://www.auctions -USA.com/ or call (260) 593–2522. Horse sales are in the spring and autumn. A number of other auctions, including exotic animals, dairy feeders, driving horses, and implements, are scheduled throughout the year.

FEES: None to enter the auction house.

CARVED STALLS. Inside Saint James Chapel at Howe Military School are individually carved stalls. The wood supposedly came from the area.

TOUR GUIDE. Fifth-grader Alex Canacci points out detail in one of the religious paintings at Saint James Chapel.

INSTRUCTOR. Detail on the stalls of Saint James Chapel is noted by Colonel George Douglass, himself a Howe Military School graduate and now an instructor in religious studies.

Saint James Memorial Chapel, Howe

HOWE—"Mr. Canacci, will you please show our visitor around the chapel."

I had arrived unannounced at Saint James Memorial Chapel on the campus of Howe Military School in the middle of a weekday afternoon. The door to the chapel was open, and, when I entered, I found Colonel George Douglass there, instructing his lower-school class in religion about ethical issues.

When I said I had not visited the chapel before, that's when the teacher dispatched one of his students, ten-year-old fifth-grader Alex Canacci from Cleveland, to be my guide.

That's all I know about Alex except for two things. Although he was in his first year at the school—fifth grade is the beginning grade of the lower school—Alex proved extremely knowledgeable about the structure and what was in it. Also, during our short tour, he seemed to me to be just about the most polite and well-mannered young man one could expect to meet.

He carefully explained how to tell which saints were which, as shown in the paintings by what else appeared in the depiction. When we went down to the crypt under the chapel, I must admit he was a little shaky about the exact histories of those persons buried there.

Our tour finished, he returned me to Colonel Douglass as the class was dismissing. That gave me a chance to talk with the instructor, himself a Howe graduate in the class of 1960.

One of the fascinating traditions about the chapel is the story of how its wooden stalls, or pews, were individually carved, each with its own symbol, so no two are the same. I use the term "tradition" because only an undocumented article in a Howe school newspaper has this account.

The story has it that a young German student showed up at Howe with no means to pay his tuition. So, a deal was struck. Since he had wood-carving skills, he carved the individual stalls in return for his tuition.

It's a romantic story, of course, but it may be at best only partially true. A brochure put together by Douglass reports that "the woodwork was carved under American supervision by carvers from Oberammergau, Germany." He has heard the story of the single carver but will only call it "tradition." *Indiana: A New Historical Guide* simply refers to the chapel's "hand-carved walnut pews."

Whatever the case, each stall has its own character. If the visitor wants to picture a young German wood-carver spending a number

THE CHAPEL. Saint James Chapel, on the campus of Howe Military School, located in northeastern Indiana.

IF YOU GO

of years meticulously preparing each stall as he comes and goes from his classes, so be it.

Frances Howe is referred to as the founder of what was then called Howe School. She founded the school for the training of Episcopalian priests following the death of her husband, John B. Howe, in 1883. When John's half-brother, James B. Howe, died in 1896, Illinois architect John Sutcliffe built the chapel in his honor. Frances died in 1904.

The cornerstone was laid on November 28, 1902. Bells in the present bell tower were a gift of James Howe and, after being moved to the tower, were first played on April 4, 1915.

The building has been enlarged several times—all of which the young Canacci explained to me. The chapel was first extended in 1903, the crypt under the building added in 1906, the chapel again enlarged along with the addition of the north extension and the organ chamber in 1909, and, finally, the south extension in 1914.

The school today has 170 coed students. Howe reports that 97 percent of its graduates go on to seek higher education.

Each weekend evening ends with vespers "to kind of wind down the day," Douglass explained. Howe residents use the chapel on Sundays at 9 a.m. and "the corps" at 11 a.m.

GETTING THERE: At Howe, go north on Indiana 9. The school is on the right after crossing Indiana 120. Saint James Memorial Chapel is at the first entrance.

INFORMATION: Visitors are welcome at any time. If the chapel is closed, go to the Administration Building for assistance. For more information, go to the Web site at http://www.howemilitary .com/ or call (260) 562–2131 or (888) 462–4693.

FEES: No charge for a tour.

NATURE CENTER. Some young park visitors wait for the park's nature center to open. It features exhibits about the park's natural and cultural history and is open daily in the summer and from Wednesday to Sunday during the school year.

Pokagon State Park, Angola

ANGOLA—It was fifty years ago that I first camped out at Pokagon State Park. Much about the park was the same when I recently visited there—although freshly painted and well kept. I wasn't aware of the popular toboggan run that first time—although it was there—and the camping area seemed less primitive than I recalled it.

The biggest change, though, was Potawatomi Inn.

What was once a typical state park inn now has expanded to become a resort and conference center. It offers 138 guest rooms and new conference and banquet rooms that can accommodate up to five hundred people. The expansion attempted to preserve the inn's original design as much as possible, although when you are in a corridor away from the lake it's more or less like being in any other fine hotel.

Naturally, given the lake setting, the recreational activities, and attractiveness of the facilities, getting rooms at the inn means planning ahead. You can book rooms two years ahead to the day, meaning you can call, for example, August 12 to request rooms for up to August 12 two years from now. The desk clerk at the inn told me most weekends are booked solid, although they do have some rooms available during weekdays. Cancellations do occur as a date arrives.

One of the inn's great assets is the view out onto Lake James as you sit on the large porch or stroll down toward the lake. Not all rooms can be on the lakeside, of course. The hotel has eight patio rooms on the ground floor, lakeside, that have direct outside access.

Twelve of the rooms are located in four buildings west of the inn in the woods near the toboggan run. No cooking, however, which usually is available in state park cabins.

An area is roped off on Lake James at the inn beach for swimming. The inn also offers an indoor pool, whirlpool, and sauna along with gift shop, dining room, courtyard cafe, rooms for activities, crafts and games, and a laundry room. Naturally, you also have access to the rest of the state park.

Seven trails—two easy and five moderate—range from one-half mile to two and one-half miles in length. One—the Bluebird Hills Trail—crosses rolling hills and grasslands and goes through a bluebird habitat. In the midst of the trail is a wetlands, restored from early farming lands.

Fishing is a popular sport at the park, and boats can be rented at the inn beach on Lake James's lower basin. No launching facilities for private boats are available in the park, but there's a pier for boats

POTAWATOMI INN. The expanded resort and conference center at Pokagon State Park is placed on a hill just beyond the Lonidaw Nature Preserve and gatehouse. Down the hill to the right is Lake James.

IF YOU GO

launched elsewhere on the Lake James chain of lakes. Saddle horses and hayrides, swimming at the beach on the upper basin, picnicking, a camp store, a nature center, and a campground complete the park's activities.

Pokagon is considered one of the Indiana state parks' winter wonderlands. The toboggan run is a 1,780-foot refrigerated twin track that's open weekends from Thanksgiving through February, with extended holiday hours. Visitors rent a park toboggan for the tracks or can use their own sleds on nearby hills.

Other winter sports include sledding, ice skating, cross-country skiing (you can rent them), camping, and ice fishing. The campground offers two hundred class A sites with electricity, toilets, hot water, and showers, along with seventy-three class B sites—everything but electricity. It also has a youth tent area—reservable May through October—where campers must be under adult supervision.

The 1,203-acre park, established in 1925, is west of Interstate 69 just before it crosses into Michigan. The southern and western park borders are Lake James's three basins and, to the northwest, Snow Lake. Angola is five miles south on U.S. 27.

GETTING THERE: Located off Interstate 69 north of Angola. Use exit 154 west into the park.

INFORMATION: The telephone number for the state park is (260) 833–2012. The number for Potawatomi Inn is toll-free (877) 768–2928. Inn reservations also may be made at http://www.indianainns.com/.

FEES: Park admission charged.

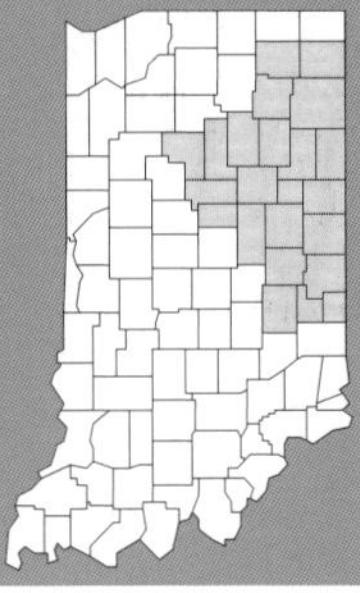

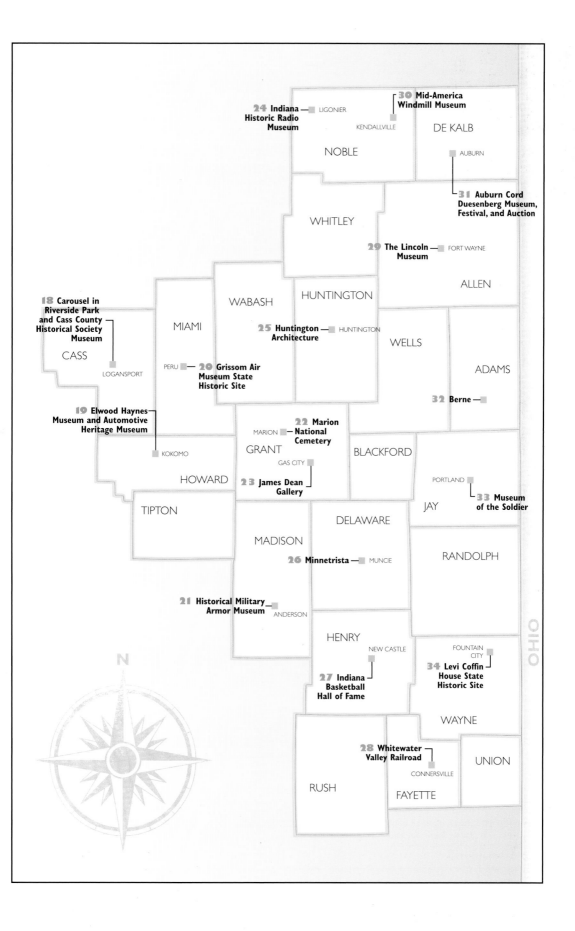

24 Indiana — Historic Radio Museum

LIGONIER

30 Mid-America Windmill Museum

KENDALLVILLE

DE KALB

AUBURN

NOBLE

31 Auburn Cord Duesenberg Museum, Festival, and Auction

WHITLEY

29 The Lincoln Museum

FORT WAYNE

ALLEN

18 Carousel in Riverside Park and Cass County Historical Society Museum

WABASH

HUNTINGTON

MIAMI

25 Huntington Architecture

HUNTINGTON

WELLS

CASS

LOGANSPORT

PERU

20 Grissom Air Museum State Historic Site

ADAMS

32 Berne —

19 Elwood Haynes Museum and Automotive Heritage Museum

KOKOMO

22 Marion National Cemetery

MARION

GRANT

BLACKFORD

PORTLAND

23 James Dean Gallery

GAS CITY

33 Museum of the Soldier

HOWARD

JAY

TIPTON

DELAWARE

RANDOLPH

MADISON

26 Minnetrista —

MUNCIE

21 Historical Military Armor Museum

ANDERSON

HENRY

NEW CASTLE

FOUNTAIN CITY

34 Levi Coffin House State Historic Site

27 Indiana Basketball Hall of Fame

WAYNE

28 Whitewater Valley Railroad

UNION

CONNERSVILLE

RUSH

FAYETTE

OHIO

N

REACHING OUT. Grabbing a brass ring gives the carousel rider a free ride.

SURVIVOR. This piano, now in the Cass County Museum, was the first in Logansport, arriving in the mid-1830s. It survived a dunking in the Mississippi River as it was being transferred at New Orleans.

WOMEN'S SOFTBALL. Softball uniform worn by Ilean Babb during Logansport's softball heyday during the mid-twentieth century.

Carousel in Riverside Park and Cass County Historical Society Museum, Logansport

LOGANSPORT—The idea is to catch the brass ring as you ride your hand-carved animal around the Dentzel Carousel in Riverside Park. Getting a ring isn't the problem. You simply stretch to the right and snag a ring from an extended holder. When the holder was loaded before the ride began, however, all the rings were silver with the exception of the brass one. The trick is to get that one so your next ride is free.

Whether you get the brass ring or not—and certainly it's a big deal to the children who ride to get one—most people seem to find the greatest pleasure in just watching the carousel as it goes round and round. After all, it is a National Historic Landmark. The animals, created by German carver Gustav Dentzel's company, are known for their size and their realistic qualities.

The big year for carousels in the United States was 1904 at the World's Fair in Saint Louis. Soon every community wanted one. Dentzel, who came to the United States from Germany in 1860, was one of the country's major carvers and builders. His carousels, mostly housed in pavilions, were created between 1870 and 1928.

The carousel in Riverside Park and its forty-two animals was first a Fort Wayne attraction before it was moved to Logansport in 1919. Its history has been traced back to at least 1902, although the carved animals may have been created even earlier.

The carousel is now housed in the McHale Community Complex, finished in 1995 with community and Indiana Historic Landmarks Foundation of Indiana support. The building has climate control to protect the wooden, hand-carved animals. They are monitored every year, with a constant restoration process in place. The carousel operates from Memorial Day to Labor Day and can be rented for special events.

A trip to Logansport also can include a visit to the Cass County Historical Society Museum, located in the Jerolaman-Long House near the downtown.

It is one of Logansport's oldest buildings, constructed in 1853 by Doctor George Jerolaman, who arrived in the city in 1832, just five years after the community was platted. The house underwent extensive remodeling in 1896 with the addition of both first- and second-floor rooms, a change in the staircase, and indoor plumbing—one of the first houses in the city with this convenience. The house was given to the historical society in 1967 in memory of Benjamin and Lucy Long, who had purchased it in 1929.

The historical society has a printed, eight-page self-guided tour for the house. The exhibits, with extensive descriptions, are spread over the basement and the first and second floors with rooms dedicated to various

MUSEUM BUILDING. Log buildings on the grounds of the **Cass County Historical Society Museum in Logansport.** To the right is a two-story cabin. Behind it is a barn with a loft.

IF YOU GO

areas, including a medical office, the Civil War, religion, music, taxidermy, the military, Native American collections, and toys.

On the first floor in the parlor are four of the society's five George Winter paintings. Winter was a prominent artist in the first half of the nineteenth century and is best known for his paintings of Native Americans and Wabash Valley scenes. The fifth Winter painting, hanging in the gift shop, is of the first Logansport mayor, Colonel Jordan Vigus.

One of the second-floor museum highlights is Logansport's first piano. It was moved by steamboat in the mid-1830s from the manufacturer in Philadelphia and shipped to New Orleans for its trip up the Mississippi River. While workmen were unloading it, the piano fell into the water, and they had to wait until the water receded to retrieve it. Some water damage still can be seen. That didn't mean it couldn't be played when it finally arrived in Logansport, however, as its owner, General Hyacinth Lasselle, enjoyed listening to its sound.

Items from the time that Logansport was widely regarded as the softball capital of the state from the 1940s to the 1960s are another museum feature. Women's fast-pitch softball often drew more than four thousand people to a game.

Two log buildings—one a two-story cabin and the other a barn with a loft—also are on the grounds, as well as a brick carriage house that contains a Revere, an automobile manufactured in Logansport.

GETTING THERE: The Cass County Historical Society Museum is five blocks west of Indiana 25 at Market and Tenth streets. Riverside Park is four blocks north along the Eel River.

INFORMATION: Carousel summer hours are Monday through Friday, 6 p.m. to 9 p.m.; Saturday and Sunday, 1 p.m. to 9 p.m. During September and October, hours are Saturday and Sunday, 1 p.m. to 5 p.m. Call (574) 753–8725. The Cass County Historical Society Museum is open Tuesday through Saturday, 1 p.m. to 5 p.m., and the first Monday of the month from 1 p.m. to 7 p.m. It is closed during January, February, and on holidays.

FEES: A charge for carousel rides. Contributions are welcomed at the museum.

ELWOOD HAYNES MUSEUM HAS BEEN DESIGNATED AN HISTORICAL LANDMARK BY AMERICAN SOCIETY FOR METALS

THIS SITE COMMEMORATES THE ACHIEVEMENTS OF ELWOOD HAYNES WHO INVENTED THE COBALT BASE ALLOYS CALLED "STELLITE" IN THE PERIOD 1899 TO 1915. FROM THEIR INITIAL APPLICATION OF METALWORKING TOOLS, THESE ALLOYS PROVIDED THE BASIS FOR THE DEVELOPMENT OF SUPER ALLOYS USED IN GAS TURBINES, AEROSPACE VEHICLES AND PROSTHETIC DEVICES.
1985

HE DEFINITELY GETS CREDIT FOR THIS ONE. Although argument exists over who first invented the automobile and stainless steel, the American Society for Metals credits Elwood Haynes with inventing stellite. This plaque is mounted on his museum home in Kokomo.

NOTICE SOMETHING DIFFERENT? The driver sits in the backseat of this 1905 Haynes automobile. It has a front "mother-in-law" seat. The car is in the sunroom of the Haynes museum.

Elwood Haynes Museum and Automotive Heritage Museum, Kokomo

KOKOMO—The Portland, Indiana, native was thirty-three years old when the Indiana Natural Gas Company in 1890 named him field superintendent with headquarters in Greentown. Within a year Elwood Haynes had come up with a way to dry gas by refrigeration to prevent pipeline freezing. The process left something called gasoline.

Determined to use this by-product, Haynes began drawing up plans for a horseless carriage operated by a gasoline-powered engine. He moved to Kokomo, hired the Apperson brothers to build his carriage, and on July 4, 1894, towed his contraption out to the Pumpkinvine Pike. Haynes started his carriage and, on a rut-filled road, drove six miles at six to seven miles per hour.

Although many claims exist over who invented the automobile, Kokomo is satisfied that Haynes's drive was the first road test of the first commercially successful automobile.

Then in 1906, Haynes discovered an alloy, called stellite, that could withstand heat and stress and virtually eliminate erosion. Stellite alloys still are in use today, for example, in the blades of the turbines powering fuel pumps in liquid-propelled missiles such as those used in the rockets fired into space. It was used for the moon buggy, and as Kay Frazer, Elwood Haynes Museum director, puts it: "Haynes's inventions go from the Pumpkinvine Pike to the Sea of Tranquility."

It was six years later, in 1912, that Haynes was told by his wife, so the story goes, to do something really useful. Mrs. Haynes was tired of polishing silver all the time, so he came up with stainless steel tableware especially for her. Again, exactly who created the first stainless steel is arguable, as a number of experiments were under way around the world at about the same time. Nevertheless, Haynes won the patent rights.

Not bad for a young Portland man—automobiles, stellite, and stainless steel.

The house where Haynes lived during the early 1900s has become the Elwood Haynes Museum. Many of the items on the first floor of the house were owned and used by the Haynes family. The house was given to the city of Kokomo in 1965 by a Haynes daughter, Bernice.

In the sunroom is a 1905 Haynes auto. The driver sits in the backseat of the vehicle, which has a front "mother-in-law" seat and, of all things for a 1905 car, a steering wheel that tilts. In the room, there's also an early traffic signal.

The second floor exhibits Kokomo-produced items, many of which contributed to the Kokomo slogan of a "City of Firsts"—pneu-

SOME GRAND CARS. A Haynes 1923 touring car, center of photo, looks ready to go. That's a 1921 Haynes automobile to the left in the Automotive Heritage Museum in Kokomo. To the right is a low-slung 1911 Haynes runabout with a 1923 Apperson Jack Rabbit, also a touring car, behind it.

matic tire, carburetor, American howitzer shell, canned tomato juice, mechanical corn picker, push-button car radio, all-metal lifeboat and raft, signal-seeking car radio, and all-transistor car radio.

Several miles north on U.S. 31 near the edge of Kokomo, in a former Big R commercial building, is the Automotive Heritage Museum, which highlights historical automobiles. It shares the building with the Johanning Civic Center, site of meetings and conventions.

In the museum, there's a facade of the house where Haynes lived as he built his first automobile. An 1897 Haynes-Apperson auto body, believed to be the fourth car they built, is one of the automotive features, along with other early cars. Most are restored models, of course, but the museum has a 1940 Chevrolet in its original condition. On loan from the Indianapolis Motor Speedway Hall of Fame Museum is a 1900 Haynes-Apperson auto.

Automobiles were manufactured in Indiana cities up through the 1960s. Although Kokomo's production ended in 1925 with 75,850 cars made, the community remained closely connected in the early twenty-first century to the automobile industry with Delphi-Delco and Chrysler plants.

GETTING THERE: At the north edge of Kokomo is the Automotive Heritage Museum at 1500 N. U.S. 31. To go to the Elwood Haynes Museum, turn west on Boulevard Street off U.S. 31. Go about two miles to the corner of Boulevard and Webster streets. The museum is at 1915 S. Webster Street.

INFORMATION: The automotive museum is open 10 a.m. to 5 p.m. daily and is closed Christmas Day and New Year's Day. Telephone (765) 454–9999 or fax (765) 454–9956. The Haynes museum is open Tuesday through Saturday from 8 a.m. to 4 p.m. and Sunday, 1 p.m. to 5 p.m. Its telephone number is (765) 456–7500.

FEES: The automotive museum has an admission charge. The Haynes museum does not have an admission fee.

A BLUE ANGEL. A Grumman FII-F Tiger aircraft used by the famed Blue Angels in aerial shows.

AND ONE SCREW. Terry L. Woodling of Warsaw, Indiana, made this Lear jet model on display at the Grissom Air Museum. He used 82,500 toothpicks and one screw. Visitors are asked to spot the screw. (Hint: Look up from directly underneath.)

A CHILD'S SILK DRESS IN AN AIR MUSEUM? In flying's early days, it was customary if a pilot lived after bailing out from a plane to use silk from the parachute for a dress for a family member. When William Kepner, a Hoosier, survived his sixty thousand-foot *Explorer* balloon descent and parachute jump in 1934, he gave the parachute silk to his seven-year-old niece, Norma Kepner. Her mother made the dress.

Grissom Air Museum and State Historic Site, Peru

PERU—He was an authentic Miami County military hero, so it's little wonder that his story is part of the Grissom Air Museum and State Historic Site at the Grissom Air Reserve Base.

In 1909 William Kepner left his Miami County home to enlist as a private in the Marine Corps. He served as an infantry captain in World War I, but it was in the skies where he ultimately became an aviation hero, first in dirigibles and balloons and then naval aircraft.

In World War II he commanded the Eighth Air Force. After the war, he was in charge of the atomic bomb tests at Bikini Atoll and of all atomic weapons development by the U.S. Air Force. He reached the rank of three-star general.

In a room of the museum, largely dedicated to Kepner's exploits, are his forty American and foreign service decorations, signed photographs from presidents and military and other world leaders, and a depiction of his best-known exploit.

That was in 1934, when Kepner commanded the balloon, *Explorer I*, as it rose to a height of sixty thousand-plus feet. When he saw the balloon's fabric beginning to rip, Kepner calmly proclaimed the mission at an end. Since the rip was near the base of the balloon, the three-man crew's emergency parachute exit wouldn't work until they reached about five thousand feet. Kepner had to force out the second crew member, caught in the escape hatch, from the rapidly descending balloon, but they all landed safely.

The *Explorer I* adventure fixed Kepner's reputation as one of aviation's pioneers. He ended his military career as commander of the Alaskan Air Command. He died in 1982 at age eighty-nine.

The museum, located on a drive exiting U.S. 31 north of Kokomo, is much more than the story of Kepner, however.

A state historic site, the museum features the story of—and actual aircraft from—World War II through the Gulf War. It's easier to see them now, since a forty-foot observation tower has been opened with a commanding view of the parked aircraft.

On the grounds are a B-17 Flying Fortress; B-25 Mitchell bomber; B-47 stratojet bomber; B-58 delta-winged Hustler bomber; C-1, C-47, and C-119 cargo planes; EC-135 airborne command post from Desert Storm; F-4, F-11, F-14, F-84, F-100, F-101, and F-105 fighters; KC-97 aerial refueling tanker; O-2 observation plane; T-33 and T-37 trainers; U-3 and YS-11 for light cargo and passengers; A-10 Warthog attack plane; and Huey and Piasecki helicopters.

Inside the museum are artifacts from military aviation history, including aviation armaments, flight trainers, uniforms, survival gear, engines,

MUSEUM AIRCRAFT. Some of the military aircraft at the Grissom Air Museum as seen from the observation tower. The museum and parking area are in the background.

art, and models. One feature is the propeller from the second Wright plane in 1908. A theater can be used for lectures and films, and the museum also has its own gift shop.

The first place youngsters head toward is the cockpit of a Phantom jet, where they can climb into the pilot's seat to let their imaginations take over.

The facility was opened in 1942 to train navy pilots but closed with the end of World War II. It was activated by the air force in 1953 as Bunker Hill Air Force Base. Later, it was renamed to honor Hoosier native Virgil I. "Gus" Grissom, one of the original seven Mercury astronauts, who died in an Apollo command module training accident in 1967. The field was realigned as an air reserve base in 1994 and became a state historic site in 1991.

Much of the former air force base now is the Aeroplex Industrial Park. Air force reserves still use the airfield, flying KC-135 aerial refueling tankers. The observation tower, at one time a security tower for the airbase, allows a long look down the runway used by the reserves.

GETTING THERE: The site is located north of Kokomo on U.S. 31.

INFORMATION: The museum is open Tuesday through Sunday, 10 a.m. to 4 p.m., mid-February through late December. For information, call (765) 689–8011. The Web site is http://www .grissomairmuseum.com/.

FEES: Admission charged and also a charge to climb the observation tower.

THE WATER TANK. First light tank used in World War I, supposedly to carry water to the front lines but actually intended to be a weapon of war. It was constructed by two builders, one fabricating the bottom and the other the top.

THREE WARS. On the grounds near the entrance to Joe McClain's Historical Military Armor Museum in Anderson are weapons used in three wars—a Huey helicopter from Vietnam, a Russian cannon captured at Kuwait City in Desert Storm, and a smaller cannon, a three-inch anti-tank gun used in World War II.

Historical Military Armor Museum, Anderson

ANDERSON—It was a collection that turned into an avocation and now has become an obsession. That's how Joe McClain explains his fascination for his Historical Military Armor Museum, located on Anderson's north side.

McClain has put together one of the top five armored museums in the nation. "Our interior space and number of pieces is larger than Fort Knox or Aberdeen Proving Grounds," he says.

Opened in 1989, the museum occupies about 30,000 square feet of the 92,000-square-foot former Lynch Manufacturing Corporation building. McClain says his purpose is "preserving history." About 10,000 people a year visit the museum.

"You can track the evolution of the light tank over eighty-five years from the beginning up to the present—World War I up to the M-551 Sheridan, a 'current issue' tank from Desert Storm. You also can follow the fifty years of history of the main battle tanks from the M-48 [1950s] through the M-60 [1960s] up to the Abrams, 'current issue,'" says McClain. The Abrams, a sixty-three-ton monster, is the only one in private hands, McClain says.

The tanks are lined up against two walls, light tanks along the west wall and main battle tanks—at almost twice the tonnage—along the east wall of the museum.

Obtaining the tanks for the museum has been no simple matter. First, McClain has to obtain a federal permit to purchase an armored vehicle. Most of his purchases come, he says, after base commanders call to say they have a vehicle.

"This is a tight-knit group," McClain says. "There aren't many of us." From notification until arrival of the equipment usually takes about two years, he notes.

One of the first vehicles you see when you enter the main museum building is the prototype of today's modern tank. The builders, to confuse the Germans in World War I, said it would be used as a "water tank" to carry water to the troops in the trenches. In fact, it was intended to be a weapon of war, and it quickly became known simply as a tank. The six-ton tank was built in 1917. It carried two men, could go 3.4 miles per hour, and had as its armament a machine gun. Only five of these tanks exist today.

The museum has on its property seven "Serial No. 1" vehicles—in other words, the first ones produced. Three currently are on display, including two amphibious track vehicles and a rocket launcher. (Two boys leaving the museum agreed the rocket launcher was their favor-

CURRENT ISSUE. Joe McClain stands next to the biggest tank in the armor museum, the more than sixty-ton Abrams, used in Desert Storm.

ite, probably, McClain theorized, because it most closely resembled vehicles they had seen on television or models they might own.)

One of the non-American vehicles is a BTR-40 Russian armored car and troop carrier. First put into use in the late 1940s, the vehicles were purchased by the Syrians and used in battles against the Israelis. McClain purchased this car from Israel, whose troops had captured it. He has restored its Russian designations.

McClain's military interests are deep-seated thanks in part to his own period of service in Vietnam with the U. S. Navy. His mother, Virginia McClain, was a nurse in World War II, creating a frontline M*A*S*H unit and serving in North Africa and Europe. She was one of the first into the German concentration camp of Dachau and was awarded the Bronze Star for her heroism.

McClain's father, Senior Master Sergeant F. J. "Mac" McClain, was one of the "Flying Sergeants," given temporary rank as officers to fly fighters in the South Pacific. McClain says his father was credited with sinking a Japanese battleship in the Battle of the Coral Sea.

Aircraft and armored vehicles are parked near the entrance to the museum. One is a Mohawk OV1 aircraft used in secret reconnaissance missions in Vietnam. "It was in perfect shape three or four years ago before they flew it into the Anderson Airport and crash-landed it," he says with a shrug of his shoulders.

Oh, yes, those boys who liked the rocket launcher. They had another favorite, too, but one that seems strangely out of place at a military armor museum.

It was Terra, an eight-year-old lioness McClain keeps at the museum. She was "the runt of a litter" when he got her as a one-day-old cub. (McClain also has an endangered species license.)

GETTING THERE: On Business Indiana 9 at the north side of Anderson, turn east at School Street. Go one block and turn south onto Crystal Street.

INFORMATION: Call (765) 649–TANK (8265). The museum is open Tuesday, Thursday, and Saturday from 1 p.m. to 4 p.m. Group tours of ten or more by appointment.

FEES: Admission charged.

SILENT CIRCLE MONUMENT. Three militiamen with rifles and flag stand guard in this monument dedicated July 23, 1888. The inscription reads "In memory of the men who offered their lives in defense of their country."

FIRST GOVERNOR. Justin H. Chapman, the first governor of the Marion National Soldiers' Home—now the Veterans Affairs Medical Center—is buried, along with his wife, Kate, in this fenced grave at the Marion National Cemetery. He was discharged from the army in 1868 and served at the Marion home from 1891 until his death in 1904.

Marion National Cemetery, Marion

MARION—If you make a trip to the Marion National Cemetery—where some eight thousand veterans are buried from America's conflicts stretching back to the Civil War—on Memorial Day, you'll notice that every grave has beside it a small American flag.

That's because volunteers from the Boy Scouts, Girl Scouts, Veterans of Foreign Wars, and the American Legion showed up at the cemetery in the early morning hours to place flags at each grave.

The Memorial Day weekend continues on Monday with the traditional 11 a.m. ceremony. The program includes a Memorial Day message and the placing of wreaths followed by lowering the flag and playing "Taps." The Indiana National Guard Reserves assist in this nationwide salute to veterans.

The Marion cemetery, one of 135 national cemeteries, is part of the National Cemetery Administration of the U.S. Department of Veterans Affairs. Since this cemetery was established in 1890, it mostly has been in the shadow of its next-door neighbor, variously referred to over the years by those in Marion as the Old Soldiers' Home or the VA Hospital and, today, by its official title as the Northern Indiana Health Care System, Department of Veterans Affairs Medical Center.

Marion got the medical center and cemetery because a local attorney and legislator, Colonel George W. Steele, convinced Congress to establish a soldiers' home in Grant County. Steele later became the governor of the Oklahoma Territory.

The Marion soldiers' home was one of the first six opened in the United States in the years following the Civil War. In 1920 the soldiers' home officially became known as the Marion Sanatorium, but it was never called that locally.

When I was a boy growing up in Marion, I made the assumption that the cemetery was there only to provide graves when veterans at the hospital died. I was right about the very early years of the hospital—long before I was born. I was wrong about the more recent past.

Some of those buried there did, indeed, die while they were at the Marion medical center. But the fact is that today any honorably discharged veteran can be buried without cost in any one of the 135 national cemeteries with available space—122 of them maintained by the National Cemetery Administration, with most of the others at battlefield sites maintained by the National Park Service. Burial includes opening and closing the grave, a headstone or marker, and burial flag.

GRAVESTONES, ROW ON ROW. Part of the markers in the Marion National Cemetery, where veterans from the Civil War on are buried. The present burial grounds are expected to be filled around 2045.

Director Brian G. Moore, who has been at the Marion cemetery since 2004, says he frequently will receive a call from a relative who thinks a veteran who was at the Marion medical center certainly must be buried in the cemetery there. "That's possible but not always true," he says.

Not everyone comes to see a loved one's grave when the cemetery office is open (8 a.m. to 4:30 p.m. Monday through Friday). To help in locating graves, a "grave locator" booklet can be found in a box outside the office door.

Eleven more VA cemeteries are to be created in the United States in the immediate years ahead, including those in Atlanta, Detroit, Miami, Sacramento, Pittsburgh, and Oklahoma City.

Moore says it's expected the Marion burial grounds of nearly forty acres will be filled by 2045 at the present rate of around five burials a week. "Then we will probably get more land expansion. That will likely be the land where these old buildings are now at the hospital since the hospital has all been moved up to the front now [toward Lincoln Boulevard]. So that land will come to the cemetery," he says.

IF YOU GO

GETTING THERE: The cemetery entrance is off East Thirty-eighth Street in southeast Marion.

INFORMATION: Office hours are 8 a.m. to 4:30 p.m. Monday through Friday and 8 a.m. to 7 p.m. Memorial Day. Call (765) 674–0284 or (765) 674–3321, ext. 3546. Fax (765) 674–4521. The cemetery office's mailing address is 1700 E. Thirty-eighth Street, Marion, Indiana 46953.

FEES: None.

TRIBUTE TO STAR. This art deco building houses the world's largest collection of James Dean memorabilia and souvenirs.

TAKE A LOOK. Visitors look over one of the six rooms of the James Dean Gallery, interpreting the career of the Marion-born actor.

THREE MOVIES. Each of James Dean's three motion pictures—*East of Eden, Rebel without a Cause,* and *Giant*—has its own display area in the James Dean Gallery.

James Dean Gallery, Gas City

GAS CITY—He made but three motion pictures, only one of which had been released at the time of his death at age twenty-four in a California automobile accident on September 30, 1955. Yet in the years that have followed, the James Dean legend of the young rebel has become a worldwide phenomenon that almost defies description.

The subject of hundreds, if not thousands, of magazine covers and articles in every imaginable language around the globe; the second Hollywood legends stamp issued by the U.S. Postal Service—only after Marilyn Monroe; the object of look-alike contests that perhaps equal those of Elvis Presley—the list about Dean's impact goes on and on.

Japanese travelers have been known to fly into Indianapolis, rent a taxi to central Indiana, visit spots where Dean hung out as a high school student, and, of course, go to see his grave site at Fairmount's Park Cemetery—and head back to Japan.

A few years ago, I talked with a woman from South America visiting in Fairmount. She was spending a week in this Grant County town because she wanted to walk the streets, eat in the cafés, and take in the sights that Dean might have. Her itinerary for her trip was New York, Paris, and Fairmount!

Now, fifty-one years after his death, visitors to Indiana are finding the James Dean story even more accessible as they drive up and down Interstate 69. The new James Dean Gallery—the former gallery was located in Fairmount—opened May 2004 at the interstate's exit 59 at Gas City/Upland.

The original gallery opened in 1988 in near-downtown Fairmount and consistently drew ten thousand visitors or more annually. The old gallery has become the "Rebel, Rebel"—named for a David Bowie song—and is the home of 1950s and 1960s memorabilia and collectibles as well as a Dean gift shop.

The Dean gallery's curator, David Loehr, says the growth of his collection and the ever-increasing popularity of the Indiana-born actor necessitated more space and more accessibility to the public. It is the world's largest Dean collection and exhibit, he says.

The gallery is housed in a 7,200-square-foot art deco building. Inside is a six-room interpretive display with three rooms dedicated to Dean's three motion pictures, a research library, galleries of memorabilia about Dean, and a thirty-five-seat theater where some of his earlier television shows and screen tests can be seen. Naturally, an extensive gift shop is also included.

RIBBON CUTTER. David Loehr, James Dean Gallery curator, cuts the ribbon at the grand opening to launch the new James Dean Gallery.

A showstopper among the Dean artifacts is the replica of Dean's 1955 Porsche 550 Spyder, which the actor was driving when he was killed in the California automobile accident.

The intersection of Interstate 69 and Indiana 22 will have other additions coming along soon. A 1950s diner and an ice cream parlor are in the works while a medical center also has been constructed. Landowner Doctor B. D. Patel says the diner and ice cream parlor "would keep up with the theme of the gallery and be a fantastic addition."

IF YOU GO

GETTING THERE: Use Interstate 69's exit 59 at Gas City/Upland. The gallery is located at the northeast corner, behind the Best Western Hotel.

INFORMATION: Call (765) 998–2080. The gallery is open 9 a.m. to 6 p.m. every day. The gallery's Web site is http://www.jamesdeangallery.com./ Telephone for "Rebel, Rebel" is (765) 948–3326.

FEES: Admission charged for the gallery.

DISPLAY ROOM. The famous RCA dog and speaker logo is in the fore-front of the main display room of the Indiana Historic Radio Museum in Ligonier. Floor models surround the center display area of the museum.

MUSEUM'S HOME. The Indiana Historic Radio Museum is located in a former automobile repair shop and gasoline station. Herbert Duesler, who owned the station for three years until 1942, chats with a visitor.

THE BEST. The "Duesenberg" of radios was this 1936 Scott radio, manufactured in Chicago. It sold for $700. The information card on the twenty-speaker, chrome-finished, tube set claims it can outperform a good number of modern radios. Museum volunteer Herbert Duesler stands next to the radio.

Indiana Historic Radio Museum, Ligonier

LIGONIER—It's Sunday evening in America. Dinner is over and the dishes are washed. Now, everyone in the family has gathered around the set. They're ready for an evening's entertainment.

But it isn't television. It's radio.

You have to be of a certain age to remember those days—the 1930s, 1940s, and early 1950s—of radio's golden age, when it brought fast-breaking news, family entertainment, and an enlarged view of a big, wide world to a nation that, in many ways, had been isolated.

It was radio that carried the voice of the British king, saying he would give up the throne "for the woman I love." It was radio where the name of Joe Louis and his "bum of the month" club captured the imagination of sports fans. It was radio that allowed the rest of the world to hear the bombs falling on London in 1940. It was radio that announced to a stunned American nation on Sunday, December 7, 1941, that the Japanese had attacked Pearl Harbor and the United States was at war. It was radio that told an equally stunned nation four years later that FDR—Franklin Delano Roosevelt—the only president many people had known, had died as World War II neared its end.

It was radio's family entertainment, however, that had the nation enthralled on Sunday nights. Walter Winchell with his "let's go to press, Mr. and Mrs. America"; Jack Benny and his self-deprecating humor; Edgar Bergen and his sidekick, Charlie McCarthy—the list goes on.

You can't recapture those days by traveling Indiana, but you can see the radio sets Americans used down through the generations when you visit Ligonier's Indiana Historic Radio Museum. It's housed in a former gasoline station and auto-repair shop that Herbert Duesler owned for three years until he went into military service in 1942.

On a trip there, I was fortunate to talk with Duesler. At the last minute, he had volunteered to staff the museum that day when the regular volunteer couldn't be there. "I can't tell you much about radios," he admitted. He did recall, though, "working on Model T Fords and selling gasoline at seven gallons for a dollar." A veteran of the Battle of the Bulge, he was a machine gunner in a unit from which four of eight survived.

In more recent years, the Ligonier building, which also houses the Ligonier Visitors Center, sat empty. The museum opened in 1998.

"We get one hundred to two hundred visitors a month," Doctor Floyd Warren, another staff volunteer, told me on another day. "Many of them are senior citizens' bus tours and schoolchildren. Frequently, the tours are from out of state."

ROWS OF RADIOS. Radios sit along one wall of the Indiana Historic Radio Museum in Ligonier, part of the total display of more than four hundred models.

IF YOU GO

More than four hundred radios are on display, including some of the first handcrafted, crystal-set models. Specialty radios are a feature, along with floor and table sets, up through transistor radios, which revolutionized the industry.

The world's first all-transistor radio, the TR-1, on display at the museum, has a solid Hoosier connection. It was produced in Indianapolis by the Regency Company in 1954 for sale during the Christmas season. It cost $49.95, or about $200 in today's money.

Some of the radios required considerable additional equipment. For example, a 1924 Atwater Kent, model 12, manufactured in Philadelphia, before its use needed a set of tubes, two B batteries, one C battery, one to four A batteries, a horn speaker, headphones, and an antenna system. The model 12 cost $105 new. Tubes, batteries, speaker, and antenna would add another $75 to $100. That was at a time when wages sometimes were no more than $5 a day and a new automobile might be purchased for around $300. So the better radios could only be afforded by the few.

Still, according to one statistic at the museum, in 1938 the 130 million people in the United States owned 38.5 million radios—or one for every three and a half people. By comparison, 165 million Russians had 350,000 radios—one for every 470 people.

GETTING THERE: Located on Indiana 5 in Ligonier, the museum is on the west at Union Street. Its address is 800 Lincoln Way South, Ligonier, Indiana 46767.

INFORMATION: The museum is open Saturday, 10 a.m. to 2 p.m., November through April, and Tuesday, Wednesday, and Saturday, 10 a.m. to 3 p.m., May through October. It is handicapped accessible. For information, call toll-free (888) 417–3562 or go to the Web site, http://home.att.net/~indianahistoricalradio/ihrp6mus.htm

FEES: Free.

ALSO BUILT IN 1904. This is the Huntington City Building. Its high towers are typical of the Richardsonian Romanesque architectural style. It is two blocks west of the county courthouse.

YES, IT'S AN OPERA HOUSE. A well-known actress, Minnie Maddern, was the first performer in the Huntington Opera House, located on the second floor of this building, constructed in 1881.

Huntington Architecture, Huntington

HUNTINGTON—Dozens of Indiana towns have historic buildings. Some even have a National Register Historic District—a large number of historic buildings concentrated in an area. But it's difficult to believe any community has a better walking-tour guide for its buildings than Huntington.

The single-sheet, eighteen-by-twenty-three-inch guide contains a walking-tour map of the Courthouse Square National Register Historic District—not that unusual. What makes it distinctive, however, are the color photographs and descriptions of many of its nineteenth- and early-twentieth-century buildings on the tour. Each is numbered to correspond with its place on the map.

The guide, which folds down to pocket size, has on the other side a map showing the greater Huntington area, again with photos and descriptions of historic buildings.

So, if you spent some time looking at these buildings, what would you see?

Probably the most important building—called the "crown jewel" in the historic district—is the Huntington County Courthouse. Built from 1904 to 1906, it is in the neoclassic style of the 1900 to 1920 period of architecture. It depicts majesty as it rises above the courthouse square—four floors, dome, and cupola. It is constructed of Bedford limestone.

Inside the courthouse, the attention to detail and design continues. Marble stairs, leaded art-glass ceilings, the dome over the central rotunda—all speak of an important building meant to be the center of the county.

Another 1904 structure is the City Building and Fire Station, located two blocks to the west of the courthouse. It is Richardsonian Romanesque in architectural style with high, pointed towers and round arches. While the courthouse occupies an entire block and is set back from the street in typical Indiana courthouse-square style, the city building is only a sidewalk away from the street.

While it might be difficult to believe today, most Indiana towns, even small ones, had an opera house at the turn of the last century. Huntington was no exception. The Opera House Building, one block north of the courthouse, opened in 1881 with performance space on the second floor and small businesses on the first. Today, the second floor has been divided into apartments.

One of the oldest buildings in the district is the former Hotel Huntington, just north of the city building. The central part was con-

HUNTINGTON COUNTY COURTHOUSE. Huntington County, named for Samuel Huntington, a signer of the Declaration of Independence, has retained its 1904 courthouse. Housed on the second floor is the restored Grand Army of the Republic Room, a repository for Civil War memorabilia.

IF YOU GO

structed in 1848, built in the Greek Revival style. Additions were constructed between 1883 and 1900. Its Market Street facade has pedimented windows—low-pitched gables extending over the top of each window. Another former hotel is the Hotel LaFontaine, a five-story structure built in 1925 and considered the most prestigious of Huntington's buildings. Now it is a senior living center, where the lobby and ballrooms have been meticulously restored to their original grandeur.

There's more—in all, thirty properties and districts are included in the tour guide. Walking around and looking at buildings isn't something that's going to appeal to everyone, of course. But what about coupling it with a stop at Nick's Kitchen on North Jefferson Street, right in the heart of the historic district? That's where Dan Quayle "historically" used to show up on election morning after he had cast his ballot.

Speaking of Quayle, the Dan Quayle Center is the home of the United States Vice Presidential Museum, the only vice presidential museum in the nation, and is another spot to visit. The museum, located in the former Christian Science Church just north of downtown, opened in 1993. Since then, thousands of visitors from all fifty states and many other countries have gone through the two public floors of the museum.

GETTING THERE: Indiana 5 goes directly into Huntington and the Huntington Courthouse Square National Register Historic District. The office of the Visitor and Convention Bureau is at 407 N. Jefferson Street, a one-way street going south.

INFORMATION: The visitor and convention office is open Monday through Friday, 9 a.m. to 5 p.m. The telephone number is (800) 848–4282, and the Web site is http://www.visithuntington.org/.

FEES: No charge for a copy of the tour guide.

IMPOSING COLUMNS. These six stone columns, all that remain from the front portico of the Frank C. Ball home, mark the entrance to Minnetrista Cultural Center.

CATALYST. Minnetrista Cultural Center, dedicated in 1988 on the site of the Frank C. and Bessie Ball home, is seen behind the newly dedicated sculpture, *Catalyst*. Minnetrista campus tours begin here.

A MYSTERY, MAYBE? Young visitors especially are fascinated by this hidden-door bookcase at the George A. Ball home at Minnetrista. It opens into a small passageway to a screened-in porch, seen beyond the regular open door.

Minnetrista, Muncie

MUNCIE—You say you want to take a half-day tour of Minnetrista so you can go along as slowly as you wish, trying not to miss anything? That's okay.

No? You don't have that kind of time? You have an hour at best? Well, that's okay, too. One of the attributes of Minnetrista tours is that they can be as short or as long as the visitor has time for.

First, some definitions may be in order.

It isn't Minnetrista Cultural Center any more. Yes, there is a Minnetrista Cultural Center—that large, interesting-looking building on the circle drive behind the six stone columns off Minnetrista Parkway. It is but one part, however, of the Minnetrista campus, extending from Wheeling Avenue on the west to Walnut Street on the east and from White River on the south to Minnetrista Parkway and Centennial Avenue on the north.

A recent decision was made to call the entire complex Minnetrista— East Central Indiana's Center for Natural and Cultural Heritage.

No one can be absolutely positive where the word "Minnetrista" comes from—the name given the area and more specifically the residence of early Muncie glass manufacturer Frank C. Ball and his family. The most likely definition is that it's a combination of words, meaning "a gathering place by the water."

Frank's residence is the only one of the five Ball brothers' homes no longer existing on the north bluff of the White River. His residence was destroyed by a fire during the night of February 28, 1967. It is remembered, however, by the six stone columns—all that remain from the front portico of Frank's home—at the entrance of the Cultural Center, dedicated in 1988.

Minnetrista campus tours usually start at the Cultural Center— with its new outdoor sculpture, *Catalyst*, and its changing second-floor exhibits; the grand home of Edmund B. and Bertha Ball, whose daughter Janice, wife of Muncie civic leader John Fisher, alone remains of the second generation of Ball family members; and the homes of brothers George A., Lucius L., and William C.—now a guesthouse owned by Saint-Gobain Corporation—as well as a smaller stone "cottage" near Wheeling Avenue.

It's George A.'s home—Oakhurst—where most visitors spend considerable time, wandering among the second-floor historical displays and outdoors at the reproduction of daughter Elisabeth's dollhouse, the log cabin educational center, and the home's extensive gardens.

NOT ALWAYS SEEN. Meeting Circle Amphitheater on the Minnetrista campus is located in the nature area, sometimes missed by visitors. It is north of Saint Joseph Street and to the east of the fairgrounds.

At the west end of the campus is a river overlook, looking downstream on the White River. At the east end of the property is the *Appeal to the Great Spirit*, dedicated as a memorial to Edmund B. by his family in 1929.

Before I run out of space, the gift shop in the center, the Minnetrista Orchard Shop with items created and grown on-site, the annual Farmers' Market, and the musical programs on the extensive lawn to the east of the Cultural Center—are all worthy of attention.

While not part of the tour, mention must be made of Minnetrista's ambitious outreach programming. It takes a large booklet to describe the current schedule. Plus there's work with Minnetrista Affiliates, representing fifteen different groups ranging from the East Central Indiana Audubon Society to the Minnetrista Camera Club.

During my recent tour, young—and highly informed—Justin Knox also took me through the nature area, between Centennial Avenue to the north and Saint Joseph Street to the south—wetlands, prairie, woodlands, Meeting Circle Amphitheater. What an unexpected delight, nestled quietly in the midst of campus, houses, and streets.

IF YOU GO

GETTING THERE: On Wheeling Avenue, turn on Minnetrista Parkway to the Cultural Center entrance, where tours begin. Go to the center's information desk. The address is 1200 N. Minnetrista Parkway.

INFORMATION: Call (765) 282–4848 or (800) 428–5887 for more information. The Web site is http://www.minnetrista.net/. A map of the campus also is available. Minnetrista is open 9 a.m. to 5:30 p.m. Monday through Saturday, and 11 a.m. to 5:30 p.m. Sunday.

FEES: Admission charged to view exhibits at Minnetrista Cultural Center.

LOOK AT THAT FOLLOW-THROUGH. A museum visitor puts up his shot to win the game with the home team behind 75–74 and time expired in the championship game.

A HISTORY TIMELINE. As the museum visitor descends the ramp to the ground floor of the museum, a history of basketball unfolds to the left. Permanent exhibits are to the right.

Indiana Basketball Hall of Fame Museum, New Castle

NEW CASTLE—Hoosiers might have an inferiority complex about a number of things: We live in one of the nation's smallest states other than some of the original thirteen, we are locked between two midwestern powerhouses, Ohio and Illinois, and we worry about our best and brightest leaving for the two coasts.

But when one subject comes up, we stand tall. Of course, that's high school basketball. So it's not surprising that we have a shrine to this sport, the Indiana Basketball Hall of Fame Museum.

New Castle won out over other cities, including Indianapolis, in the competition about where the hall of fame would be constructed. The hall opened in 1990 and in 2003 had more than ten thousand visitors.

The stories about the visitors themselves could fill a book. One eighty-year-old came to the hall in a limousine as a birthday gift. A high school team from South Africa once showed up to tour the facility. High school, college, and professional players from every part of the country have been here. One Chicago band member wanted his buddies to see his brick in the courtyard, so he had his flashlight out at three in the morning to prove it was there.

Perhaps the outstanding visitor, however, was famous coach John Wooden. He came with his family to see the museum and especially the projection mannequin through which Wooden delivers a three-minute "locker room" speech about basketball and life. The Martinsville native set the record with ten national championships as head coach at UCLA.

This exhibit is a continuous film loop of Wooden projected onto a sculpted head. In taping the speech, Wooden had to remain perfectly still with a black shroud around his head and could not use his glasses. He did it just right on the second take.

The visitor is greeted at the museum with the pennants of all the state finalists and semifinalists from the previous March waving in the breeze in the courtyard of the entrance. In the courtyard walkway, bricks forming an outline of the state of Indiana are surrounded by an outlined basketball. The bricks were purchased by patrons of the museum as a fund-raiser.

Articles about the more than 1,100 teams that have played in the state tournament are available in office files. Team memorabilia are rotated in the museum from the extensive archival room in addition to the six permanent displays purchased by their sponsors—Muncie Central, Milan, Crispus Attucks, Crawfordsville, Attucks's Oscar Robertson, and East Chicago.

Everyone and everything is included. Out in the lobby are photos of the most recent inductees into the Hall of Fame as well as the Silver

HOOSIER HYSTERIA. The entrance to the Indiana Basketball Hall of Fame Museum in New Castle. Bricks forming the outline of the state can be seen in the walkway, surrounded by a giant basketball. Pennants of all of the previous year's finalists and semifinalists fly in the breeze.

Anniversary team. There's a room of all previous hall inductees and sections devoted to sportswriters and sportscasters, cheerleaders, girls' basketball, and referees. A history of the game timeline begins as you move to the ground level, walking through the pennants of all the state champions from 1911 to the present.

Two interactive displays draw considerable attention. In one, you have the ball as the seconds tick down in the final game. It's up to you to hit the shot at the buzzer. In the other, you try to outleap Robertson and Stephanie White. A strobe light catches you at the height of your leap, but you have a real challenge: Robertson's vertical leap measures nine feet, six inches.

Film footage of all state championship games since 1947, including the beginning of the girls championship in 1976, can also be viewed.

The hall also sponsors the Hall of Fame Classic each December at next door's New Castle Fieldhouse, the largest high school basketball gymnasium in the world, and the men's annual Hall of Fame induction on the Wednesday preceding the state championship games. The women's annual banquet is in April of each year.

Maybe basketball began with a peach basket up on a wall in a Massachusetts YMCA, but Indiana boys and girls have made it into a legend. The Indiana Basketball Hall of Fame Museum is the story of that legend.

IF YOU GO

GETTING THERE: Turn east off Indiana 3 at Trojan Lane at the south side of New Castle. The Hall of Fame Museum is on the left.

INFORMATION: Call (765) 529–1891. The Web site is http://www.hoopshall.com/. The museum is open Tuesday through Saturday from 10 a.m. to 5 p.m. and Sunday from 1 p.m. to 5 p.m. It is closed on Thanksgiving, Christmas Eve, Christmas Day, New Year's Eve, New Year's Day, and Easter. Guided tours are available with advance notice.

FEES: Admission charged.

PASSENGERS IN CAR NUMBER 9. Some happy campers set out for Metamora on the Christmas Walk Special. A few minutes later, they were excited to see a deer running in a field next to the train.

Whitewater Valley Railroad, Connersville

EN ROUTE TO METAMORA—"Look, there's a deer! See it! It's running right beside the train!"

For the moment, the two young teenage girls, caught up in applying eye shadow and lip gloss while gazing approvingly in their pocket mirrors, pause and join everyone else in Car Number 9 watching the deer. A little later though, most of us—including me—miss another three deer standing in the woods between two farms.

We are on the Whitewater Valley Railroad's five-passenger-car train headed from its home station in Connersville sixteen miles down to Metamora for an evening of shopping and eating.

This is the Metamora Christmas Walk Special that leaves Connersville at 4 p.m. on the four weekends following Thanksgiving. After arriving in Metamora around 5:30 p.m., passengers have three hours before the train whistle blows—four times—for its 8:30 p.m. departure back to the Connersville station.

The railroad is manned entirely by volunteers with the exception of its office manager. Car Number 9's conductor, a woman, had driven up from Cincinnati to work the Connersville–Metamora run this first Saturday evening of the season. She collects tickets, but mostly chats with passengers. Her most oft-asked question? What's the best place to eat in Metamora? She offers several possibilities.

The train ride follows the route of the nineteenth-century Whitewater Canal's towpath as it crosses and recrosses Indiana 121. (One crew of the railroad's volunteers is in a truck out ahead of the train to serve as flaggers at nonsignal crossings. That's not difficult given the train's slow speed.)

The train passes by Alpine and Laurel on its way to Metamora. It stops in Laurel to pick up any additional passengers.

In the case of our group of passengers, with several small children included, we were worried on this brisk Saturday evening whether the passenger cars would be heated. They are, by steam. By the time the trip was over, we had peeled off our sweaters.

When the train reaches Metamora, everyone is hungry. (Note for passengers with children: Metamora is not well lighted at night, and vehicles are permitted on the streets. You're advised to keep a close rein on the kids.)

A short three hours later, it feels good to be back on the warm train after the sun, which had long since set, has been replaced by the chill of the evening.

GETTING HIS ORDERS. The engineer of the Metamora Christmas Walk Special receives his orders just before the Connersville-based train leaves on its sixteen-mile journey to Metamora.

You might think by now that everyone would be wiped out and most would be asleep for the return trip. Not so. It reminds me of trains I had taken during World War II: much commotion, people talking loudly, singing, just generally having a good time—at least as I remember it now, more than fifty years later. One jokester observes that, indeed, the railroad cars may be the *same* ones we rode in more than a half century ago. Actually, they could be, since all the cars were built between 1926 and 1934.

When we roll back into Connersville after the return trip, people still are swapping stories, joking, exclaiming about the farmhouse "with more than 1,000 lights," according to the woman conductor. (Probably more than several thousand, most of us agree.)

At the station, the kids are handed up into the train engine to look around and, no doubt, pretend they are running the train. Everyone has a last look around the station and its gift shop, uses the restrooms, and then heads home.

While it was lights on and lots of conversation while we were on the train, at least in our vehicles on the way home it is lights out and lots of sleeping.

IF YOU GO

GETTING THERE: In Connersville, when Indiana 1 turns to the left, continue south on Western Avenue, which becomes Grand Avenue. The Whitewater Valley Railroad depot is on the left.

INFORMATION: Operating season begins in May, running Wednesday, Thursday, and Friday, and in October on Thursday and Friday at 10 a.m. The train operates on Saturday and Sunday at 12:01 p.m. from the first Saturday in May until the last Sunday in October. Call (765) 825–2054 Tuesday through Saturday during the operating season.

Web site is http://www.whitewater valleyrr.org/.

FEES: Admission charged. A dinner train leaves the first and third Friday at 6 p.m. May through October and stops at the Laurel Hotel restaurant for dinner.

THE BACKWARDS AXE HAN-DLE. When the statue in front of the Lincoln National Life Insur-ance Company offices on Harrison Street was unveiled in September 1932, one keen observer noted that the axe handle held by Lincoln was backwards. "It would chop off your foot if you used it that way" was the comment. A year later, a properly mounted axe handle was in Lincoln's hands, and the backwards axe handle now rests in the Lincoln Museum, where it can't do any harm.

FORT WAYNE—It only takes a moment to figure out why the admission charge to the Lincoln Museum is $3.99 for general admission. That's so you can be returned a Lincoln penny.

There's more history in this museum than most of us are prepared to take in even during a long visit. For instance, the shiny Lincoln penny given the visitor comes attached to a card that explains the penny was first minted in 1909 on the one hundredth anniversary of Lincoln's birth, was the first to depict a U.S. president (all previous coins featured eagles, shields, and such), and that the penny last was redesigned in 1959, the one hundred fiftieth anniversary of Lincoln's birth. The coin contains a depiction of the Lincoln Memorial, which replaced two stylized heads of wheat.

And that's just for starters.

The Lincoln Museum holds the world's largest privately owned Lincoln collection. Its eleven galleries, eighteen interactive computer exhibits, four theaters, and museum store contain 30,000 square feet. In them are:

300 documents signed by Lincoln

18,000 books about Lincoln and his times

7,000 nineteenth-century prints, engravings, and newspapers

5,000 original nineteenth-century photographs

350 sheet-music titles

scores of period artifacts and Lincoln family belongings

As Fort Wayne residents know, the museum has gone through a number of transformations and, in recent years, its directors considered taking it to a bigger city.

It was first established in 1928 and given a permanent home in 1931 on the fourth floor above the Lincoln National Life Insurance Company headquarters. It was moved to larger space on the first floor in 1960 and then into nearby bi-level space in 1977. In the early 1990s, the Lincoln board was ready to move the museum so "it could be shared with a greater audience." But local citizens raised such a ruckus that the decision was made to build a new facility in Fort Wayne. The two-floor museum—permanent displays on the first level and temporary on the lower—opened in downtown Fort Wayne in 1995. Today, the museum attracts about fifty thousand visitors annually.

The first level exhibit is organized to give the visitor three major insights—Lincoln's life, his times, and his legacy. His life stretches from Indiana youth to prairie politician to Ford's Theater. (There's a lock of his hair and a fragment of a bandage taken from Lincoln's deathbed.) His times are highlighted by The American Experiment and Civil War exhibits. His legacy is found in Remembering Lincoln and The Experiment Continues.

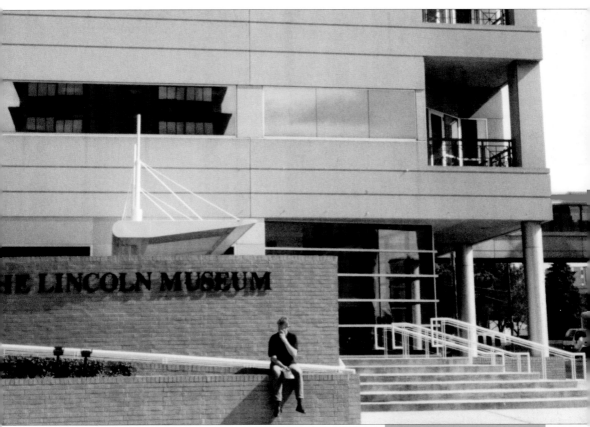

CORNER OF CLINTON AND BERRY. The Lincoln Museum is located in downtown Fort Wayne. It occupies the first and lower levels of this building, formerly the Lincoln National Life Corporate Center, before it moved to Philadelphia.

Of course, there's also Lincoln at the Movies, including his portrayals by Raymond Massey and Henry Fonda, among those better known.

Plus, acquisitions keep coming. Recently, the museum purchased one of forty-eight replicas of the Emancipation Proclamation signed by Lincoln. The original is housed at the National Archives in Washington. Lincoln signed these forty-eight copies as a fund-raiser in 1864 for a civilian charity that supplied medical personnel and supplies for Union soldiers during the war. Fewer than half are believed to exist today. Only eight have been displayed, and the Lincoln Museum's is the only one in the world on permanent display. No cost of the acquisition has been made public, but it is known that Malcolm Forbes purchased a copy in 1984 at an auction for $297,000.

The visitor comes away from the museum with three impressions. First, you know you are in the presence of greatness. Of all American presidents, Lincoln, along with perhaps one or two others, towers among the world's most revered figures. Second, at least for me, I am reminded of the battlefield at Gettysburg: So much to see and understand, so much need for quiet reflection and meditation, so much feeling of awe and reverence, so deeply emotional. Third, Hoosiers ought to be aware of Lincoln's deep Indiana roots, for it was here he grew up to become the man he was.

You cannot touch the life of Lincoln without touching humanity and the ages.

IF YOU GO

GETTING THERE: In downtown Fort Wayne, go north on Barr Street, one-way north, for three blocks. Turn left on Berry Street, one-way west, and into the museum parking lot.

INFORMATION: Open from 10 a.m. to 5 p.m. Tuesday through Saturday and 1 p.m. to 5 p.m. Sunday. Call (260) 455–3864; e-mail theLincolnMuseum@LNC.com; Web site, http://www.theLincoln Museum.org/; fax (260) 455–6922.

FEES: Admission charged.

POST WINDMILL. This windmill was constructed so the steps can be picked up and the windmill turned on a track to catch the wind. It is a replica of the Robertson Post Windmill, built in England and used as a gristmill for grinding corn.

MODELS, TOO. Windmill models are also part of the display at the Mid-America Windmill Museum near Kendallville.

IN SECTIONS. Some of the windmills at the Mid-America Windmill Museum are inside the historic bank barn. The windmill on the right is a sectional windmill. As the wind velocity increases the windmill's sections open through centrifugal force so the wind isn't hitting each blade equally, limiting the windmill's speed.

Mid-America Windmill Museum, Kendallville

KENDALLVILLE—The volunteers and board of directors of the Mid-America Windmill Museum every year expect another good season. The museum opens for weekends at the beginning of April and then returns to a full schedule in May until it closes again in October.

"We had twice as many people last year as the year before," Betty Jones, museum volunteer, told me recently in keeping with the expectation.

The volunteer—"one of the Jones girls"—said the museum has a large number of school groups among its visitors who come to learn about windmills and their history.

The museum is the result of business leaders in Kendallville seeking a tourist attraction concept that would fit their community. Windmills seemed to be the answer.

In the 1800s, during the windmill's heyday in America, some ninety-six manufacturers were producing windmills within an eighty-mile radius of this county seat. One of the most prominent was Flint and Walling Company of Kendallville. Of its eleven models, ten are on the grounds of the museum.

Certainly there's plenty to see at the thirteen-acre site. The museum has forty-eight windmills on display, a barn museum (a story in itself), a video room, gift room, and a red barn that can be rented for community events, receptions, and similar activities. A nine-minute video introduces the visitor to windmills and the story of wind power. "It was produced at a sixth-grade level," Jones explained, "so it's easy to understand."

Windmills date back to Persia more than 1,600 years ago. They replaced man as a source of power, but they were in turn replaced, first by steam power and later by electrical power and the gasoline engine.

Their greatest use in the United States came during migration into the western lands because surface water was less available, causing a need for low-cost, reliable, and self-regulating windmills. By the years following World War II, however, they had largely disappeared from use, with the wind-powered turbine electrical generator most commonly in use today.

Each of the museum's windmills has a nearby plaque that explains its history, how it operates, what sizes were produced, and the manufacturers.

A bonanza for the museum occurred in 2000 when a collection of fifty-five windmills became available in Texas. "Several of our gentle-

OUTSIDE EXHIBITS. Part of the windmills on exhibit at the Mid-America Windmill Museum.

IF YOU GO

men took a semi to Texas where they picked up the collection," Jones said. "Some were in perfect shape; others needed a lot of repair."

Another fortuitous event occurred when a historic bank barn became available on the Walter Klinger farm near Avilla, south of Kendallville. The barn, which opens on two levels, was built in 1889 of hand-hewn timber and constructed without the use of nails, but rather using pegs.

When the museum board was alerted to the barn's availability, it was dismantled and reassembled during a cold February in 1994 by Amish workers. That's the building that today houses the museum with its windmill exhibits and artifacts. The entire museum operation functions using volunteers, including a twenty-person board of directors plus the people who staff the museum.

GETTING THERE: East on U.S. 6 from Kendallville to Allen Chapel Road (1000E) and south about three quarters of a mile to museum on the right.

INFORMATION: Open weekends in April. The May through October schedule is Tuesday through Friday, 10 a.m. to 4 p.m.; Saturday, 10 a.m. to 5 p.m.; and Sunday, 1 p.m. to 4 p.m. For further information, go to the Web site, http://www.midamericawindmillmuseum.com/, or call (260) 897–9918.

FEES: Admission charged.

A "DUESY." One of the exhibits at the Auburn Cord Duesenberg Museum is this restored 1931 Duesenberg. It's parked in front of a display recounting the career of E. L. Cord, president of the Auburn Automobile Company.

BUILT FOR SPEED. This 1932 Auburn racing car had a copper cooling coil for its V-12, 160-horsepower motor. Auburns were built through the 1936 model year; Cords and Duesenbergs through 1937. In the background is a 1933 Duesenberg with a 420-cubic-inch, 265-horsepower engine. Cars built on Duesenberg chassis sold for $14,000 to $20,000—in the 1930s.

Auburn Cord Duesenberg Museum, Festival, and Auction, Auburn

AUBURN—No question about it: The Auburn Cord Duesenberg Festival includes the biggest car show around. In early September, some 5,000 cars go up for auction each day, with crowds estimated at 150,000 on the grounds and in town. The Kruse International Classic and Collector Car Auction claims more classic cars are sold here than at all other events of its kind combined.

You can't miss the Kruse auction site as you're driving along Interstate 69. It's just off the interstate at Auburn exit 126.

But while you're in Auburn for the auction, the grand parade, or other festival events, it would be a shame not to take some quieter moments to visit the Auburn Cord Duesenberg Museum at the south edge of town, a couple of miles north of the auction park. The museum and festival are operated by separate not-for-profit organizations. The auction, of course, is a for-profit business.

The present museum building was the center of the 1930s automotive empire constructed by E. L. Cord, mastermind of the Auburn Automobile Company, who gave his name to what many consider the best designed of all American cars, the Cord.

Unfortunately, his empire and his dream were short lived. Cord commissioned the art deco, sixty-six thousand-square-foot building to showcase his cars and to provide his design and administrative headquarters for the future. The year was 1930 when the Auburn company moved into the building. World events, however, took over—the Great Depression had just begun. Seven years later, the Auburn Automobile Company went out of business.

The two-story building became the home of the Auburn Cord Duesenberg Museum in 1974. It is on the National Register of Historic Places. Today, more than one hundred cars await the visitor. They represent a panorama of automotive history's golden age during the early part of the twentieth century, but focus mostly on cars produced in Indiana.

Plus, there's information that car aficionados probably know all about, but the rest of us would not. For example, one display tells the visitor that most cars built between 1910 and 1930 were not manufactured; they were assembled. Manufacturers produced "off-the-shelf" components and subassemblies, such as engines, axles, chassis, and the like. Then automobile makers, without the high costs of design and manufacturing, put the parts together in their own special way. Of Indiana's more than one hundred auto producers, that's how most of them did it—they assembled cars.

JEAN HARLOW RODE IN ONE. This re-created 1931 front drive Cord is like one bought by Paul Berns, husband of Jean Harlow, the famous movie actress of the 1930s. The Cord was first displayed at the Paris Automotive Art Show in 1931. It had an in-line, eight-cylinder, 297-cubic-inch engine.

The museum features galleries of Auburns, Cords, and Duesenbergs, as well as cars built in Auburn and other Indiana cities.

For example, tiny Albany in Delaware County was where two automobiles were assembled—the Albany, 1902 to 1904, and the Cory, 1907. Anderson led all east central Indiana manufacturers, with nine different cars built there between 1899 and 1920.

Other museum exhibits include automotive fine arts, restored design and clay model studios, advertising offices, and Cord's presidential office, along with other exhibit areas completed in a $3 million addition.

One car of special interest is the Avanti, which the Studebaker company in South Bend introduced in 1963 as a two-door sports coupe, first designed with a glass fiber body, in a last-ditch effort to save the northern Indiana automobile builder. Studebaker thought that perhaps a bold new sports car image would turn around the company's fortunes. It didn't.

If you like cars, this is a place to linger. You don't want to hurry through this museum.

IF YOU GO

GETTING THERE: At Interstate 69 exit 126, take County Road 11A to Highway 427 North, which becomes Wayne Street. Cross the railroad tracks and proceed to the stoplight at Auburn Drive. The museum is on your right as you pass Auburn Drive. The parking lot is on the north side of the building.

INFORMATION: The museum is open every day except Thanksgiving Day, Christmas Day, and New Year's Day from 9 a.m. to 5 p.m. Its telephone number is (260) 925–1444. The best Web site for information is http://www.acdfestival.org/, with links to the museum and other information about Auburn and the festival. The museum's Web site is http://www.acdmuseum.org/.

FEES: Admission charged.

FLOWERS AND MUSIC. Berne's main street during the summer months is filled with flowers and music (Swiss Alps yodeling).

IT'S A BIG ONE. This two-ton beam lowered to press apples into cider is as big as it looks.

Berne

BERNE—It's a curious place: Side-by-side are Amish in their horse-drawn carriages next to community-perfected tourism. Throw in furniture makers, publishers, and all the trappings of your usual Indiana small town and, yes, it's a curious—and interesting—place.

Berne got its start in the mid-1800s when seventy Mennonite immigrants from Switzerland moved to Indiana. Later, other church fellowships from the Jura Mountain area in Switzerland—including the Amish, Reformed, and Christian Apostolic—also settled here. One of the largest Mennonite churches in the United States is in Berne at the intersection of U.S. 27 and Indiana 218.

First noticed by most visitors to the Berne area are the Amish carriages moving slowly along the highway with their red triangular signs on the back, warning motorists to exercise caution. (Incidentally, the Amish request their photographs not be taken, although pictures of their outdoor surroundings are welcomed.)

Two Berne attractions that most people know about are Swiss Heritage Village and Amishville USA.

Swiss Heritage Village, Museum, and Nature Center, a not-for-profit facility operated by the Swiss Heritage Society, is located just north of downtown Berne between MacIntosh Road and Parr Road along Swiss Way. Open May 1 to October 31, its twenty-six acres contain twelve historic buildings along with a wildlife and bird sanctuary. The museum's visitor center offers a ten-minute video for background prior to a tour.

The museum has a four thousand-square-foot Celebrating Our Heritage exhibit, telling the story of the settlement of southern Adams County from the early 1800s until the present.

An attractive twenty-eight-page booklet available at the village describes the history of each building. One of them, a pioneer cabin nestled back in the woods, was built in the 1840s. It actually came from Adams County, where it had been dismantled and each hewn log marked, and was reconstructed here in 1995. Guides lead tours of the buildings.

Probably the most intriguing part of the village is the cider press, one of the largest in the world. The beam lowered to press the apples measures thirty by thirty inches and is thirty feet long. Weighing an estimated two tons, it is from a tree believed to be three hundred years old when it was cut down about 1860.

The Nature Center is another village feature. It contains a second-growth woods, wetland, pond, and meadow. A 1965 tornado took down

MADE OF HEWN LOGS. When this log cabin was dismantled in Adams County, it was one and a half floors. Reassembled at Swiss Heritage Village, the 1840s cabin was reduced to one floor.

all but a few of the original trees, but the center now is "healing." A one-mile trail with its identified trees is part of the nature center, too.

South of Berne just off County Road 900S and 000 (running north and south) is Amishville USA. It, too, has restored buildings along with a gift shop, buggy rides, camping, and the Essen Platz restaurant (its specialty, apple dumplings). I recall our family going there for Sunday lunch more than thirty years ago. Today, it is very much as I remember it. Camping, primitive and modern, is available from April through October but reservations are recommended for holiday periods.

People who know the Berne area are aware that the furniture business is also an integral part of the community. But what may be less well known are the two furniture manufacturers—Smith Brothers and Berne Furniture Company. Berne Furniture offers tours; call (260) 589-2173 for an appointment.

Also not so well known—and offering tours of its plant—is the House of White Birches publishing company, located on Parr Road just south of Swiss Heritage Village. If you're into crafts, sewing, or cooking, the publications you read probably come from here; call (260) 589-8741 for information.

GETTING THERE: U. S. 27—North and South—and Indiana 218—East and West—intersect in Berne.

INFORMATION: The Berne Chamber of Commerce has a visitor center in downtown Berne. Telephone (260) 589–8080; fax (260) 589–8384; Web site is http://www.bernein.com/. Swiss Heritage Village hours are 10 a.m. to 4 p.m. Monday through Saturday, May through October.

FEES: Swiss Heritage Village asks an admission charge. No fees to enter Amishville USA, but fees for services and products.

MOUNTAIN GUN. This Hotchkiss mountain cannon fired a two-pound shell, seen on the ammunition case at the right. The shell recently was found by a military dealer. The French-designed artillery piece was first used during the Spanish-American War. It is on loan from the Indiana War Memorial in Indianapolis.

BALL FOUNDER'S HATS. These officers' hats are believed to have belonged to Edmund B. Ball, one of the founding brothers of Ball Brothers glass company. Jim Waechter, left, museum president, is researching the hats that he thinks Ball wore as a major in the Indiana Guard early in the twentieth century. Brian Williamson, museum vice president, holds the second hat, showing its gold braid.

Museum of the Soldier, Portland

PORTLAND—The roof leaks. The building has no heat or air-conditioning. Money is in short supply. They're plugging away, however, with two sections of the old Coca-Cola building renovated.

No matter. The Museum of the Soldier is serious about its mission to "recognize and honor the service and sacrifice of those who served and supported the armed forces of the United States."

Located in the donated former Coca-Cola bottling plant on East Arch Street, the museum now uses about eight thousand square feet of the building's total twenty-six thousand square feet.

"It's a wonderful brick building but it is in need of some repairs and remodeling," the museum's newsletter says of the 1938 structure.

"The roof's pretty bad," says Jim Waechter, museum president, more to the point. "We can only be open during the summer months because we have no heat. We can't use most of the space that we have. So, we're looking for more funding." The fund-raising goal for building renovation, establishing a research library, and maintenance of the artifacts collection is $750,000. To date, just under $150,000 has been raised, according to Waechter.

The museum offers memberships, has matched a $10,000 grant from the Portland Foundation, and has started an endowment fund.

An earlier $1,000 grant from the Jay County United Way provided funding for an inside wall in the southwest corner of the building to set off the present exhibit space. That allowed the museum to open in November 1998.

It isn't that the museum suffers from the lack of knowledgeable leadership. Waechter, who served with the army engineers in Vietnam, is the exhibits director of the Lincoln Museum in Fort Wayne. Brian Williamson, museum vice president and a member of the Indiana National Guard, is technical director of the Museum of Art in Fort Wayne.

What separates their museum from others, they believe, is the identification of most exhibit items with individuals. A uniform is not merely displayed. Usually, they know who wore it, where he—or, in some cases, she—wore it, and the "trail" of how it arrived at the museum.

"We want to put the names and faces along with the history of our exhibits," says Williamson. "Because they are donated by the person involved, or a family member or someone from around here, we usually can do that."

A recent example are two officers' hats found in the wardrobe of Muncie's Civic Theater. Inside the hatband of both is written the name "E. B. Ball."

KOREAN WAR. Uniforms worn by American service personnel during the Korean War are featured at Portland's Museum of the Soldier.

IF YOU GO

"We're still researching it, but we believe the cofounder of what was then Ball Brothers was a major in the Indiana Guard prior to 1912," says Waechter. The theater parted with the hats in an agreement to use other museum properties when needed for staging its shows.

Wayne Derby from Indianapolis donated his "tiger stripe" shirt and trousers, worn on long-range reconnaissance patrols in Vietnam. The right sleeve was cut away below the elbow when he was wounded. He later cut the other sleeve to match.

Jay Miller of Portland gave the museum items from his father, Earl, who served in World War I with the First Gas and Flame Regiment in France. Roger Markley, formerly of Portland, donated his uniform, a .32-caliber revolver, and other World War II gear. He piloted a glider in the D-Day invasion of France. In addition to the many donations, acquisitions are obtained through military dealers, loans, and "keeping an eye out."

Waechter and Williamson know they are in for a long tour of duty to get the museum near what they have in mind.

"We're not here to celebrate war, but we are here to honor the dedication of those who served their country," says Williamson.

GETTING THERE: In Portland, from U.S. 27, go to Arch Street and turn east four blocks to the museum.

INFORMATION: The museum is open the first and third weekends of each month, April through November, from noon until 5 p.m. Telephone (260) 726–2967, the Web site is http://www.museumofthesoldier.com/.

FEES: Admission charged.

FALSE BOTTOM. This wagon had a false bottom—note the sacks near the front rest on boards, leaving space underneath—so that escaped slaves could be transported along the Underground Railroad. It is in the barn at the Levi Coffin House.

Levi Coffin House State Historic Site, Fountain City

LEVI COFFIN AND A "FREE LABOR DESK." A portrait of Levi Coffin, the Underground Railroad's "conductor," is in his Fountain City home. Coffin, a Quaker business-man, shipped this desk to an Indiana customer after Coffin moved to Cincinnati. The desk was produced by "free labor," as opposed to slave labor.

FOUNTAIN CITY—The Levi Coffin House tour guide was explaining that Coffin had a simple strategy to thwart hunters looking for escaped slaves in this Wayne County area north of Richmond.

If it seemed that a slave-hunting party was close and an effort might be made to search Coffin's home for escaped slaves, Coffin resorted to the law: Get a search warrant and show proof of ownership, Coffin would say. Slave hunters might produce documents showing "ownership" but getting a search warrant was another matter. That meant a trip from Newport—today's Fountain City—to Centerville (the county seat from 1814 to 1873), thirteen miles to the south, and back.

Any slave hunter knew that if escaped slaves were in Coffin's house, they certainly would not be there when the hunter got back from a twenty-six-mile horseback journey, even if he could obtain a warrant.

If the worst came, the Coffins had a space—a garret—behind a small door in an upstairs bedroom. A bed could be pulled in front of the low door, which would not be visible. There, under a sloping roof that extends down over the south porch, it is believed as many as fourteen persons could be hidden.

From 1826 to 1847, when Levi and Catharine Coffin were "conductors" for the Underground Railroad, their home was never searched.

It was called a "railroad" because, much like a railroad, slaves would make stops along their escape route at homes and barns of those opposed to slavery, the "conductors." "Underground" meant it worked without authority and through the efforts of sympathizers.

Escaped slaves reached the Coffin home by following little-known back roads and trails from Cincinnati, Jeffersonville, or Madison. "Follow the North Star" was the advice.

Since it was against federal law to aid an escaped slave, obviously no careful records were kept by the Coffins. So far as is known, they helped some two thousand slaves pass to eventual freedom in Canada by keeping them in their house, sometimes for extensive periods of time while they rested and regained their strength.

What is amazing is, again given the information available, not one slave was ever captured, even though slave-hunting parties combed Indiana. Later, when the Coffins moved to Cincinnati at the request of abolitionists to manage a warehouse of goods produced by "free labor," they were said to have aided another thousand escaped slaves.

Exasperated slave hunters are said to have coined the phrase, "There must be an Underground Railroad and Levi Coffin must be the President and his house the Grand Central Station."

LEVI COFFIN HOUSE. The Coffins helped an estimated two thousand escaped slaves during the twenty years they lived in Newport, living eight years in this house that they had built in 1839.

The Levi Coffin House Association, which operates the state historic site in agreement with the state of Indiana (its owner), was fortunate when it began restoration of the house in the 1960s. A built-in bookcase for the library was found dismantled in the attic. Almost all of the wavy windowpanes were still in place. Doors, door panels, pieces of baseboard, and two original windows also were either in the garret or stored elsewhere. Plus, later owners had kept the house in good repair.

Making the house a historic site was the first project in 1882 of the Wayne County Historical Society. It took almost a hundred years—it opened in 1970—but today it is listed as a National Historic Landmark, and Coffin is one of four "conductors" cited by the U.S. Park Service in its official map and guide of the Underground Railroad.

Recently, the association has purchased a nearby house, which will become the Levi Coffin Interpretive Center. The building's street-front facade is to be restored, while the structure will offer space for education and research.

IF YOU GO

GETTING THERE: The Levi Coffin House is on the southeast corner of U.S. 27 and Mill Street in Fountain City.

INFORMATION: The house is open from June 1 to August 31, Tuesday through Saturday, 1 p.m. to 4 p.m.; September 1 to October 31, open Saturday 1 p.m. to 4 p.m. For information call (765) 847–2432. Tours are made on an "as-requested" basis.

FEES: Admission charged.

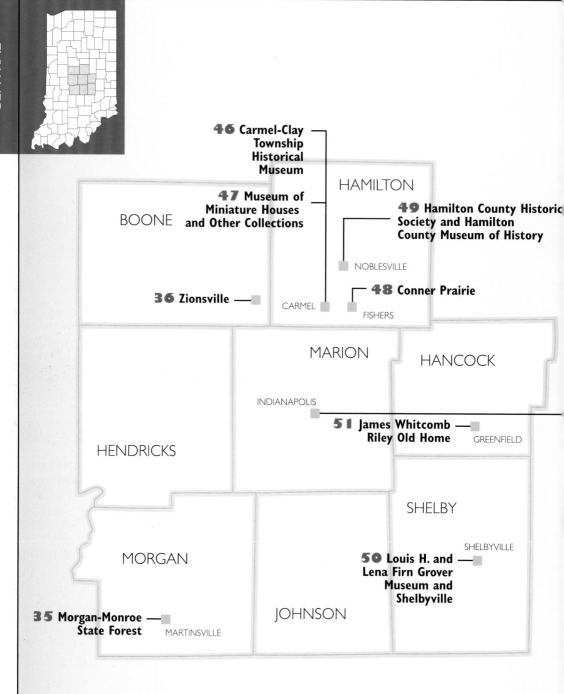

46 Carmel-Clay
Township
Historical
Museum

HAMILTON

47 Museum of
Miniature Houses
and Other Collections

BOONE

49 Hamilton County Historic
Society and Hamilton
County Museum of History

NOBLESVILLE

36 Zionsville

48 Conner Prairie

CARMEL

FISHERS

MARION

HANCOCK

INDIANAPOLIS

51 James Whitcomb
Riley Old Home

GREENFIELD

HENDRICKS

SHELBY

SHELBYVILLE

MORGAN

50 Louis H. and
Lena Firn Grover
Museum and
Shelbyville

JOHNSON

35 Morgan-Monroe
State Forest

MARTINSVILLE

OHIO

N

A PLACE OF BEAUTY. One of the many, many places in Morgan-Monroe State Forest with trees reaching to the sky, sunlight filtering through to the ground, and nothing but solitude.

EVERGREEN. This solitary evergreen towers above nearby trees at the Morgan-Monroe State Forest south of Martinsville.

UNFORTUNATELY, IT'S CLOSED. The fire tower at Morgan-Monroe State Forest is closed because of needed repairs. It was placed on the National Register of Historic Places in 1999.

Morgan-Monroe State Forest, Martinsville

MARTINSVILLE—Folklore has it that Cherry Lake in Morgan-Monroe State Forest once was stocked with fish by state forest employees so that Indiana governors "holding meetings" in a nearby cabin could be certain to always have a good day fishing.

Maybe it's true and maybe it's not. Whether it ever was true, it doesn't appear to be so today, insofar as everyone on the premises seemed to know when I talked with them during a visit.

Nevertheless, "the governor's lake" is what one man called it when I talked with him as he walked his dog near the lake.

Whatever the truth, it makes a good story.

I can't vouch for the fishing in the forest's three lakes. (A fourth lake, Beanblossom, is dry since a levee failed after heavy rains in 1993.) Several pickup trucks were parked along the roads near the lakes when I was there. One man nodded "yes" when I asked him if the fishing was any good.

Morgan-Monroe State Forest, seven miles south of Martinsville, is the state's second largest. As with other state forests, it likely appeals to the more rugged outdoors type than do the state parks, for example.

Camping is class C, primitive, at the Mason Ridge Campground with a picnic table and grill at each site. Seasonal drinking water is available. The Scout Ridge Youth Tent Campground for Scouts and other youth groups has bigger sites with picnic tables and grills and a nearby picnic shelter. Its peak use is around holidays, I was told.

If the nineteen sites at Mason Ridge are filled, campers can use the ten sites at the Oak Ridge Campground, considered an overflow. Campers register at the forest office.

Picnic tables and four shelters are scattered throughout the 23,680 acres of the state forest. They are on a first-come, first-served basis without fees.

Both of the forest's longer hiking trails are termed rugged. There's a .6-mile Pathfinder Orientation trail and a one-mile Tree Identification trail, which are marked easy, and three moderate trails, ranging from .5 to 3.1 miles. But the two long ones—Three Lakes Trail, 10.2 miles, and Low Gap Trail, 10 miles—are loops and go through some hilly country.

Hikers are advised to wear hunter orange or some other bright color during hunting season. Firearms are not supposed to be used, however, in safety zones or within two hundred feet of recreational areas.

The steps of the forest's fire tower and support structure are in need of repair, unfortunately, so the tower is closed. From the ground it looks as if it would offer a grand view of the forest.

SHELTER HOUSE. This large shelter house is at the Scout Ridge campground at Morgan-Monroe State Forest. No reservation is needed for its use.

When you leave Indiana 37 to go into the forest, you might be surprised to see a number of private residences. That's because the main forest block doesn't actually begin until you've gone a mile or so off the highway. You'll know you're there when you come to an intersection and see a large state forest sign. Even then, it's about another five miles to the forest office, campgrounds, and fire station.

Like other state and national forests, mostly it seemed quiet. It reminded me of nearby Yellowwood State Forest: If it weren't for the occasional automobile, you could just as easily be back in the days of Daniel Boone.

There's something to be said for that.

THE GOVERNOR'S. This is the desk where the twenty-seventh governor of Indiana, Samuel M. Ralston, a Boone County native, worked. It was restored by the Sullivan Museum Guild in 1994.

ADDIE WINNER. Created for the museum's twenty-fifth anniversary, this papier-mâché cow, made from advertisements of farms for sale, won two Addie awards from the American Advertising Federation in 1998. The theme was the demise of the Hoosier farm.

Zionsville

ZIONSVILLE—I've never quite known whether our nation's fascination with certain even-numbered anniversaries stems from the human spirit or is something journalists have created. For example, few seem to note a forty-ninth wedding anniversary, but the fiftieth gets lots of attention.

So it is, too, with any 150th anniversary, and that's what Zionsville celebrated throughout the year 2002. The living out of the year probably changed very little for most people in Zionsville from the preceding year, but, still, it was likely to be at least somewhat different. It was an "anniversary" year.

Zionsville, of course, probably was similar to any other middle America community marking its 150th anniversary in the twenty-first century. A year with appropriate pomp and ceremony could be expected.

This town's yearlong celebration officially began on January 26, Founders Day, with a social and dance at the Zionsville Methodist Church, a recently built church. The original church was founded in Eagle Village in 1838 and moved to Zionsville in 1854.

The history of the first white settlement of the region goes back to the 1820s, but it wasn't until the late 1840s that William Zion, a Lebanon businessman, saw the need for an additional railroad station midway between Indianapolis and Lebanon. He convinced Elijah and Polly Cross that a town should be built on their Eagle Township land. It was on January 26, 1852, that a report and chart of the proposed town were filed with the county recorder.

An event still recalled in Zionsville is the time in 1861 when president-elect Abraham Lincoln's train stopped here. Lincoln came to the rear platform and spoke briefly to the crowd. The site now is Lincoln Memorial Park.

What Zionsville probably is best known for across the state, however, is its antique and art shops, mostly gathered along the nineteenth-century brick Main Street.

An integral part of any anniversary would be the Patrick Henry Sullivan Museum and Genealogy Library at 225 W. Hawthorne Street and its next-door neighbor, the Munce Art Center at 205 W. Hawthorne. Both operate under the Sullivan Foundation.

The museum was dedicated in 1973 as a gift from Iva Etta Sullivan to honor her great-grandfather, Patrick Henry Sullivan, thought to be the first permanent white settler in the region in the 1820s. Iva, a Zionsville native, worked in libraries and as a historian before going to

P. H. SULLIVAN MUSEUM. A foundation supports the Patrick Henry Sullivan Museum and Genealogy Library in Zionsville as well as the Munce Art Center, located next door.

Hollywood to work as historian for Cecil B. DeMille in his early talking movies. She apparently invested her money wisely.

When she died in the early 1960s, her will set aside funds to build the museum. It fulfilled two of her interests: family history and a desire to do something for her hometown. Her will had a stipulation about her bequest, however: the 1850 Boone County census report—both volumes—had to be on display at all times.

A key feature of the museum building is its genealogy collection.

"It's a fine collection about Boone County and central Indiana, particularly those counties that touch Boone County; but also of the migration states from the East Coast that came into Indiana and Illinois. We've been working on this for many, many years," says Marianne Heath Doyle, genealogist and Boone County historian.

"We consider ourselves a community archive. We strive to keep history alive. We make sure we're going to be here for a long time," she adds.

Regardless of what is on display around the town, you can rest assured—and so can Iva—that the 1850 county census books are just inside the genealogy room on a top shelf and ready for instant inspection.

IF YOU GO

GETTING THERE: In Zionsville, turn onto Hawthorne Street to the museum and art center.

INFORMATION: For the museum, telephone (317) 873–4900; Web site is http://www.sullivanmunce.org/. For the art center, (317) 873–6862. For the Chamber of Commerce, (317) 873–3836; Web site, http://www.zionsvillechamber.org/. The museum and art center are open Tuesday through Saturday, 10 a.m. to 4 p.m., and Thursday night until 8 p.m.

FEES: No charge to visit.

VUKOVICH ROADSTER. Bill Vukovich drove this roadster to victory in the 1953 and 1954 races.

JUNIOR IS THE DRIVER. A thrill for youngsters visiting the museum is to be photographed in an Indy race car.

FIRST WINNER. Winner of the first race in 1911, the Marmon Wasp was supposedly the first car to use a rearview mirror. Because of its tail and yellow coloring, it was nicknamed the Marmon Wasp. The Marmon automobile, along with the Stutz, Cole, National, and Duesenberg, was built in Indianapolis.

Indianapolis Motor Speedway Hall of Fame Museum, Indianapolis

INDIANAPOLIS—Quick, all of you 500-mile race fans. Why was Bill Vukovich's Number 14 race car, winner of the Indy 500 in 1953 and 1954, called a roadster?

A trip to the Indianapolis Motor Speedway Hall of Fame Museum can supply the answer. Or, more correctly, Donald Davidson, museum historian, can. Look at the grill of Vukovich's car. Because the grill looked so much like the grill of the Kurtis-Kraft automobile of the early 1950s, Vukovich's racer was dubbed a roadster. It's that simple.

Of course, there's much more to see than Vukovich's roadster in this West Sixteenth Street museum, owned by the Indianapolis Motor Speedway Corporation. One surprise might be that the motor displays include passenger and foreign cars, as well as some of the famous racing cars of the past.

For example, one early auto on display is the 1886 Daimler, built in Germany, that could obtain a top speed of ten miles per hour from its one cylinder. Another Daimler historical note: Shortly after Gottlieb Daimler died in 1900, his successors agreed to build sportier, faster cars. A distributor ordered thirty-six with the agreement that the cars would be named for his twelve-year-old daughter. Her name was Mercedes.

Something new is on the floor most of the time. Other cars and artifacts are stored, to be rotated onto the main museum floor. Some of the storeroom cars are under restoration, while others are just being held for space on the main floor. Sometimes, cars are loaned out for special occasions.

For photo buffs, you can have it both ways. Bring your camera if you wish, or you can order pictures from the four million-plus negatives owned by the Speedway. The photo department can make prints of any size. (Call [317] 492–6771 or fax [317] 492–6470 to place an order.) In the Tony Hulman Theatre, you can watch a twenty-two-minute history of the track. It has been reedited in recent years, so it's less on crashes and more on history.

If you want to know how you would look at the wheel of an Indy race car, you can be photographed sitting in the cockpit of Number 1. It's a 2000 Dallara and is a popular photographic spot in the museum.

Another attraction is a tour of the track. Tours are held between 9 a.m. and 5 p.m. If the track is not in use, the tour runs around the track itself. On occasion, when the track is in use, then it's a "behind the Indy scenes" tour of garages and other off-track highlights.

INDIANAPOLIS MOTOR SPEEDWAY HALL OF FAME MUSEUM. A circular fountain in front of the museum greets visitors driving in under the track from the West Sixteenth Street entrance.

Of course, the museum has a gift shop—actually, two gift shops, one to the right and a second to the left—just inside the main entrance. Both carry nearly identical merchandise, but are needed at times of high attendance. As you can imagine, visitors come from all over the world, sometimes by the busload.

Golfers know there is an eighteen-hole championship course with four of the holes inside the track infield and the other fourteen outside. Racing enthusiasts also are aware that the Allstate 400 and the United States Grand Prix racing events have been added to the track's schedule in recent years.

If racing is your thing, you easily could spend hours in the museum. Don't be thrown off when you approach the building, however. For some reason, the facade lettering doesn't identify it as the Hall of Fame Museum but simply as the Hall of Fame.

IF YOU GO

GETTING THERE: On West Sixteenth Street, turn north under the track—the main entrance. The museum is at the top of a short incline. Hours are 9 a.m. to 5 p.m. (6 p.m. during May), and the museum is open every day but Christmas. The address is 4790 West Sixteenth Street.

INFORMATION: Museum, (317) 492–6784; gift shop, (317) 492–6760 or (800) 955–INDY; golf, (317) 492–6572. The Indianapolis Motor Speedway Web site is http://www.indianapolis motorspeedway.com/.

FEES: Admission charged for the museum; separate charge for the track tour.

DILLINGER'S GRAVE. John Dillinger Jr. is buried at Crown Hill Cemetery in the family plot. The simple headstone—the third at the site—has been chipped away over the years.

THE INDIANAPOLIS SKYLINE. Some two and a half miles away to the south, this is the downtown Indianapolis skyline as viewed from the grave site of James Whitcomb Riley.

Crown Hill Cemetery, Indianapolis

INDIANAPOLIS—The young man and woman sit atop a nearby boulder just below the open canopy monument at the grave of Hoosier poet James Whitcomb Riley. It's apparently a hot summer day—they're holding an umbrella to ward off the sun. You can see Riley's grave behind them. They're not paying much attention to that, however. Their thoughts are likely more about each other as they cuddle together and smile for the camera.

Their photograph, reproduced in the Crown Hill Cemetery tour book, was taken more than seventy-five years ago.

So I'm far from the first person to be impressed with the surroundings at Riley's grave, located at the cemetery's highest point—the very top of Crown Hill. The cemetery straddles Thirty-eighth Street, west of downtown Indianapolis.

What strikes me, though—and give the young couple credit, perhaps they liked what they viewed, too—is the panoramic scene from Riley's grave site.

To the south, two and a half miles away, is the Indianapolis skyline. To the west are the Indianapolis Museum of Art and the muffled sounds from Dr. Martin Luther King Jr. Street. To the north is Butler University. To the east are high-rise condominiums.

What's most surprising, however, are the trees. I am in the middle of a major metropolitan city and, in every direction, spreading out below, are forests of trees.

Probably it makes some difference as to the time of day when one stands near Riley's grave to take in this 360-degree view of Indianapolis. Of course, it is a cemetery, but, nevertheless, the solitude coupled with the grandeur of what can be seen make it, in my book, one of the most awe-inspiring scenes to be found in Indiana.

This view alone, however, isn't all that a trip to Crown Hill Cemetery offers.

With its more than 555 acres, it's the third largest nongovernmental cemetery in the United States. Among those buried here in the 185,000 graves are a U.S. president, three vice presidents, eleven governors, fourteen U.S. senators, fourteen mayors, and thirteen Civil War generals.

Down at the southern end of Crown Hill is the burial place of Benjamin Harrison, the twenty-third president of the United States, and his wife, Carolyn Scott Harrison. He was in the White House from 1889 to 1893, and his wife died there in 1892. Harrison's death came in 1901.

THE TOP OF CROWN HILL. Hoosier poet James Whitcomb Riley is buried under this open canopy monument at the highest point of Crown Hill Cemetery.

The cemetery was opened in 1864 as the Civil War entered its last two years. Among its dead are 1,616 Confederate soldiers who perished at Camp Morton, a federal prisoner of war camp at present-day Twenty-second and Delaware streets. They were first buried at City Cemetery, but their remains were put in the Confederate Burial Mound at Crown Hill in 1931. Ten bronze plaques, dedicated in 1993, list the names of all the Confederates who died at the camp.

The list of the famous buried at Crown Hill is a long one. It includes pharmaceutical founder Eli Lilly; authors Meredith Nicholson, Kin Hubbard (the creator of Abe Martin), and Booth Tarkington; and vice presidents Thomas A. Hendricks, Charles W. Fairbanks, and Thomas R. Marshall.

If you want to tour the cemetery and be certain to see those graves on your list, you can do it in one of two ways.

You can do what I did: Show up, get a map, and start driving and walking, creating your own tour. If you buy the more comprehensive tour book, it includes driving and walking tours that you can follow.

Or you can take one of the special tours scheduled throughout the year. These tours include those centered on the Civil War, heritage, pioneers, authors, cemetery art and architecture, famous funerals, African Americans, Crown Hill celebrities, politicians, actors/artists/architects/musicians, and others.

WHITE RIVER GARDENS. One of the attractions of the nearly twenty features of White River State Park is White River Gardens, with 3.3 acres of interior and exterior flowers, plants, and trees.

MILITARY PARK. A fourteen-acre green space is Military Park, once a Civil War encampment and training field, as well as the first site of the Indiana State Fair. Today it is a popular place for picnics, reunions, and runs.

White River State Park, Indianapolis

INDIANAPOLIS—It's not your father's state park.

White River State Park in downtown Indianapolis has water, picnic areas, grassy hillsides, trees, and walks, but that's where any resemblance to the traditional state park ends.

Rather than putting up your tent, you're invited to spend the night at a nearby hotel. Instead of birding, swimming, or tramping through the forest primeval, you more likely will watch the 70mm IMAX movie on a six-story screen, see the Indianapolis Indians play at Victory Field, visit White River Gardens, spend your time in either the Eiteljorg or the Indiana State museums, or take in the 350 species of animals and other features in the cageless Indianapolis Zoo.

It's an urban state park with all that implies. You're next to the NCAA national headquarters and Hall of Champions, only a block from the state capitol building, two blocks from the Indiana Convention Center and the RCA Dome, and adjacent to Indiana University–Purdue University Indianapolis campus and sports facilities.

It boasts within minutes of the park more than two hundred restaurants and bars, two hundred places to shop, twenty-two memorials/parks/gardens, ten live theaters, thirty-six museums and galleries, four pro sports teams, nine major sports complexes, ten performing arts theaters, and twenty-four hotels with more than 5,400 rooms—and more coming.

If all of this seems overwhelming, it's because it is. You simply need to realize when you arrive at White River State Park that it's a different kind of park—attractions for everyone that can be enjoyed singularly or together, placed in a major urban setting.

You probably will want to make several trips to this state park. It wouldn't be a bad idea to go the first time just to acquaint yourself, find a parking spot you like—there's a huge underground parking facility off Washington Street—and maybe do one thing. For example, see one of the special exhibits in the expanded Eiteljorg Museum of American Indians and Western Art, or the butterflies—in season—at White River Gardens, or attend one of the numerous festivals, concerts, or other activities on the grounds.

Of course, you also can enjoy walking, jogging, or skating along the canal, pedal boating in the canal, strolling along the river promenade, or picnicking. Walkers and runners these days are in abundance along the park's paths and pedestrian-safe bridges.

The best place to begin your visit to the park, however, is by going to the visitor center where the former Beveridge Paper Company

A QUIET TIME IN THE BIG CITY. Walks along the canal, which goes through White River State Park, offer a chance for some contemplative moments. Downtown workers use it during noon hour; others all the time.

plant stood. Here you can pick up information and have your questions answered. Perhaps an even better idea is to call or e-mail before you head to Indianapolis and ask for a map and guide for specific information.

The zoo, of course, is its own major attraction. Events are scheduled throughout the year—a biggie is the annual holiday light show—in addition to animals on an African plain, an Amazon rain forest, a safari-oriented family roller coaster, and a watery playground for the kids. It anchors the west end of White River State Park and has its own parking lot.

More recently open is the Indiana State Museum with its own busy schedule and exhibits. Hoosiers of a certain age will enjoy relaxing in the L. S. Ayres Tea Room, a replica of the former and famous downtown dining room.

The park also is the home of Victory Field, where the Indianapolis Indians play. When I was walking through the park one summer afternoon, I could hear the cheers from the nearby baseball park. For that moment, I felt a part of the game. I suspect the park designers would like that.

IF YOU GO

GETTING THERE: In downtown Indianapolis, go west on Washington Street and cross West Street at the Eiteljorg Museum. The underground garage is just a short distance to the right. The visitor center's parking lot is another short distance on Washington Street and again a turn to the right at Schumacher Way.

INFORMATION: You can reach White River State Park at (800) 665–9056 or its Web site at http://www.inwhiteriver.com/; IMAX Theater (317) 233–4629, http://www.imaxindy.com/; Eiteljorg (317) 636–9378, http://www.eitel jorg.org/; Indianapolis Zoo (317) 630–2001, http://www.indianapoliszoo.com/; Indianapolis Indians (317) 269–3542, http://www.IndyIndians.com/; White River Gardens (317) 630–2001, http://www.whiterivergardens.com/; Indiana State Museum (317) 232–1637, http://www.indianamuseum .org/; and NCAA Hall of Champions (317) 916–4255 and http://www.ncaahallofchampions.org/.

FEES: No fee to enter the park. All the attractions charge.

THE GLASS DOME ABOVE THE ROTUNDA. Looking up at the glass dome, three floors above the center rotunda at the statehouse.

Indiana Statehouse, Indianapolis

INDIANAPOLIS—If you were more than 115 years old, you probably would have gone through several "restorations," too! So it's no surprise that Indiana's statehouse has had a number of updates over the decades, often dependent upon how much money was available.

You can get a good understanding of these changes by visiting the venerable 1888 building in downtown Indianapolis, especially if you have in hand two brief but informative—and free—publications. A sixteen-page booklet, *The Indiana Statehouse*, provides a self-guided tour. The second, *Indiana State House Design and Restorations*, also explains in eight pages the building's various remodelings. (Note the two spellings of "statehouse." Some dictionaries insist it is two words, but the Associated Press Stylebook and one of the booklets have it as one.)

Of course, Indiana's first territorial capital wasn't in Indianapolis at all. It was at Vincennes from 1800 to 1813, when this was the Indiana Territory. The second capital, and first state capitol building, was in Corydon until state government moved to Indianapolis in 1825. An early Indianapolis statehouse stood on the south capitol grounds, facing Washington Street.

When the roof fell in on that structure, it seemed to be time to think about another building. Finally, two contractors and several lawsuits later, the new statehouse was completed in 1888. You'll see a plaque on the main floor reporting that the building was constructed for $1,980,969.18. That's good, because the Indiana General Assembly had mandated that the cost could not exceed $2 million.

In 1931 it had been forty-three years since any attention had been paid to the outside of the building. It was steam cleaned to remove what was called "a black coat of soot" caused by coal furnaces, prevalent at the time, and exhaust fumes from early automobiles.

Almost no work was done on the building during the Great Depression. The major renovation came in time to celebrate the centennial of the statehouse in 1988. Literally acres of plaster were removed, more acres of limestone cleaned, marble floors taken up and re-laid, the wood on more than two hundred doors stripped and refinished, the rotunda glass restored and cleaned, and on and on.

Other changes in the statehouse occurred over time. For example, if you go into the House and Senate chambers on the east and west sides of the third floor, you will notice that the rooms have no windows. A 1948 renovation created walls inside the existing chambers, making room for offices between the walls and the windows. Total cost? $10,937,292.00, or five times the cost of the building's original construction.

INDIANA'S STATEHOUSE. View of the state capitol building from the southeast, at the corner of Washington Street and Capitol Avenue.

IF YOU GO

The building houses all three branches of state government. Most executive offices are on the main floor, the legislative chambers and supreme court on the third, legislative galleries, judges' offices, and committee rooms on the fourth. (A single-sheet layout of the building also can be picked up at the information desk.)

One of the building's major features is the open atrium extending from the main floor up 105 feet to the glass-topped dome, high above the fourth floor.

That's probably the most dramatic view in the building. You can stand on the main floor and look as I did—no doubt gawking like a tourist—up through the atriums on either side of the beautifully restored glass dome. It is illuminated by a reflective structure with high intensity lights in the room of the exterior dome above it.

That dome, 235 feet high, is covered with copper and serves as the base for a 1,200-pound flagpole.

You might also want to look at the first floor. Today, media offices are located there, replacing the building's old press shacks. The building's services offices are there, too, along with rooms dedicated for committee hearings and a snack bar. In the old days, it was the stable for legislators' horses and buggies.

If you're in Indianapolis and you want to tour the statehouse, you can pick up the self-guided tour booklet at the information desk outside the rotunda or in Room 220. You also can go on one of the guided tours. On the day I was there, tours were scheduled at 9 a.m., 11 a.m., 1:30 p.m., and 3 p.m.

GETTING THERE: The statehouse is two blocks west of Monument Circle in downtown Indianapolis.

INFORMATION: Telephone (317) 233–5293 for information about tours and hours. The e-mail address is captours@idoa.state.in.us.

FEES: None.

TOP OF THE MONUMENT. *Victory* stands atop the Soldiers and Sailors Monument on the Circle in downtown Indianapolis. Her sword symbolizes victory, her torch the light of civilization, and the eagle on her brow, freedom.

Soldiers and Sailors Monument, Indianapolis

VIEW TO THE NORTH. Looking north up Meridian Street from the observation balcony of the Soldiers and Sailors Monument. Christ Church Cathedral is seen at the lower right.

INDIANAPOLIS—When you went on a school field trip to the Soldiers and Sailors Monument on the Circle in Indianapolis, you probably decided to go up the 330 steps—maybe even ran—to the top. Today, if you're like me, you would use the elevator.

Frankly, I had never been inside the elevator until I visited the monument recently. While I didn't have a tape measure with me, it's difficult to believe that the floor inside the elevator is much more than three feet square. Still, six people emerged when it reached the ground floor as I waited for it before I took my trip to the top.

Even if you do take the elevator, you will still need to walk up a few steps to reach the small observation balcony, enclosed in glass, located 321 feet above the ground. The view, though, is worth it.

I was there on a sun-splashed weekend afternoon, and the view of Meridian Street to the north was the most dramatic. It was unobstructed as far as the eye could see, beginning with Christ Church Cathedral—a church that was there before the monument was built—immediately to the right.

Most Hoosiers have some knowledge about the monument. We know that it was constructed to honor Indiana's veterans and war dead from the Civil War. Of the men of military age in the state, no less than 74.3 percent—210,487—served in the Union armed forces, and 24,000 of them died.

Before the monument was completed, its mission had been changed to honor those who had served in the military up through the Spanish-American War.

The site first had been selected for the construction of the governor's home in 1827 after the central city square mile had been laid out by Alexander Ralston. Tradition has it that no governor ever lived there because no governor's wife was about to hang out her washing to dry in the middle of the city for everyone to see.

After the house deteriorated and was demolished in 1857, the Circle became a grazing ground for livestock, and a city park was planned. That changed, however, when a monument to Civil War veterans was proposed in the 1860s.

A monument commission decided to hold a design competition, which was won by architect Bruno Schmitz of Berlin, Germany, in 1888. It was another fourteen years before the monument was finally completed and dedicated on May 15, 1902. At the dedication ceremony, according to *Indiana; A New Historical Guide*, General Lew Wallace presided; James Whitcomb Riley recited a poem he had written,

PEACE. *Peace reigns in the statues displayed on the west side of the Soldiers and Sailors Monument.*

"The Soldier"; and a John Philip Sousa march, "Messiah of the Nations," was performed.

The statistics of the monument are impressive.

The monument is 284 feet, 6 inches tall; by comparison, the Statue of Liberty stands 306 feet, 8 inches.

Its complete cost was slightly less than $600,000. It is estimated it would cost at least $500 million to build today.

The monument is constructed of gray oolitic limestone, quarried in Owen County.

The statue on top has been called Miss Indiana, but her actual title is Victory. It stands 38 feet tall and weighs 19,300 pounds.

Much of the story of the monument is told in the stone statues on all four sides of the monument.

For example, on the east is the depiction of *War* with *The Dying Soldier* directly above the fountain. *War* includes a battle scene of cavalry and infantry charges, the goddess of war urging them on, while Columbia, in the background, holds the Stars and Stripes. On the west is *Peace* with *The Return Home*. A soldier is reunited with his family, Liberty holds the flag, and at her feet a freed slave lifts his broken chains as the Angel of Peace holds aloft a wreath of victory and an olive branch.

"The monument," as it often is called, is worthy of a studied look you may not have given it in the past. Also, don't miss the Colonel Eli Lilly Civil War Museum in the basement.

GETTING THERE: The Soldiers and Sailors Monument is on Monument Circle at the intersection of Meridian and Market streets in downtown Indianapolis.

INFORMATION: The telephone number for the Indiana War Memorials Commission (where an attendant can answer questions) and the Colonel Eli Lilly Civil War Museum gift shop is (317) 232–7615. The monument and the museum are open Wednesday through Sunday from 10 a.m. to 6 p.m. during spring and summer. During winter hours, they are only open on weekends until March 5.

FEES: Minimal charge for an elevator ticket. It can be purchased at the museum gift shop. The Lilly Civil War Museum is free.

The former home of onetime Indiana governor James Brown Ray is thought to be one of the oldest, perhaps even the oldest, existing house in Indianapolis. It was built by Ray, who served as governor from 1825 to 1831.

This home on North Vermont Street was built about one hundred years after many in the Lockerbie Square neighborhood but was designed to fit in with existing houses. It won a New Construction Award from Historic Landmarks Foundation of Indiana.

Lockerbie Square, Indianapolis

INDIANAPOLIS—If you use your imagination, you can visualize the scene from the early 1900s.

The older gentleman comes out the front door of the Italianate home where he is a paid boarder, descends the steps to the cobblestone street, and sets off for an office he has at the Union Trust Bank, not too many blocks away in downtown Indianapolis. Later in the day, he retraces his steps, arriving at 528 Lockerbie Street after a brisk walk home.

Frequently, neighborhood children fall in step and accompany him part of the way. Children have an instinct about these things. They like the man. Maybe it's because he tells them a story or two, or, more likely, he recites some verse. If it's verse, he probably wrote it, for the well-dressed walker is James Whitcomb Riley, the Hoosier Poet.

According to stories told about those times, Riley also would often walk to a neighborhood store, buy some candy, and give it to the children who followed him.

Partly because Riley lived here and partly because of the homes built on Indianapolis's near east side, historic Lockerbie Square, with its Queen Anne, Federal, and Italianate homes, has been placed on the National Register of Historic Places.

The square, originally platted between 1847 and 1850, includes structures built mostly in the 1855 to 1930 period. Revitalization began in the 1960s, which resulted in the first historic district preservation area in Indianapolis. It was listed on the National Register of Historic Places in 1973 and enlarged in 1987.

Happily for us, the Lockerbie Square People's Club, in cooperation with the Historic Landmarks Foundation of Indiana, has produced a walking-tour guide. It identifies twenty-five historic buildings plus five newer residences that have been constructed in recent years but which were built to blend into the neighborhood. Almost all of the buildings are residences, with a few exceptions. One is Lockerbie Square United Methodist Church at the corner of East and New York streets; the other is Clemens Vonnegut Public School Number 9, now converted into an office complex.

The Lockerbie Square historic district stretches from Michigan Avenue on the north to New York Street on the south and from East Street on the west—yes, that's right—to Davidson Street on the east. It's an area you can comfortably walk in an hour or two.

The centerpiece is the James Whitcomb Riley Museum Home, where the poet spent the last twenty-three years of his life. Actually, the house was built in 1872 by John Nickum, an Indianapolis baker. His daughter, Magdalena, married attorney Charles Holstein, and they continued living

The Hoosier Poet James Whitcomb Riley lived as a paying guest for twenty-three years in this home at 528 Lockerbie Street in Indianapolis. It's the best-known home in the Lockerbie Square historic district.

in the home. It was the Holsteins who in 1893 invited Riley to live there. He shared the household expenses and purchased items for the house.

Since most of the Lockerbie Square homes are private residences, the stroller can only see them from the outside. Not so the Riley Museum Home, however. It's operated by the Riley Children's Foundation and has regular hours plus tours on request. You can see the second-floor bedroom where Riley worked at his corner desk, the wicker chair where he spent considerable time following a 1911 stroke, and the bed on which he died on July 22, 1916.

Because it is a preservation museum, just about everything in the house is as Riley knew it, with the exception of the kitchen, much of which is a restoration.

Across Lockerbie Street at 517 is the Reading-Kindell cottage. It's a small, one-story frame house built in 1856. That's where Katie Kindell, the Riley home housekeeper, lived.

Two of the newer homes are across Vermont Street from each other. The more spectacular is the house at 628, built in 1992–93. It features what the tour guide calls "an abundance" of windows facing the street.

The Lockerbie Square historic district also has what is believed to be one of the oldest, if not the oldest, homes in Indianapolis. It is the Governor James Ray-Buscher house at 302 N. Park Avenue. Built in 1835 where the Marion County Jail now stands, it was moved here in 1977.

You can also walk down neighborhood alleys and find some run-down garages and sheds that may be about as old. In a few years they'll probably be gone, replaced by garage apartments, which are becoming quite popular.

IF YOU GO

GETTING THERE: In downtown Indianapolis, go east five blocks from Meridian Street on New York Street to Lockerbie Square.

INFORMATION: The Riley home is open for guided tours from 10 a.m. to 4 p.m. Tuesday through Saturday and noon to 4 p. m. Sunday. The last tour begins at 3:30 p.m. Call (317) 631–5885 to make arrangements for group tours. Walking-tour guides can be found at various city locations or at the Indianapolis City Centre in the Circle Centre Mall. Call toll-free (800) 323–4639 for information. Call (317) 638–9368 to have a tour guide mailed to you.

FEES: Admission charged for Riley home tours. The walking-tour guide is free.

NOT GARFIELD. This statue is of Major General Henry W. Lawton, who died "in front of his troops while leading a charge" in the Battle of San Mateo in 1899 in the Philippines during the Spanish-American War.

A CYCAD. It's one of the more spectacular trees in the conservatory at Garfield Park in Indianapolis.

IN CONSERVATORY. This waterfall and surrounding plant life and trees fill the far end of the Garfield Conservatory in Indianapolis.

Garfield Park Conservatory and Sunken Gardens, Indianapolis

INDIANAPOLIS—The imposing statue overlooking Garfield Park's Conservatory and Sunken Gardens is that of President James A. Garfield, for whom the city park is named, right?

Wrong. It's true the near-south-side complex was named for the former U.S. president after he was assassinated in 1881. The statue, however, is that of Major General Henry W. Lawton, who died in battle in the Philippines during the Spanish-American War. The statue originally stood at the old Marion County Courthouse but was moved to the park in 1915.

The park—the city's oldest and "only 10 minutes from downtown Indianapolis," according to the park's brochure—was established in the late 1800s on the site of a failed horse-racing track. Its 136 acres include, in addition to the conservatory and sunken gardens, wooded areas, greenway trails, creeks, and athletic and recreational areas along with an art center, picnic sites, and shelters. It since has been listed on the National Register of Historic Places.

Dedicated in 1916, the gardens early on gained a reputation in the Midwest for its fountains and floral displays. Its three acres include graceful fountains, paved walkways, and benches to complement its European classical garden formations.

Time was not kind, as the gardens deteriorated over the decades. Restoration efforts have been successful in recent years, and the gardens were rededicated in 1998. The battle for sufficient funding continues, however. The conservatory maintains a Friends of Garfield Park Conservatory fund-raising campaign to manage its upkeep. (A brick, placed on the plaza between the conservatory and the sunken gardens, costs the donor $80.) There's also a Friends of Garfield Park Inc. that raises funds for the entire park.

Other than the park's outdoor recreational facilities, it is the conservatory that draws the most visitors. The first conservatory opened on this site in 1915 and was replaced in 1954 with an all-glass and welded-aluminum structure of ten thousand square feet. It, too, has undergone renovation, this time in the 1990s.

A self-guided tour takes the visitor into the gazebo room and follows an oval-shaped path among the conservatory's plants and trees. Midway through the tour, at the south end of the conservatory, is a waterfall. Large group guided tours also are available.

An extensive summer program begins in May and continues through August. Summer concerts in the gardens are another feature.

FOLLOWS EUROPEAN DESIGN. The sunken gardens at Garfield Park were designed to follow the European classical form.

The conservatory also offers Environmental EdVentures for children in preschool through fifth grade, one of five city parks to do so. The curriculum-based environmental education programs focus on the rain forest, use of the five senses as related to nature, plants, bugs, and trees. Then EdVentures students can go to the sunken gardens to tour some more, relax, or have lunch.

IF YOU GO

GETTING THERE: On Interstate 65 South in downtown Indianapolis, exit west at Raymond Street and turn south to the park on Shelby Street at the first traffic light on Raymond.

INFORMATION: Call (317) 327–7184 for more information and tours or go to the park's Web site at http://www .garfieldgardensconservatory.org/. The address is 2505 Conservatory Drive. Conservatory hours are daily from 10 a.m. to 6 p.m. Memorial Day to Labor Day, and 10 a.m. to 5 p.m. during the winter. Sunken gardens hours are 10 a.m. to 10 p.m., daily, April 15 to October 15, and 10 a.m. to 5 p.m. during the winter.

FEES: Admission charged for the conservatory.

MEMORIAL CENTER. The Bona Thompson Memorial Center now is the art and cultural center for Irvington on Indianapolis's east side. Early in the twentieth century it was the Butler University library.

STEPHENSON LIVED HERE. The front portico of this Irvington house was added when D. C. Stephenson, Grand Dragon of the Ku Klux Klan, bought it in 1923.

BEAUTIFUL HOMES. One of the well-maintained homes in Irvington, this one is located on South Audubon Road.

Bona Thompson Memorial Center and Irvington, Indianapolis

INDIANAPOLIS—The project was to return the Bona Thompson Memorial Center "to its former glory." It was going to cost $800,000 to make the 1903 neoclassical building a community arts and cultural center.

A daunting project, but the Irvington Historical Society did it.

Rededicated in 2002, the building was the recipient of the 2003 Historic Landmarks Foundation of Indiana's Neighborhood Award. The award noted the building gives "the east side a historic showplace in which to gather and exhibit art and history."

It is that, indeed. A recent tour of the Indianapolis suburb of Irvington ended with a reception at the Thompson Center. In appearance and cleanliness, it looks as if it were built yesterday. Yet it's been there for a hundred years and continues hosting a multitude of events, one of them being the annual Irvington Ice Cream Social and Art Fair each August.

The center formerly was the library for Butler University from 1903 to 1928 when the campus was located in Irvington before its move to the north of downtown Indianapolis. Edward and Mary Thompson donated money and land for its construction in memory of their daughter, who died shortly after her graduation from Butler.

As imposing as the Bona Thompson Memorial Center is, Irvington has even more to offer the visitor. A self-guided tour of approximately a mile and a quarter is available at the center. Homes in Irvington range from mansions of the day to Sears mail-order houses. That's right—Sears offered do-it-yourself, precut mail-order houses. One, a Stratford Tudor Revival cottage, can be seen at 822 N. Campbell Avenue. It was built in 1933, while the last Sears models were available into 1940.

Only a block south of the Thompson Center on Downey Avenue is the elegant Benton House, restored by the Irvington Historic Landmarks Foundation as a place for parties, meetings, and receptions. It, too, has guided tours by appointment. All its furnishings have been donated by Irvington residents and organizations.

The Benton House was one of the first homes built in Irvington, a suburb settled largely by abolitionists after the Civil War, many of them Quakers and members of the Disciples of Christ. Benton House is a one-and-one-half story French Second Empire structure built in 1873 as a speculative property. Allen R. Benton, twice president of Butler University, and his wife, Silence, owned the house from 1886 to 1907. Benton later became the first chancellor of the University of Nebraska.

Former fraternity and sorority houses, now mostly converted into residences, and houses that at one time were the homes of university

BENTON HOUSE. The house is located on the northwest corner of Ohmer and South Downey avenues in Irvington and is termed "an example of what an area can do to preserve its past," according to the Benton House Association. The association was formed in 1969 to maintain and arrange use of the historic house.

IF YOU GO

professors abound in the Irvington historical district, bordered on the north by Pleasant Run Parkway, on the east by Arlington Avenue, on the south by Rawles Avenue, and on the west by Emerson Avenue.

One of the houses has a more notorious past. That's the onetime Phi Delta Theta fraternity house, originally built on University Avenue in 1889 by W. H. H. Graham, a Civil War veteran and American counsel to Canada. In 1923 the Graham family sold the house to D. C. Stephenson.

Stephenson was the Grand Dragon of the Ku Klux Klan, who once claimed, "I am the law in Indiana." He added an Ionic portico to enhance the house's image. Everything came crashing down for Stephenson, however, when he was convicted of the assault that ended in the death of another Irvington resident, young Madge Oberholtzer.

On a more pleasant note, the Irvington Historical Society and Irvington Historic Landmarks Foundation take care of another community point of interest, a giant bur oak tree, estimated at the time of the American bicentennial in 1976 to be 350 to 400 years old.

The tree, across from a house at 5940 Beechwood Avenue, is called the Kile Oak and is 87 feet high with a crown spread of 123 feet. The International Society of Arboriculture and the National Arbor Association recognized the tree in the bicentennial year "as having lived during the American Revolutionary period."

GETTING THERE: The Bona Thompson Memorial Center is about two miles west of Interstate 465 and East Washington Street. It is three blocks south of Washington Street and one block west of Ritter Avenue at the intersection of south Downey and east University avenues. Parking is to the north of the center.

INFORMATION: The Bona Thompson Memorial Center is open Saturday from 1 p.m. to 3 p.m.; Sunday, 2 p.m. to 4 p.m.; Wednesday, 1 p.m. to 3 p.m.; or by appointment. Its street address is 5350 E. University Avenue. Call (317) 353–2662 for more information. The Benton House is open by appointment. Call (317) 357–0318.

FEES: None for tours.

GARRISON RESTAURANT. Lunchtime at the conference center's Garrison Restaurant at Fort Harrison State Park. An evening "Hoosier supper buffet" is served on Saturday.

Fort Harrison State Park, Indianapolis

INDIANAPOLIS—It's almost as if it were just waiting to become a state park.

When the federal government decommissioned most of Fort Harrison in 1991, it meant an officers' club, three officers' homes, a building to house special guests, an eighteen-hole golf course, and one of the largest tracts of hardwood forests in central Indiana were available for other use.

The fort had been an active station for nearly a hundred years. It was dedicated in 1906 by President Theodore Roosevelt, in honor of the nation's twenty-third president, Benjamin Harrison.

In 1995 the U.S. Department of the Interior approved transferring 1,700 of the fort's 2,500 acres to Indiana for use as a state park. Today Fort Harrison State Park is a popular golf resort, conference center, and site for outdoor exercise.

Located three miles east of Interstate 465 South and north of Fifty-sixth Street, the state park offers the outdoor enthusiast biking, fishing, golf, picnicking, and trails for hiking and horseback riding. The three hiking trails are all easy to moderate and from two to two and one-half miles in length. Horse rentals are available from March through October. If you're interested in fishing, you will need a state license, available at the park office.

The Lawrence and Fall Creek hiking trails go through wooded uplands and ravines, while the Harrison Trace Trail has been covered with asphalt for walkers, bicyclists, joggers, and in-line skaters. Bicycles are allowed only on the Harrison Trace Trail. Because of its streams, the two nonasphalt trails can be muddy or even wet at times.

The trails don't offer all the scenes of some of the state parks in southern Indiana—for example, deep ravines, rocky outcroppings, steep hillsides. But they do offer wildflowers in season, peaceful wooded tracts, and a kind of rustic beauty only a few minutes removed from downtown Indianapolis.

The park has three shelter houses and three picnic areas that have tables, grills, toilets, playground equipment, and play fields. The shelters can be reserved by calling the park office.

An interpretive center is part of a park office complex, located on its south side near Fifty-sixth Street. It includes the park office, saddle barns, a natural resources education center, and the interpretive center. Staff interpreters at the center mount displays and offer programs telling about the park's natural and cultural history.

Fort Harrison is considered a day-use park, so it closes at dusk.

FORMER OFFICERS' CLUB. The Fort Golf Resort and Conference Center is headquartered in the former officers' club at Fort Harrison on the east side of Indianapolis.

The seventy-two-par golf course was redesigned by Pete Dye in the mid-1990s. It features rolling hills, tree-lined fairways, and an award-winning wetlands design. The course is located at the eastern side of the state park and is off-limits to those other than golfers.

The Fort Golf Resort and Conference Center offers multiday "play and stay" golf packages. Men's and women's locker rooms, a pro shop, and a driving range also are available.

Overnight facilities make use of lodging that was provided for special military guests and officers. They include Harrison House, which formerly served as VIP lodging for military visitors. Harrison House now is made up of two-room suites and single guest rooms. Additional housing consists of three furnished former officers' homes, each with three bedrooms and two sofa beds.

One of the former officers' dining rooms, now the Garrison Restaurant, serves lunch Monday through Saturday, 11 a.m. to 2 p.m.; dinners, Friday and Saturday, 5 p.m. to 8:30 p.m.; and a Sunday brunch from 11 a.m. to 2:30 p.m. The building includes banquet facilities for up to four hundred people.

A cozy fireplace in the restaurant lobby is a good place to end a meal with a cup of coffee.

IF YOU GO

GETTING THERE: Turn east off Interstate 465 South in Indianapolis on Fifty-sixth Street to Post Road and go north to the state park entrance.

INFORMATION: The Web site is http://www.in.gov/dnr/parklake/ properties/park_fortharrison .html. The state park number is (317) 591–0904. The Fort Golf Resort and Conference Center number is (317) 543–9592, or you can write the center at 6002 N. Post Road, Indianapolis, Indiana 46216. For restaurant reservations or information also call (317) 543–9592. The number for the interpretive center is (317) 591–0122.

FEES: Admission charged.

PHOTO MONTAGE. These historic photos, Keys to the Past: Our History in Residential Architecture, make up one of the displays at the Carmel-Clay Township Historical Society's museum in Carmel.

Carmel-Clay Township Historical Museum, Carmel

CARMEL—The Carmel-Clay Township Historical Society has only been on the job for about thirty years. That's not very long as historical groups go, but this one has made some serious progress during that time.

With the nation's bicentennial coming up in 1976, folks in this community north of Indianapolis thought it was time to begin "documenting, preserving, and presenting our rich local history." So they got themselves organized and turned toward their first project. That was to raise funds to buy the abandoned Monon railroad station with the idea of turning it into a city-township historical museum.

Incidentally, why were those Monon stations painted as they were? You'll find the answer at the end of the column.

By 1980 the historical society had the money. The next task was to move and restore the station, located on the old Monon tracks near downtown Carmel. Fortunately, most of the original timbers of the station were in good shape for the move.

"It had been maintained and kept up over the years," according to Carmel-Clay Township historian Tom Rumer. In the years that followed, historical society members and volunteers added a kitchen, a restroom, and some additional space, where they now have an old-time schoolroom on display.

As you might expect, the Old Monon Depot Museum is still a work in progress. When I visited there, historian Rumer was up on a ladder inside the museum, doing some manual labor. We held a conversation about the historical society, the museum, and writing as he kept working. It turns out that Rumer is an author as well as the much-appreciated historian for the historical group, after previously working for the Indiana Historical Society.

The township historical society has been working on its displays for the past decade. (It may be difficult to appreciate the amount of time needed by such an organization that depends entirely upon volunteers to gather artifacts, organize them, find financing, and work up displays. It can easily stretch into years.)

Among recent improvements to the station, built in 1883, have been a furnace and air-conditioning, made possible by the Clay Township trustee; a copier, provided by the Legacy Foundation; and a computer, purchased by society members.

Rumer said the group constantly is on the lookout for additional material. He showed me donated materials from the estate of Eleanor Murphy Hunt, including a wedding dress and old photo albums. One

OLD MONON DEPOT MUSEUM. After the Carmel-Clay Township Historical Society purchased the old Monon railroad station, it was moved across the tracks to become the society's museum.

of the photographs shows part of Carmel under water during the 1913 flood.

Donations of documents, manuscripts, reference books, photographs, and other historical artifacts are always sought. At the same time, and like practically every other historical museum, display space is at a premium.

One prized possession is one of the nation's first automatic traffic signals. It was invented in Carmel by Leslie Haines in the early 1920s and once controlled traffic at a Main Street intersection.

The historical society's operation actually extends into two buildings. Next door to the depot museum is a second building that houses the archival collections. To visit it, you first go to the depot for admission.

Among the group's events are a Halloween Tour to an area cemetery; a County Christmas Bazaar, held on a Saturday late in October; a Historic Home Tour on a Friday and Saturday in early December; other special programs of music, field trips, speakers; and publication of the society's newsletter.

Those Monon stations? According to Rumer, passenger trains and stations for a brief period following World War II were painted crimson and cream to honor Indiana University, while freight trains and stations were painted gold and black for Purdue.

Today, the station is red.

IF YOU GO

GETTING THERE: In Carmel, stay on Range Line Road and go to First Street SW. The address is 211 First Street SW. Turn west to the museum at the old Monon tracks, now the Monon Trail.

INFORMATION: The museum is open Friday, 9 a.m. to noon and 1 p.m. to 5 p.m.; Saturday, 10 a.m. to 4 p.m.; and the first Sunday of each month, 2 p.m. to 4 p.m. The telephone number is (317) 846–7117.

FEES: Donations accepted.

MORE THAN 140 YEARS OLD. This 1861 dollhouse is on permanent loan from a descendant of the builder. A handwritten poem found in a wall panel when it was cleaned tells of its construction by Thomas Russell "as a memento for my niece, S. Ward."

WHERE THE PRINCESSES DANCED. A children's favorite at the museum is Silver Woods by Suzie Moffett, taken from the fairy tale, "The Twelve Dancing Princesses."

Museum of Miniature Houses and Other Collections, Carmel

CARMEL—Those are the kinds of friends to have.

Money for operations is usually a tight squeeze for any museum. When extra funding becomes available, that's a welcome gift beyond expression.

Some additional financial help was on the way recently to the Museum of Miniature Houses and Other Collections Inc. All proceeds from two auctions at the Philadelphia, Pennsylvania, Miniature Show and Sale—$12,000—were given to the Carmel museum.

It's a way in which the national show helps not-for-profit miniature museums around the country. That assistance was in addition to support for the museum that comes from admission fees, the Friends of the Museum group, grants, and sales at the museum shop.

The Carmel museum celebrated its eleventh anniversary in late August 2004. Founded in 1991 by Suzie Moffett, Suzanne Landshof, and Nancy Lesh, the museum opened two years later in a renovated building previously occupied by a law firm.

Each of the rooms was compartmentalized when the museum bought the building and that has worked out well.

Since it opened, the museum has had more than forty thousand visitors from all fifty states and a number of foreign countries. The museum is a favorite for touring groups, too, including schools and senior groups.

It's a not-for-profit organization operated by a board of directors along with about forty volunteers who help run the museum.

The museum's purpose is to preserve and exhibit quality miniatures and other collections, to provide educational forums and workshops, and to show relationships to history, architecture, and decorative arts.

The museum has more than fifty different dollhouses, miniature houses, and room boxes, spanning from 1861 to the present day. As visitors enter from the back parking lot, the rooms they will see include:

Room 1, filled with dollhouses from 1861 to the 1950s

Room 2, dedicated to deceased cofounder Lesh, includes two houses she built, which are replications of her former homes

Room 3, which recently featured a Route 66 display and permanent larger displays

Rooms 4 and 5 contain items from the permanent collection

Room 6 exhibits change every three or four months, including those from local collectors and are not necessarily miniatures—part of the

THE MUSEUM'S HOUSE. The Museum of Miniature Houses in Carmel formerly housed attorneys before it was renovated in the early 1990s for the museum.

rest of the museum's name, "and Other Collections." At the time of my visit, the display was of early American silhouettes, a collection dating from the late 1700s to the 1860s.

The museum also houses a reference library with books and periodicals about miniatures along with the small museum shop featuring miniatures, many handcrafted by well-known artisans.

Works by artisans also are shown in a case of highly crafted miniatures made to specific scale. These works represent the finest in various art forms, including paintings, silversmithing, ceramics, furniture and cabinetry, and textiles.

IF YOU GO

GETTING THERE: In Carmel, turn east from Range Line Road onto Main Street—One Hundred Thirty-first Street—one block to the museum. The address is 111 E. Main Street.

INFORMATION: Open Wednesday through Saturday 11 a.m. to 4 p.m. and Sunday 1 p.m. to 4 p.m. Telephone is (317) 575–9466. Web site is http://www.museumofminiatures .org/.

FEES: Admission charged.

LEAVE 1836 PRAIRIETOWN. Walking through the Cedar Chapel covered bridge, one enters 1886 Liberty Corner. The bridge was moved from De Kalb County thirty years ago. Notice the cupolas on the bridge roof.

IT'S BIG. The size of the beehive oven at the William Conner home at 1836 Prairietown at Conner Prairie can be seen in this photo. It extends out at the left corner of the front of the home.

THEY'RE TYPICAL. The bedrooms in the 1886 Zimmerman house are typical of the era. Washbasins, chamber pots, and no electricity are some of the features. But the beds look comfortable!

Conner Prairie, Fishers

FISHERS—You've been to Conner Prairie, visited the museum center, and walked around 1836 Prairietown. So, that about does it, right?

Hardly.

On your computer, go to the museum's Web site. Check out the calendar of events. When I did, no less than sixty-two different activities were scheduled over several months. The fact of the matter is that the living history museum has so much to do, so many things to learn about our past, and so many ways to enjoy yourself that the real task is to be selective in picking those of greatest interest.

The major recent event has been Weekend on the Farm at the 1886 Zimmerman family farm. Guests take part in a two-day farm weekend.

Now, before you say too quickly, "Oh, boy, life on the farm. Won't that be wonderful," do a little thinking about farm life in the late 1800s. For starters, there is no electricity, so no hairdryers, refrigerators, or electric lights. No indoor plumbing. No telephones. Plus, whoever said farm work was easy? You have such chores to complete as taking care of the livestock and preparing meals.

It isn't all work, of course. A barn dance, parlor games, baseball games when the weather cooperates, and, naturally, lots of visiting and conversation are also part of your activities.

But let's back up a minute because the Zimmerman farm itself is one of the newer aspects of Conner Prairie.

The farm is part of the 1886 area, added to Conner Prairie to complement 1836 Prairietown—in other words, fifty years later. It's part of Liberty Corner, a Victorian crossroad with a district school, a Quaker meetinghouse, and the farm.

The visitor "crosses over" fifty years by entering Liberty Corner via the Cedar Chapel covered bridge. The bridge, originally constructed in De Kalb County in 1884 by George Woentz and son, is unique with its signature cupolas that have been carefully restored.

The other connection between the eras is Susannah Zimmerman, once a young innkeeper at the Golden Eagle Inn at Prairietown in 1836 and now, fifty years later, living with her son and his family at the farm.

All the roles are performed by costumed staff. They are composite characters, according to Daniel Schoeneberg, manager of 1886 Liberty Corner, because the historical program wanted "representative persons and didn't want to put words in the mouths of real people."

Among the numerous educational programs during the summer months is a behind the scenes tour. Its nature changes from week

BEEHIVE OVEN. A Conner Prairie costumed staff member opens the beehive oven next to the hearth at the William Conner home. It took a lengthy preheating and a cleaning out of all the ashes before the oven, much larger than it appears in this photo, could be used.

IF YOU GO

to week. The Friday I visited, it dealt with hearth cooking. We moved from place to place, examining hearth cooking and the use of the first cooking stove in the county at the doctor's home. Eventually, we ended up at the William Conner home for an explanation of beehive oven cooking, so called because the oven extends in the form of a beehive outside the house.

Follow the North Star was scheduled for that evening, a tour in which guests—now escaped slaves out in the dark of the night—try to make their way to freedom by avoiding bounty hunters. The next day, it was wagon rides, a visit by an Indian agent, Lenape cooking and food, ornament signing, and a repeat of escaped slaves following the North Star program.

So it goes, day after day. The best thing to do is to check the calendar of events.

Coming soon will be a second historical update, a 1943 working farm equipped with an 1898 metal trestle bridge to provide another "gateway," this time into the twentieth century. Another generation of Zimmermans will be living on this farm.

GETTING THERE: Located on Allisonville Road north of Fishers.

INFORMATION: Call (800) 966–1836 or visit the Web site at http://www.connerprairie.org/. The historical program closes after November and reopens in April, but the museum center, shop, restaurant, and other special programs continue year-round. Open Tuesday through Saturday 9:30 a.m. to 5 p.m. and Sunday 11 a.m. to 5 p.m. Closed on major holidays.

FEES: Admission charged.

RESTORED PARLOR. The Hamilton County Historical Society has restored this parlor on the first floor of the old Hamilton County sheriff's home on the courthouse square.

Hamilton County Historical Society and Hamilton County Museum of History, Noblesville

NOBLESVILLE—The 1925 conviction of D. C. Stephenson, head of the Indiana Ku Klux Klan, for second-degree murder in the rape and death of a young woman essentially spelled the end of the Klan's power in Indiana. His sensational trial that attracted national attention in the mid-1920s was moved from Indianapolis to Hamilton County.

"That's where Stephenson was held for trial—in one of the older cells," says Diane Nevitt, museum director for the Hamilton County Historical Society, pointing upstairs toward cells located at the back of the former sheriff's residence.

The society's county museum today is in the old sheriff's home and jail adjacent to the county courthouse in downtown Noblesville. Cells built in 1940 are behind a steel door connecting them to the residence.

I was lucky this late Saturday afternoon. Nevitt was putting things in her car, about ready to close the museum for the day, but she was gracious enough to show me through the museum, even though we finished well past the normal 4 p.m. closing time.

The rest of the Stephenson story, apart from his confinement in the jail, took place next door in the courthouse in a second-floor courtroom. The courtroom, which has been restored to its appearance at the time of the Stephenson trial, now is usually locked.

"You can go across the hall to the assessor's office and someone there probably will unlock the door for you," Nevitt says. Since it was Saturday afternoon when I was visiting, the courthouse was closed, of course. She says Noblesville Main Street or the Chamber of Commerce also can arrange tours of the courtroom. (I did go into the courtroom during a later visit.)

When the courthouse was constructed in 1877, a tunnel connected the next-door jail to the new courthouse. Now the tunnel has been filled. The sheriff's residence and jail were built at a cost of $28,474 the year before the courthouse was started. The historical society has renovated the home portion of the Old Sheriff's Residence but not the jail.

The building was leased to the historical society in 1979, and the exterior renovation was completed in 1993 with county government funds. Restoration of the residence's interior was funded by the historical society.

The building's interior follows a familiar pattern of homes built in the late 1800s. A family parlor is to the right of the front entrance. Behind it are the dining room and the kitchen. The formal parlor is to the left. Bedrooms are on the second floor.

SHERIFF'S RESIDENCE AND JAIL. The former Hamilton County sheriff's residence and jail are in the foreground—the jail is the limestone addition to the rear of the residence. The Hamilton County Courthouse, built soon after the residence was constructed, towers behind it.

IF YOU GO

At the back of the residence is the room where prisoners were brought in a side door and booked—the "book in" room, Nevitt calls it. That's where the stairs lead up to the older cells, one of which housed Stephenson.

The historical society has made the second-floor landing of the sheriff's home into an office area. One bedroom has been restored, while a second is used for the society's office and a third for a library and genealogy research. The house has a basement and attic, which today are used for storage.

Either the sheriff or his first deputy lived in the residence until 1972, while the jail was in use through 1977. The sheriff's or deputy's wife cooked the prisoners' meals, and it's said the children of the house sometimes served the food.

Stephenson wasn't the only notorious prisoner in the Hamilton County jail. Mass murderer Charles Manson was held at one time as a young escapee from the Indiana Reformatory.

Another recent guest was motion picture actor Gene Hackman. He stopped to see if this was the home he had visited in 1940 when his parents were friends of a sheriff at the time. The actor thought he remembered spending the night in the sheriff's home.

Even though they agreed this probably wasn't where Hackman's family spent the night, Nevitt still got him to sign the guest book.

GETTING THERE: The museum is at the southwest corner of the courthouse square in downtown Noblesville.

INFORMATION: Open Thursday, Friday, and Saturday, 10 a.m. to 4 p.m. or by appointment. Call (317) 770–0775.

FEES: Free but donations accepted.

THE BEARS OF BLUE RIVER. Balsar Brent, the hero in Shelbyville native Charles Major's *The Bears of Blue River,* is depicted holding two bear cubs in this statue that stands on the north side of the town's square.

STREETS OF OLD SHELBY. Built to represent a typical scene from the 1900–1910 era, these street scenes are on the main floor of the Grover Museum in downtown Shelbyville.

Louis H. and Lena Firn Grover Museum and Shelbyville

SHELBYVILLE—He didn't go from a log cabin to the White House, but he got as close as you can without sitting in the Oval Office.

Thomas A. Hendricks, who grew up in Shelby County before his family moved to Indianapolis, was elected vice president with President Grover Cleveland in 1884. Unfortunately, Hendricks died less than nine months after taking office.

He was one of five United States vice presidents who were elected from Indiana.

Know the other four? Their names are at the end of this article.

Hendricks did live here in a log cabin, built around 1822 by his father, John Hendricks. The reconstructed cabin now is on the grounds of the Shelby County Fairgrounds. It's about as big as a moderately sized bedroom in a modern American home. According to *Indiana: A New Historical Guide*, the present cabin was rebuilt in 1962 from many of the logs of the original structure. Hendricks later lived in more plush surroundings in Shelbyville before moving to Indianapolis, where, as a lawyer, he became an Indiana governor, senator, and then vice president.

The cabin is one of Shelbyville's historical features.

Downtown on the city square is a second. Today, probably very few know of the book *The Bears of Blue River*, by Shelbyville resident Charles Major. Early in the twentieth century, it was a great favorite of Hoosier schoolchildren. A bronze statue of the story's hero, Balsar Brent, holding aloft his two bear cubs, Tom and Jerry, stands at the north edge of the square.

At the center of the square, now a parking lot also used as a site for community events, is the Joseph Memorial Fountain. It honors Julius Joseph, a German immigrant who bequeathed funds at his death for the erection of the fountain on the square. Another recent downtown feature has been the conversion of the Porter Memorial Swimming Pool into facilities for the Welcome Center, Shelby County Chamber of Commerce, and MainStreet Shelbyville.

The centerpiece of historic Shelbyville, however, is the Louis H. and Lena Firn Grover Museum, maintained by the Shelby County Historical Society, a block south and two blocks west of the square. The building was formerly the downtown headquarters of the Elks Lodge, but was dedicated in 1980 as the county museum.

Like other county museums, it has both permanent and changing displays. Many years of volunteer labor have created Streets of Old Shelby, which is located on the museum's main floor.

RECONSTRUCTED LOG CABIN. Logs from the original log cabin built by the father of Vice President Thomas A. Hendricks were used in the reconstruction of the cabin, located at the Shelby County Fairgrounds.

The museum's brochure calls it a "generic village of the 1900–1910 era." In other words, it is not exactly what Shelbyville looked like at the time—it's a representation. What a representation it is. Spread over three town streets, you will see most of the business establishments of an Indiana town at that time: a hotel, saloon, hardware store, blacksmith, livery stable, woodworker's shop, post office, printer's office, dressmaker, lawyer's office, barbershop, butcher shop, jail, grocery store, telephone exchange, tobacco store, emporium, bank, doctor's office, photography studio, church, schoolroom, cemetery, and even an outdoor privy!

They're only storefronts, of course, but behind them are artifacts, mostly those that have been donated by Shelby County residents. Tools in the woodworker's shop, for example, include a lathe from Morristown and a workbench from the Hodel Furniture Factory. On some weekends, a printer actually is at work in the print shop, while on other weekends you can buy a root beer float at the emporium.

The museum also is home to an annual quilt display and luncheon, Christmas tree exhibit, and Christmas tea and workshops.

Those other vice presidents? There's Dan Quayle, of course, who served under George H. W. Bush and was elected in 1988, but did you also know the names of Schuyler Colfax, Ulysses S. Grant's vice president in 1868; Charles W. Fairbanks, who served with Theodore Roosevelt, 1904; and Thomas R. Marshall, who served two terms with Woodrow Wilson, 1912 and 1916?

IF YOU GO

GETTING THERE: In Shelbyville, turn west on Broadway to the museum at 52 W. Broadway Street. The Shelby County Fairgrounds is on the northeast side of town.

INFORMATION: Call the museum at (317) 392–4634; the Web site is http://www.grover museum.org/. The museum hours are 10 a.m. to 4 p.m. Tuesday through Saturday. Group tours by appointment.

FEES: None for the museum, but donations accepted.

VIEW FROM THE KITCHEN. The sitting room and parlor of the Old Riley Home. Across from the parlor was attorney Reuben Riley's law office.

RILEY MUSEUM. A photograph of an older James Whitcomb Riley is next to a smaller picture of Riley at age twenty-five in the Mitchell home, which houses a Riley museum. Next to the photos is one of the signs Riley painted before his work became famous and he settled in Indianapolis.

James Whitcomb Riley Old Home, Greenfield

GREENFIELD—When New Yorkers bought tickets for the February 26, 1894, program at Madison Square Garden, the featured speaker—listed in boldface type on the ticket—was James Whitcomb Riley, the Hoosier Poet.

Given second billing was another author of some note—Mark Twain.

History has turned things around a bit today so that Twain's work is best known while Riley's popularity has waned. Not so a hundred years ago, however, or even now in the hearts of residents of this quiet Indiana town who revere their native son. (Riley returned the compliment in 1898, calling Greenfield "the best town outside of Heaven.")

Located at 250 W. Main Street is the James Whitcomb Riley Old Home, open to the public. It was built by Reuben Riley, the poet's lawyer father who was a handyman, if not a craftsman, with building tools. It isn't where Riley was born on October 7, 1849—that was in a log cabin on the same property. But Reuben knew the cabin was inadequate for his family of five and, over a period of three years, built a new home. He used logs from the cabin where he could—for example, in constructing a winding stairway leading to the second floor.

The front porch stairs led up to Reuben's law office on the right and the family's front parlor on the left. The family lived here until 1870, when they were forced to give up the house as Reuben's law career never quite recovered from his absence during the Civil War. He had helped raise a company of militia from the Greenfield area and served as captain.

Later, after several decades of modest income when young James Whitcomb Riley worked mostly as a newspaper reporter, sign painter, and medicine-show performer, his writing began to catch on, especially his verse.

He drew upon life as he knew it in Greenfield, using the dialect of the day for some of his best-known work, such as "The Old Swimmin' Hole," "When the Frost Is on the Punkin," "Little Orphant Annie," and "The Raggedy Man." (There really was an orphan who came to stay with the Rileys when James was a small boy and apparently, while telling them about witches and goblins, warned them "The Gobble-ins 'll get you Ef you don't watch out!" And Greenfield did have a ragman who came to town, working for Reuben Riley chopping wood, feeding the horses, milking cows, and spading the garden.)

With sufficient funds available from his published works, lectures, and readings, Riley bought back the old family home in 1893 but never

RILEY HOME. When Reuben Riley's family expanded in the mid-1800s, he started building this house, using logs from the cabin on the property where James Whitcomb Riley was born.

lived there again, continuing to live in a friend's residence in Indianapolis on Lockerbie Street. However, Riley's brother, John, and his wife, Julia, lived in the Greenfield house, and Riley visited them on a regular basis.

Now, several thousand people a year visit the Old Riley Home, as well as the adjacent Mitchell home, which has been converted into a Riley museum. The two houses now are referred to as the Riley complex. John Mitchell was a Greenfield printer, and his publishing firm printed many of Riley's poems. (It's in this home that the 1894 Riley-Twain ticket is displayed.)

Both houses are owned by the city of Greenfield and operated by the city and the Riley Old Home Society. The distinction between the two homes is that the old Riley home is maintained as it might have looked in the mid-1800s, while the Mitchell home is a museum commemorating Riley's lifetime. The gardens behind Riley's home are especially interesting in spring and summer.

Riley and his contemporary, Booth Tarkington, were considered at the time as the two greatest authors of Indiana's golden age of literature. However, just as Twain has overshadowed Riley at the national level, so has Theodore Dreiser's *Sister Carrie*, according to Hoosier historian James Madison, eclipsed Riley's Indiana literary reputation.

But not in Greenfield.

IF YOU GO

GETTING THERE: The Old Riley Home is on the right at 250 W. Main Street, west of Main Street's intersection with Indiana 9.

INFORMATION: Call (317) 462–8539. Open Monday through Saturday from 10 a.m. to 4 p.m., April 5 through November 6. Closed on Sunday.

FEES: Admission charged.

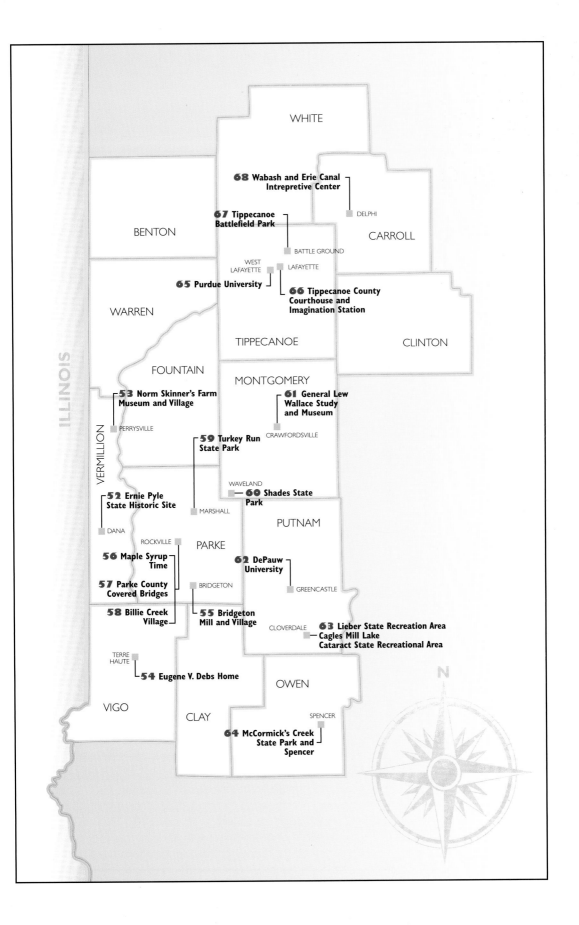

WHITE

BENTON

CARROLL

68 Wabash and Erie Canal Intrepretive Center

DELPHI

67 Tippecanoe Battlefield Park

BATTLE GROUND

WARREN

WEST LAFAYETTE

LAFAYETTE

65 Purdue University

66 Tippecanoe County Courthouse and Imagination Station

TIPPECANOE

CLINTON

FOUNTAIN

MONTGOMERY

ILLINOIS

53 Norm Skinner's Farm Museum and Village

61 General Lew Wallace Study and Museum

VERMILLION

PERRYSVILLE

59 Turkey Run State Park

CRAWFORDSVILLE

52 Ernie Pyle State Historic Site

WAVELAND

60 Shades State Park

DANA

MARSHALL

PUTNAM

ROCKVILLE

PARKE

56 Maple Syrup Time

62 DePauw University

57 Parke County Covered Bridges

BRIDGETON

GREENCASTLE

58 Billie Creek Village

55 Bridgeton Mill and Village

63 Lieber State Recreation Area Cagles Mill Lake Cataract State Recreational Area

CLOVERDALE

TERRE HAUTE

54 Eugene V. Debs Home

OWEN

SPENCER

VIGO

CLAY

64 McCormick's Creek State Park and Spencer

N

REMEMBER THESE? Ernie Pyle's portable typewriter on which—using two fingers—he typed his famous columns about the unsung warriors of World War II in Africa, Europe, and the Pacific.

PYLE ON OKINAWA. This diorama shows Pyle at day's end while he was covering the war on Okinawa. The all-purpose Jeep is in the foreground. A few days later he went to the nearby small island of Ie Shima, where he was killed.

Ernie Pyle State Historic Site, Dana

DANA—The fighting was intense as the Americans attempted to take the small island of Ie Shima from the Japanese in the closing months of World War II. The U.S. forces held the beach and a few hundred more yards, but that was about it. Cautiously, small groups were moving inland.

As the machine-gun fire started, the four uniformed men, moving toward a hill, dove into a ditch. When the gun stopped, for some inexplicable reason, one man raised his head. That's when the Japanese machine gunner shot him.

Ernie Pyle was dead. He would have been forty-five in four months.

Word came down the line on the island that Pyle, the most famous American war correspondent of all time, had been killed, but the fighting seemed too fierce to go into the area to retrieve a body. A chaplain and four volunteers went anyhow.

Two days later, Pyle was buried on the island along with other slain Americans. Then, in 1949, he was reburied at Punchbowl Memorial Cemetery in the Hawaiian Islands.

Pyle, who was born in a farmhouse near Dana, was remembered fondly by his fellow Hoosiers over the decades, but no serious efforts were made to save the Pyle birthplace until the early 1970s. The farmhouse had been built and owned by the Elder family in 1851, with the Pyles living on the farm briefly at the time of Ernie's birth on August 3, 1900. It was the widow of a great-grandson of the builder who suggested relocating the house into Dana. The state took over operation of the house as a historic site in 1976.

Two large Quonset huts—made of curved, half-circle corrugated metal that form both the sides and top of the structure—were added in 1998. Most of the Pyle displays now have a home in these huts, joined by a passageway. The house represents a home of the early 1900 period. Only three of its items actually are from the original furnishings—the clock on the living room mantel, a rocker, and an egg basket in the kitchen.

The displays mostly trace Pyle's career during World War II. Actually, he was a well-known writer before the war, especially as an aviation writer and the author of columns about America—"The Hoosier Vagabond"—as he traveled across the country writing about people he met and places he visited.

But it was World War II that really brought Pyle to the attention of Americans on the home front. He left the day-to-day battle reporting

PYLE BIRTHPLACE. This house was moved from the farm where war correspondent Ernie Pyle was born in 1900. Now located on the south edge of Dana, it is an Indiana state historic site.

to others. Instead, he focused on the human face of war—what life was like for the soldiers, sailors, marines, and fliers who carried out the orders and fought the war.

One of the displays in the Quonset huts tells the story of Pyle's column about the death of Captain Henry Waskow in Italy. It was included in his series of columns that won the Pulitzer Prize; over time it has become perhaps his most popular. In the column, Pyle relates how Waskow's men came to the body and stood or sat, looking into his face, holding his hand and, in some cases, talking to the dead officer.

The column begins, "Dead men had been coming down the mountain all evening, lashed onto the backs of mules. They came lying belly-down across the wooden packsaddles, their heads hanging down on the left side of the mule."

The people who knew him well said when Pyle went to the Pacific following the victory over Germany, he seemed to have a premonition he wouldn't be coming back. Soon, he, too, came down from the front, not lashed to a mule but carried on a litter.

Bill Mauldin, the equally famous war cartoonist and fellow Pulitzer Prize–winner, said it best: "The only difference between Ernie's death and the death of any other good guy is that the other guy is mourned by his company. Ernie is mourned by the Army."

IF YOU GO

GETTING THERE: The Ernie Pyle State Historic Site is located on Indiana 71 in Dana.

INFORMATION: The historic site is open from April to mid-November, Thursday through Saturday from 9 a.m. to 5 p.m. and Sunday from 1 p.m. to 5 p.m. Closed Monday, Tuesday, and Wednesday. Call (765) 665–3633 or write P.O. Box 338, Dana, Indiana 47847-0338.

FEES: Admission is free.

MOVED BARN TO FARM. Norm Skinner recently moved this round barn to his farm from Illinois.

METHODIST CIRCUIT RIDER. John Wesley Parrett used this octagon-shaped building for his justice of the peace headquarters at Newport, Indiana. According to names in a register, 441 couples were married here between 1850 and 1910. A wooden windmill stands behind the building.

BUILT IN 1844. This brick house was moved three miles by historian Norm Skinner in 1979 from the intersection of Indiana 63 and 32 to his farm museum and village north of Newport. The bricks were handmade on site by David and Barbara Wittenmyer, Skinner's great-great-grandparents, who moved to Indiana from Pennsylvania in 1831. The house weighs about 250 tons, according to Skinner.

Norm Skinner's Farm Museum and Village, Perrysville

PERRYSVILLE—It will be a once-in-a lifetime visit if you attend the annual Steam and Gas Show at Norm Skinner's farm on a Saturday or Sunday in late August.

It will be like visiting the farm of an older uncle you've heard about but never seen—stories of all the stuff he has accumulated over the years that's stashed away in various barns and outbuildings. Relatives who have been there have told you, "You have to see it to believe it."

It's true.

The basic difference between this theoretical relative and Skinner, however, is that while your "uncle" may have lost track of what he has in those buildings, Skinner appears to know exactly what he has and where it is.

"Do you know where most of this stuff is?" I asked him during my visit. His simple answer was, "Yes."

His farm, nestled close to the Illinois border in western Vermillion County, hosts this show once a year. Other times, the county historian has his farm open to visitors "by appointment and by chance." (I found him at his farm one Sunday afternoon "by chance.")

Skinner has so much to be seen, it can't begin to be described in this article. Among the items are:

A set of scales, used to weigh freight off the Wabash and Erie Canal, imprinted with the name Fairbanks and bearing the legend, "Patent No. 1."

A 250-ton, 1844 brick home—interior and exterior walls three-brick thick with three fireplaces and all walnut woodwork—that Skinner moved three miles to his farm in 1979.

A wooden crane used to pull freight overhead in a river and canal warehouse.

Six log cabins, only one identified as to age—built in 1826 and moved from its original Wabash River site. (One other "I've torn down but haven't been able to put it back together yet," Skinner says.)

A treadmill that used horses on each side to power a threshing machine.

A round barn moved from its Illinois site.

An 1830 tavern, in some places with nothing remaining but the latticed walls, which was also used as part of the Underground Railroad. It has an opening in the ceiling that leads into a large room where runaway slaves might be hidden.

Ancient wagons, sleighs, automobiles, and various kinds of farm machinery.

OLD TRACTORS AND CARS. They are lined up in a shed on the Norm Skinner farm in Vermillion County and are part of the display at his annual Steam and Gas Show.

What Skinner and his wife, Dorothy, don't know for sure is who will come to the farm each year to be part of the show.

"We've planted several acres of oats to thresh and put through a hand-fed bailing machine," Dorothy told me about one year's show, "and we hope to plow with old tractors, have steam-engine-powered wood sawing, fodder shredding, and rock crushing. We may have an oxen team pulling an 1851 Conestoga wagon, a blacksmith, weaving, and spinning. If they do old crafts, we try to get them here."

But it "all depends on who shows up," she adds.

IF YOU GO

GETTING THERE: Take Indiana 32 all the way to almost the Illinois line. The museum is on the right at Country Road 200W, about three miles west of the Indiana 63 intersection. The farm's address is 1850 W. State Road 32.

INFORMATION: The show is open from 8 a.m. to 6 p.m., usually on the third Saturday and Sunday in August. Call (765) 793–4079 or (765) 793–3022, which has an answering machine, or check the Web site at http://skinnervillage.eshire.net/.

FEES: Admission charged.

RILEY'S ROOM. Hoosier poet James Whitcomb Riley was a frequent overnight guest at the Debs Home. This second-floor bedroom now is the James Whitcomb Riley Bedroom.

DEBS'S AWARD WINNER. John L. Lewis, longtime head of the United Mineworkers Union, was the first recipient of the Eugene V. Debs Award in 1965. This bust of Lewis was a gift to the Debs Foundation by its sculptor, Ben Goodkin, in 1970.

ONE OF THREE. This bust of Debs by renowned sculptor Louis Mayer is in the Debs Home. A second is in the Debs collection at the Indiana State University Library and a third in the Smithsonian Institution. The photos at right show Mayer working on the bust, first as a plaster cast.

Eugene V. Debs Home, Terre Haute

TERRE HAUTE—Hoosier poet James Whitcomb Riley would frequently visit and stay overnight. Even today, one of the second-floor rooms is called the James Whitcomb Riley Bedroom. Abraham Lincoln biographer Carl Sandburg was another close friend. Later, the house became the home of an Indiana State University professor. Still later, it was a fraternity house and an apartment building before it was rescued in 1962 by a newly created foundation and given status as a state and national historic landmark.

Perhaps the most amazing fact about the house's builder and first occupant, however, was that he received nearly one million votes—6 percent of the total vote—for U.S. president in 1920 at age sixty-four while he was imprisoned in the Atlanta Federal Penitentiary.

He was Eugene Victor Debs, an American pioneer labor leader and champion of social justice. Five times he ran for president. In 1920 his fifth and last run came while he was in the midst of a ten-year jail sentence under the World War I sedition act. "For President . . . Convict No. 9653" read one campaign button.

He had made a dramatic antiwar speech in Canton, Ohio, in 1918, arguing against this country's involvement in World War I. He was tried in federal court for violating the nation's wartime sedition act. First imprisoned at the Moundsville, West Virginia, state prison, he was transferred to the federal prison at Atlanta two months later.

According to his biography, Debs's humility, friendliness, and willingness to assist anyone in need won him the respect of his fellow prisoners. At his home are gifts from other prisoners, including a desk and a carved cane. Debs was released after President Warren G. Harding commuted his sentence to time served on Christmas Day 1921.

It wasn't Debs's first jail sentence. He served six months for leading a sympathy strike of railroad workers in support of striking Pullman Company workers in 1894 and for contempt of court. That came after Debs had put together the first industry-wide union—the American Railway Union—in 1893. When the union struck, it faced the full force of the railroads, the government, and a hostile press. The union was broken and its leaders sent to jail.

Debs and his wife built their home here at 451 N. Eighth Street in 1890, five years after the couple's marriage. Because his wife, Kate, had an inheritance from an aunt, they were able to furnish the house in a somewhat affluent manner, which brought criticism of Debs for not living a working-class lifestyle. For example, a first floor fireplace has cobalt blue porcelain tile imported from Italy. The couple's complete

DEBS'S HOME. Standing in the shadow of Indiana State University buildings at Terre Haute is the 1890 home built by Eugene V. and Kate Debs. It is a national historic landmark.

IF YOU GO

set of Haviland china has been preserved and much of their furniture restored. Their mahogany dining suite and parlor furniture are in the house today.

But Debs's memorabilia are of particular interest to the visitor. They range from items related to his early work in Terre Haute to his two terms as city clerk and one term in the Indiana General Assembly, to his organizing the American Railway Union and to his work with the Socialist Party of America.

Also on display are some of Debs's books, among them those signed by Sinclair Lewis, Upton Sinclair, Irving Stone, and Emma Goldman. Although Debs left school at fourteen to become a railroad painter and fireman, much of his life revolved around books and writing. Most of his personal library is housed in the Indiana State University special collections, along with about four thousand of his letters.

The house's third floor, unused by Debs and his wife—although Theta Chi members slept there when the building was a fraternity house—now is a meeting room with the walls covered by murals painted by John Laska, an Indiana State University art professor. The work took three years and traces the story of Debs's life and also depicts others associated over the years with the labor movement.

Among the causes Debs pursued, the government has enacted into law rights for women, children, and minorities; safe working conditions; unemployment and welfare benefits; and an eight-hour workday.

Debs died in 1926 and his wife ten years later. He was cremated and his ashes buried at Highland Lawn Cemetery. His funeral sermon was given by Norman Thomas from the front porch of Debs's home. An estimated five thousand people attended.

GETTING THERE: In Terre Haute, take U.S. 41 (Third Street) north to Wabash Avenue. Turn left at Ninth Street, a one-way north. One-half block past Chestnut Street, turn left into Parking Lot No. 15 at Indiana State University; the home will be visible in the northwest corner of the lot. The Debs Home parking lot is south of the house.

INFORMATION: Go to the Web site at http://www.eugenevdebs.com/ or call (812) 232–2163. Visiting hours are Wednesday through Sunday, from 1 p.m. to 4 p.m.

FEES: Free.

CLOSING IN ON TWO HUNDRED YEARS. The Bridgeton Mill has been in business since 1823. It operates on a restricted production schedule these days.

MAIN STREET. Bridgeton Road is the main street of this historic Parke County community.

Bridgeton Mill and Village, Bridgeton

BRIDGETON—It has survived two fires that gutted buildings and a dust explosion that destroyed part of another, as well as the loss of its waterpower. Still, the owners of the Bridgeton Mill lay claim to having the oldest continuously operating mill in Indiana and possibly in the Midwest, even though its schedule these days is on a limited basis. Together with the nearby waterfall, and the town's historic buildings, this "authentic old mill town" remains one of Parke County's major tourist attractions.

What doesn't remain, at least for the present, is the historic Bridgeton covered bridge, lost in 2005 to an arsonist. Plans are moving ahead for its rebuilding, however, but more on that later.

Lockwood Mill was built in 1823, shortly after the first settlers moved into the area around Big Raccoon Creek, probably for sawing timber. Fire ravaged it, and a log structure used both as sawmill and gristmill also was destroyed by fire in 1869. The present frame building was constructed in 1870. A dust explosion took out some of the west end in 1951, at the same time damaging the waterpower machinery. From then until 1969 the building served as a feed mill.

With a flood control project in the offing, and with it the permanent loss of continuous waterpower, a streetcar engine was brought in to become the power source to turn the top millstone in the grinding process. In 1970 a set of forty-eight-inch French buhr stones was installed. They weigh more than two thousand pounds.

If the mill is operating, visitors can watch the stones at work, turning wheat into flour and corn into meal. Naturally, visitors can buy the mill's fresh stone-ground products along with gift items and souvenirs.

The present owners say they know the building is "not in excellent shape, but in good shape at this time." When they took possession, most of the window glass was gone, the roof had holes, and termites had eaten part of the lower floor. Today, "it's safe and sound," they report.

Only a few feet away is the main street of Bridgeton. Its first two blocks south from the river were placed on the National Register of Historic Places in 1992. One of the town's highlights is the 1878 Bridgeton House, where crafts, gifts, and antiques are sold. It features a Christmas room. Nearby is the Case 1822 log cabin, which was moved to its present site. It is available for special occasions.

Another village highlight is the Bridgeton Country Store. Built from 1884 to 1886, with additions in 1891 and 1892, it features collectibles,

HOPEFULLY, IT WILL LOOK LIKE THIS AGAIN. High on the list of sights for visitors in Parke County's Bridgeton was this covered bridge, lost to an arsonist in 2005. In this photo, taken prior to the arson, water was flowing over only part of a dam. Residents plan to rebuild the bridge.

antiques, gifts, food, and ice cream. The Mitchell House and Bridgeton Museum is only open during the annual Parke County Covered Bridge Festival and other special events, as are a number of other shops that offer crafts, antiques, gifts, handicrafts, and food.

Now, about the covered bridge.

The double-span bridge of 267 feet was built in 1868 by J. J. Daniels, who built nine of Parke County's bridges—out of thirty in the county with twenty still open to traffic. It had a Burr arch truss, as do most of the state's covered bridges. It was bypassed in 1967, so was closed to vehicular traffic.

Then, late one night in April 2005, flames swept through the bridge over Raccoon Creek. The bridge was largely destroyed by the time firefighters arrived. Within days, residents, armed with blueprints of the structure, announced plans to rebuild it.

The waterfall, next to where the bridge was located, goes over a nine-foot dam that stretches 225 feet. It is only totally covered in periods of high water.

IF YOU GO

GETTING THERE: At Rockville on U.S. 36, turn south at the first stoplight and left one block later to follow the "red" route south to Bridgeton. This becomes the Bridgeton Road.

INFORMATION: Go to Web site at http://www.bridgetonmill .com/ or http://www.covered bridges.com/bridgeton/ or call the mill at (765) 548–0106 or the Parke County Convention and Visitors Bureau (765) 569–5226. The mill is open April through November, Thursday through Sunday, from 10 a.m. "'til tired." The 1878 house is open some weekends through the summer, all special events, and during the Covered Bridge Festival. The country store also is open for special events and the Covered Bridge Festival.

FEES: None to visit.

THAT'S A SPILE. George Humphrey of Meece Sweetwater Farm at Rockville holds one form of a spile, which is inserted into a hard-maple tree to draw off its sugar water.

LOTS OF STEAM. Steam comes off the evaporating tank during the processing of maple syrup. In the foreground, placed on the concrete blocks, is a slice taken from a fallen hard-maple tree at Meece Sweetwater Farm.

ALWAYS TESTING. Gayle Meece pours sugar water into a tester during the evaporation portion of the processing of maple syrup.

Maple Syrup Time, Parke County

ROCKVILLE—It's called sugar water, and that's what it looked like to me—water—as it was poured from one of the buckets that caught it as it drained from a hard-maple tree. A few processing steps later, it would become a staple of the American breakfast—maple syrup.

Hoosiers interested in watching the procedure have only a short time each year to do so. The season begins when those who process the syrup believe that winter's last hard freeze has come and gone—usually sometime around mid-February. It only lasts a few weeks, sometimes as short as two or three and hardly ever more than six.

The length of the season depends on the weather. When the temperature reaches the 60s and 70s and stays there for several days, the sugar water stops running, and the season is over. When I visited Parke County in mid-February, the maple syrup people thought the season probably was about over. If you miss the maple syrup time here, however, consult the current edition of *Indiana Festival Guide* for other opportunities around the state.

One of the best times to watch the maple syrup process is during the Parke County Maple Syrup Fair. Parke County prepares a map that will guide you to the sites. You can pick up a copy by stopping at the visitor center in Rockville. Camps throughout the county make maple syrup by different processes. For fairgoers, other highlights of the Parke County affair are meals, crafts, and antiques at the 4-H Fairgrounds.

The size of the syrup operation depends on the number of trees tapped. For example, at Meece Sweetwater Farm, just north of Rockville, some 2,500 trees are available, although the time I was there sugar water was gathered from only about 1,800, according to Gayle Meece.

The process involves putting a hole into a hard maple and inserting a spile, a small metal cylinder that allows the sugar water to drip into a bucket or bag, usually holding around three gallons. The best time to catch the most water is when the nights are cold and the days are warm.

The next job is gathering the buckets or bags from the trees and pouring their contents into a large transportable container that holds three hundred or more gallons. That's taken to the camp where the sugar water is processed. It's placed in a heated evaporator tank so the syrup can be drawn off at the far end. Then it flows into a finishing tank. The evaporating part is accompanied by considerable steam escaping from the tank as the syrup forms, separating from the water.

PART OF PROCESS. Sugar water is poured into a larger container at Smiley Brothers near Rockville. This three-gallon bucket just seconds before had been removed from a hard-maple tree.

A camp operator needs to be on hand to frequently test the temperature and the evaporating and finishing stages of the syrup.

Early in the season, about fifty or sixty gallons of sugar water are needed to make a gallon of maple syrup. It generally is light in color and mild in taste. As the season progresses, it may take as many as ninety gallons of sugar water to make a single gallon. This syrup is darker with a stronger taste. Both kinds have their adherents who believe one taste superior to the other.

Some camps bottle their product on site, while others ship the syrup to be placed in containers for sale.

Maple syrup. It tastes great, and it's also a sure sign that spring is just around the corner.

GETTING THERE: To attend the Parke County Maple Syrup Fair, follow U.S. 36 into Rockville.

INFORMATION: Call the Parke County Convention and Visitors Bureau at (765) 569–5226 or go to its Web site at http://www.coveredbridges.com/.

FEES: None to follow the maple syrup tour.

THE COUNTY'S LONGEST. The West Union Bridge, a double-span structure over Sugar Creek, at 315 feet, is the longest in Parke County.

THE COUNTY'S OLDEST. Crooks Bridge over Little Raccoon Creek is the county's oldest, built in 1855–56, although it was rebuilt in 1876. It's 132 feet long and still in use with a three-ton weight limit.

Parke County Covered Bridges, Rockville

ROCKVILLE—Maybe it's the arch—or, rather, the absence of one—that does it for Barb Pefley.

The covered bridges tour expert was explaining as we drove around Parke County that her favorite of the county's then thirty-one covered bridges—the most of any county, possibly in the world—is the forty-three-foot Phillips Bridge that spans Big Pond Creek. It's the shortest bridge in the county and the only one that doesn't have a Burr arch—oak beams bent by using steam to form arches for both sides of the bridges.

She explains that bridge building in the 1800s was no easy task. Timber for most of the bridges—planks, sides, roof—usually was cut from poplar trees on the spot. Oak generally was hauled in by horse-drawn wagons for fashioning the trusses, uprights, and arches. Builders needed from six months to a year to complete a bridge.

Probably most readers know that covered bridges were not built to protect their passengers; they were to protect the bridge itself from rotting out. The major nemeses of the bridges, though, were vandals and floods. Back in the 1941 flood, waters were so high that rescuers went through, not under, the Mecca covered bridge in their motorboats. Some bridges had to be replaced several times.

Of Indiana's remaining ninety-one covered bridges, thirty-nine are in Parke and Putnam counties. Twenty of Parke County's thirty covered bridges continue to bear automobile traffic. Others have been bypassed over the years by rerouting roads and, in a few instances, have been dismantled and moved to new sites.

This part of the state used to be coal mining country. Several of the smaller communities prospered as company towns. Rosedale, for example, at one time was supposed to have twelve working mines and, in town, eleven saloons. In the first fifty years of the twentieth century, some thirteen million tons of coal were shipped out of Parke County. But the coal eventually played out. With the coal gone, many of the towns have slipped back to hamlet size.

Today, everyone in Parke County understands that tourism is one of the county's major businesses.

While covered bridges are reminders of America's past, they have everything to do with Parke County's present. More than eighty festivals, special days, tours, and shows are scheduled annually in Parke County, most of them centered around its covered bridges.

The big one is the Parke County Covered Bridge Festival. Hundreds of thousands of people descend on western Indiana for this

THE MOTORBOATS WENT THROUGH. In the 1941 flood, when disaster relief workers came to the Mecca Bridge, they went through it rather than under it because of the high water. It crosses Big Raccoon Creek and is bypassed—not in use—today.

ten-day event, with Rockville as its headquarters. Rockville residents open their homes to visitors who also stay as far away as Indianapolis or across the state line in eastern Illinois.

The bridges have been divided up on a map by Parke County Inc. into the red, brown, black, blue, and yellow routes to give visitors a sampling of bridges and communities. They all begin at the tourism center in Rockville.

One thing to remember while you're driving around Parke County's back roads visiting the bridges: With the exception of major highways, there's only one engineered—that means reasonably straight—road in the county. The rest meander around, turning this way, twisting that way.

Of course, if you have Pefley at the wheel, no problem. She admits she drives down the middle of the road—"everyone does"—and turns to talk with her guests as she whips around the sharp turns and up and down the hills. But, then, if you're a Parke County native like Pefley, you probably could drive them with your eyes shut—no, not a good idea.

IF YOU GO

GETTING THERE: The major east-west route into Parke County and Rockville is U.S. 36; north-south it is U.S. 41.

INFORMATION: Call the Parke County Convention and Visitors Bureau for information and brochures about bridges and tours, (765) 569–5226. Its Web site is http://www.coveredbridges.com/ or write, P.O. Box 165, Rockville, Indiana 47872.

FEES: No fees to visit covered bridges except those in Billie Creek Village, where admission fees are charged during village operational hours.

MARKS CENTENNIAL. The Leatherwood Covered Bridge was a hundred years old in 1999. It was dismantled and moved to the village in 1981.

Billie Creek Village, Rockville

ROCKVILLE—It started with a letter to the editor.

In 1956 former Parke County native Leila (Cole) Sanders came home with two friends to see the covered bridges. They could hardly locate them—in fact, they only found twenty of the forty-one then still standing. In a letter to the *Rockville Republican*, she recommended a better job of promoting the county's bridges, its natural beauty, and its heritage.

One year later came the beginnings of the Parke County Covered Bridge Festival—hundreds of thousands of people show up each autumn now—and the concept of Billie Creek Village.

The village was organized by Parke countians as a not-for-profit organization, and the goal was to re-create a turn-of-the-century village and living museum. It opened in 1969 with ten buildings. Over the next several years, most of the nearly thirty structures that now make up the village were moved there. Included in the move were two covered bridges to give the village three within a half-mile of each other—the most covered bridges in the world in such a small area.

Today, many directors, volunteers, and efforts later, the Billie Creek Village idea seems to have succeeded. More than fifteen events are scheduled annually at the village, located a mile east of Rockville on U.S. 36. The biggest of them is the mid-June Civil War Days, when reenactors carry out the state's largest battle reenactment. In 2001 more than eighteen hundred reenactors came from twenty-six states.

Nearly nine thousand schoolchildren visit the village each year during spring's School Days, autumn's Sorghum and Cider Days, Covered Bridge Festival, and winter's Billie Creek Village Christmas and Maple Fair. In all, more than fifty thousand visitors come to the village in a typical year. Some stay at the village's inn—modern but with a nostalgic touch.

What they see is a village re-created along Williams Creek, but called by everyone Billie Creek. The tract of land purchased by the county citizens' organization already had one covered bridge, lots of woods, and lay along U.S. 36.

A covered bridge, constructed in 1906 and the survivor of two arson efforts, serves as the entrance to the village. It was dismantled at its Roaring Creek location and moved to the village in 1980. The Leatherwood Station bridge also was moved to the village; at seventy-two feet, it's the longest of the three. The only bridge actually on the site, the Billie Creek bridge, was built in 1895 as part of the Plank Toll Road—the "ocean to ocean" highway, old U.S. 36.

ENTERING THE VILLAGE. Saint Joseph Catholic Church is one of the first buildings visitors see as they enter the village. That's a pre-1900 post office to the right. Barely visible at the left is the Beeson-DePlanty cabin built on Roaring Creek in the 1830s and later moved ten miles to the village.

IF YOU GO

In the village, visitors see among the many structures:

The 1886 Saint Joseph Catholic Church, moved from Rockville after a last-second gift to move it came from Mary Fendrich Hulman in Terre Haute just before the building was about to be demolished.

The Union Baptist Church, built in 1859 at nearby Hollandsburg and sawed in half to be moved.

The Burr Mill, restored and moved after a tornado hit it near Alamo, Indiana.

The Governor Joseph Albert Wright house (Indiana's tenth governor from 1849 to 1857), probably built around 1840 in Rockville.

The "flagship" building is the Billie Creek General Store, constructed in Annapolis, Indiana, during the 1850s. The store is in its original condition except for the addition of screen doors.

The latest building, not an original but newly constructed, is a chautauqua-style structure for instructional and artistic programs. It opened in 1999.

Parke countians have more than taken Sanders's advice to heart. Brightly colored brochures and advertisements herald the county's attractions, including Billie Creek Village. One map for the Covered Bridge Festival, held each autumn, not only identifies all the remaining bridges and every building at Billie Creek Village but even has the names and locations of vendors, craft booths, and food shacks on the courthouse lawn, and—oh, yes—restrooms and telephones.

GETTING THERE: Billie Creek Village is one mile east of Rockville on U.S. 36.

INFORMATION: For the village and inn call (765) 569–3430; for the general store call (765) 569–0252 or fax (765) 569–3582; Web site, http://www.billiecreekvillage.org/. The village's mailing address is Box 357, 1659 E U.S. Highway 36, Rockville, Indiana 47872. Hours are 9 a.m. to 4 p.m., full operation, Friday, Saturday, Sunday, holidays, and Memorial Day weekend through Halloween weekend. Gates and general store open at 9 a.m.

FEES: Village admission charged. Parking free.

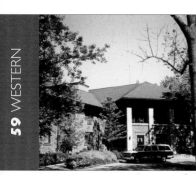

TURKEY RUN INN. The inn's sixty-one air-conditioned rooms, oak lobby with fireplace, pool, gift shop, game room, and dining room make it a favorite of park visitors.

RETURNED TO NATURE. A park naturalist is ready to release a turtle into Sugar Creek during one of the presentations made by the staff of the Nature Center. After a moment or two of hesitation, the turtle quickly acclimated itself and swam away.

Turkey Run State Park, Marshall

MARSHALL—I looked at the Turkey Run State Park map and tried to figure out how to go to Richard Lieber's cabin. The cabin is located on Trail 6—a half mile in length and termed "moderate" in difficulty—and it seemed to make no difference whether I started from the inn to the left or to the right.

It turned out that it did.

I elected to go to the left. Maybe I made a wrong turn, although state park trails usually are well marked. All I know for certain is that I found myself in Turkey Run Hollow trying to cross a creek. Stepping on a log and then a stone, I made a misjudgment, and the next thing I knew my shoe, sock, and pants leg were soaked.

Not seeing any easy way to go forward out of the hollow, I retreated back toward the inn—crossing the creek this time without incident. Since it was a warm Sunday morning, within half an hour I dried out. Sitting by the fireplace in the inn's lobby in a comfortable chair and sipping a cup of coffee helped—at least my disposition.

The next time out, I went to the right. Wouldn't you know it? Lieber's cabin was but a short distance behind the inn.

The cabin actually was a shed that Lieber stumbled across during a thunderstorm. Located about three miles from the park, it had been built in 1848. He made a deal with its owner to have it moved to the park for use as an administration building.

When the cabin, mostly made of tulip poplar logs, was reassembled, everything could be saved except the chimney. An old-timer in the area directed the construction of a new chimney in the "cat and clay" style. Its stones came from an old bridge abutment. The sticks that give it support were butternut, but since have been replaced with sassafras. Today, the cabin houses displays about Lieber and the state parks.

Lieber, born in 1869 in Germany, became the first director of Indiana state parks and was a fierce advocate of land preservation. He was largely responsible for starting the park system—McCormick's Creek being the first and Turkey Run the second. He died at McCormick's Creek in 1944.

No one can be positive how the park got its name. One theory is it was inhabited by wild turkeys who would gather in the canyon bottoms—runs—to stay warm. Another is that pioneer hunters would herd turkeys into these runs so that they would be easy targets.

The park's 2,382 acres include hiking and bridle trails, a saddle barn, a nature center that offers interpretive programs, a swimming pool, picnicking sites, shelters, playgrounds, and camping with 213 class A

YES, IT SWAYS. The suspension bridge over Sugar Creek does sway a bit as people walk across it. This view is from the Rocky Hollow Falls Canyon Nature Preserve side with its more rugged terrain.

IF YOU GO

GETTING THERE:
Located on Indiana 47 south of Crawfordsville.

INFORMATION: The Nature Center is open May through August from 9:30 a.m. to 4:30 p.m. and September through April from 10 a.m. to 4:30 p.m.; closed Tuesday and Wednesday. Park gate closes at 11 p.m. Call the park at (765) 597–2635, or the inn toll-free at (877) 500–6151.

FEES: Admission charged. Call the inn for room rates.

sites, as well as the comfortable inn with its sixty-one air-conditioned rooms and dining and meeting rooms. The inn also operates twenty-one sleeping cabins.

One of the park's highlights is its suspension bridge. It crosses Sugar Creek to the Rocky Hollow Falls Canyon Nature Preserve. Some of the trails into this area, especially the 1.7 mile Trail 3, are really rugged. It weaves in between steep walls of old growth timber, gorges, and waterfalls.

The suspension bridge was built in 1917–18 and offers excellent views down Sugar Creek. The creek itself is termed extremely hazardous and swimming is prohibited, although canoes are allowed.

The eleven trails are posted "Dangerous cliffs surround this area. Stay on marked trails." Only one trail is "easy," Number 11, but even it has sheer drop-offs. It leads to the Lieber Memorial and the Log Church—where Sunday morning church was in progress when I visited.

The park is located in northern Parke County and is only a few miles from the county seat, Rockville, the "covered bridge capital of the world," and another good reason for a trip to Turkey Run State Park and the vicinity.

IF IT LOOKS LIKE A LANDING STRIP. If it looks flat enough, wide enough, and long enough to be an airplane runway, that's because it is. This is the Roscoe Turner Flight Strip at Shades State Park, at one time the only park airstrip in the state, but no longer in use.

ENTRANCE TO PINE HILLS. Its four narrow ridges, or backbones, are remnants of glaciers. This nature preserve was given to the state of Indiana by a nature conservancy in 1961.

DEEP RAVINES. Shades State Park has numerous drop-offs and other rough ground. Some of its trails are considered rugged.

Shades State Park, Waveland

WAVELAND—Shades State Park doesn't have the creature comforts of a number of the other state parks such as Turkey Run, only a few miles away. No air-conditioned inn, no restaurant, no swimming pool. Some recreational opportunities aren't part of the park's offerings to the visitor, either. No saddle barns, no class A campsites, no boat launching ramp.

What it did have, however, until recently, was an aircraft landing strip! While the strip still is there, it is no longer in use. The park never made a big deal about the landing strip. The annual *Indiana Recreational Guide*, which includes information about state parks among other state recreational facilities, carried the simple entry, "airstrip," as part of the Shades State Park facilities.

It was called the Roscoe Turner Flight Strip, named in honor of the Mississippi native who was instrumental in developing the Indianapolis airport and who held a number of speed records during his career.

The 3,000-foot runway—120 feet wide—was for use by light planes during daylight hours. Once a plane had landed, the pilot walked over to the nearby park gatehouse to pay landing and park fees.

I was there the last year the strip was used. I saw one single engine plane parked near the airstrip. Later in the afternoon, I watched it take off. For a non-flyer like myself, there's still a fascination in watching a plane taxi into position on a landing strip, listening as the motor revs up, and then following the plane as it roars down the runway and becomes airborne.

The airstrip was not all that Shades offered, of course.

Ten trails invite the serious hiker. Most are moderate to very rugged, in and out of ravines, creek beds, steep climbs, and timber. Some are impassable at certain times of the year. Only two, each of one-half mile, are termed easy. One two-and-a-half-mile trail begins at the parking lot and extends to the backpack camp. It's moderate in difficulty.

Hikers find inspiring vistas throughout the park. Perhaps the best known are the waterfalls at Silver Cascade and Prospect Point, rising 210 feet above Sugar Creek.

While Shades has no class A camping, it does offer 105 class B sites. That means a picnic table, fire ring, parking spur, drinking water nearby, and restrooms with showers.

Shades appeals to the daytime user with picnic tables, three shelters, and playground equipment. You also can fish in Sugar Creek, which runs through the property.

PARK ENTRANCE. This prominent sign marks the entrance to Shades State Park in western Indiana.

The park takes its name from one of many legends. One is that an Indian battle took place here, with the deep shadows of its valleys symbolizing the death that came to many. Another is that of an early settler killed by Indians. Yet another is that of a settler's wife burying an ax in her husband's head. Finally, the "shades of death"—for whatever reason—was shortened to "shades."

In the late 1800s a health resort, complete with a forty-room inn, occupied Shades. Joseph W. Frisz is credited with saving the land and trees by purchasing the health association and adding even more land into the 1930s. A holding company—Save the Shades—bought the land from his heirs in 1947 until the Shades became Indiana's fifteenth state park that year.

Adjacent to Shades proper, across Indiana 234, is the Pine Hills Nature Preserve.

If you're in Shades, you can walk the one and a half miles of Trail 10 to the preserve as I did—although it seemed farther than that to me on a warm Sunday afternoon. Or you could use some good sense, look at the map, and see that parking is available at a lot directly across Indiana 234 from the preserve's entrance.

Pine Hills is the state's first nature preserve—organized in 1961. The 594-acre part of Shades is well known for its rugged typography, narrow stone ridges or backbones, and its stands of evergreen and hardwood trees.

IF YOU GO

GETTING THERE: From Indiana 234 go west for about six miles to County Road 800S, which goes a short distance to the state park.

INFORMATION: Call (765) 435–2810. The mailing address is Route 1, Box 72, Waveland, Indiana 47989. Trails close at dusk.

FEES: Admission charged.

WHERE THE BEECH TREE STOOD. This statue of General Lew Wallace—seen in the middle of the photograph—was placed on the grounds of his study at the spot where a large beech tree stood in the nineteenth century. It was under the tree's shade that Wallace wrote much of *Ben-Hur.*

LEW WALLACE STUDY. The military leader, author, inventor, diplomat, artist, and musician designed and supervised the construction of this study near his home in Crawfordsville.

General Lew Wallace Study and Museum, Crawfordsville

CRAWFORDSVILLE—Ask historian Joann Spragg what her most thrilling experience has been at this west-central Indiana museum and I'm fairly certain I know her answer. I even know the date.

September 23, 1993. That's when Judah Ben-Hur came calling. Or rather—and maybe even better—that's when Charlton Heston, the Hollywood star who played the Ben-Hur role in the epic movie, came calling.

Heston had been in Indianapolis making a speech. He was anxious to see the place where General Lew Wallace had written much of the novel *Ben-Hur: A Tale of the Christ.* The book previously had been made into silent motion pictures in 1907 and 1925. Heston's 1959 version was a blockbuster and still can be seen on cable channels.

A special viewing of the museum, which had served as Wallace's study during the last years of his life, was arranged for Heston. A photograph of the actor, standing outside the study during the time of his visit, now hangs above the museum's entrance.

"Perhaps the greatest pleasure was in just meeting the man. He was so pleasant, so easy to talk to—just like your next-door neighbor. He was very interested in what we had in the museum," Spragg recalls.

As fascinating and interesting as Heston may be, he is no more so than the man who wrote the book. More than one writer has termed Wallace a true Renaissance Man. Not a bad judgment, considering his accomplishments.

Wallace wrote seven books, including *Ben-Hur,* published on November 12, 1880, and reputed to be the best-selling novel of the nineteenth century. It's still in print, 125 years later.

He fought in the Mexican War and served as colonel of the Eleventh Indiana Volunteer Infantry during the Civil War, rising to the rank of major general. Wallace is credited with saving Cincinnati from Confederate occupation and also with helping to prevent the capture of Washington, D.C., at the Battle of Monocacy.

Wallace was second in command at the court martial of the Lincoln assassination conspirators, and he was president of the court that tried Henry Wirz, the commander of the infamous Southern prison at Andersonville, Georgia. He also served as governor of the New Mexico Territory and as U. S. minister to Turkey.

Wallace was a talented musician, making some of the violins he played. He painted, sketched, and sculpted with his work displayed around the country. In addition, he held eight U. S. patents, including one for a fishing rod with a built-in reel.

HISTORICAL MARKER. It relates the highlights of Wallace's career, including that he "organized the state for war" during the Civil War.

IF YOU GO

It was *Ben-Hur,* however, that brought lasting fame for Wallace. While he finished the book in New Mexico, Wallace wrote much of it, he recalled, while "at home, my favorite writing place being beneath an old beech tree near my house." Wallace lived around the corner from where his study later was built, but only two rooms of the house remain.

That's more than remains of the beech tree. The dying tree was cut down in 1908. Two years later, however, the spot was marked with a bronze statue of Wallace, cast from the original that stands in the National Statuary Hall in Washington, D.C.

The Crawfordsville study, personally designed and its construction supervised by Wallace from 1895 to 1898, is filled with his library of more than a thousand books, memorabilia from and about his life, and artifacts from the stage and Hollywood productions of *Ben-Hur.* For example, a drawing can be seen of an elaborate treadmill device to go under the stage to simulate the book's famed chariot race.

The Wallace study, set on three and a half acres and entirely enclosed by a high brick wall, is a National Historic Landmark and also is listed on the National Register of Historic Places. It remained in the Wallace family until 1941. Today, the Crawfordsville Park and Recreation Department is in charge of operating the museum.

Another Wallace site to visit is his grave site at the north edge of Crawfordsville in Oak Hill Cemetery. He died in 1905 at the age of seventy-seven. The grave is marked by a thirty-five-foot-high obelisk.

GETTING THERE: In Crawfordsville, while on U.S. 231 (Washington Street), turn east on Pike Street and follow the signs around the property to the parking lot off Elston.

INFORMATION: The museum is open April through October, Tuesday through Sunday, 1 p.m. to 4:30 p.m., with extended hours during the summer. Tours by appointment can be made year-round. For information or appointments, call (765) 362–5769. The Web site is http://www.ben-hur.com/, and the e-mail is study@wico.net.

FEES: Admission charged.

THE HUB. The dining facility located in the Memorial Student Union Building on the DePauw University campus.

CENTER FOR THE ARTS. This center for performing arts at DePauw University houses a 1,500-seat auditorium, a 400-seat theater, and a 220-seat recital hall.

DePauw University, Greencastle

GREENCASTLE—DePauw University mostly advertises its academic credentials: sixteenth in the list of the nation's undergraduate colleges as the baccalaureate school for PhD degrees in all fields, having 58 percent of its freshmen come from the top 10 percent of their high school classes, and being ranked in the nation's top tier of liberal arts colleges by *U.S. News & World Report* when I visited the campus in 2002.

What gets less discussion is the feeling the visitor to the campus has of being in the midst of a picture-postcard, Norman Rockwell-like college environment.

It's all here.

First, there's the setting. Greencastle is a small, graceful, tree-lined community complete with attractive homes, a modest but relatively busy downtown, and the close-by-campus Walden Inn, a prominent hotel with meeting and banquet rooms known throughout the state. Among the town's historical record, it was here that young businessman Eli Lilly opened his first drugstore shortly before leaving for service with the Eighteenth Indiana Battery in the Civil War.

The campus has its own history, too, stretching back to 1837 when the school was chartered by the state of Indiana as Indiana Asbury University. Greencastle got the campus because the community raised $25,000 to convince the Methodist Episcopal Church to locate the school in what was described as a "rough, frontier village." The school started with one professor and five students. (A recent year's enrollment was 2,385.) The name was changed to DePauw to honor Washington C. DePauw, who gave $600,000 toward a building program in the 1870s.

The oldest building on campus, East College, stands even today as an important academic structure, housing the departments of economics, history, and modern languages. Begun in 1871, it took eleven years to complete. It underwent a $2 million restoration in the early 1980s that kept its architectural design and nineteenth-century details. Its Meharry Hall, with original pews, woodwork, and balconies, represents the grand style of old-time college assembly halls.

It was in East College early in the twentieth century that Eugene C. Pulliam and a group of his fellow students organized the journalism fraternity Sigma Delta Chi, which has become the Society of Professional Journalists. The Indiana Journalism Hall of Fame also is located there.

DePauw isn't simply old buildings, however. In more recent years, the campus has added the Richard E. Peeler Art Center, the Percy Lavon Julian Science and Mathematics Center, the Holton Memorial

EAST COLLEGE. Historic East College is the oldest building at the DePauw University campus at Greencastle. It underwent restoration in the early 1980s.

IF YOU GO

Quadrangle, Rector Village student residence halls, and a state-of-the-art Track and Tennis Building, in addition to other modern structures.

One of them is the Eugene S. Pulliam Center for Contemporary Media, opened in 1991. The school's mass communications programs are headquartered here. Eugene S. was a prominent newspaper publisher, as was his father, Eugene C., the journalism fraternity founder.

The $7.2 million Lilly Physical Education and Recreation Center was completed in 1982. It includes Neal Fieldhouse and Erdmann Natatorium. It is the home of intercollegiate athletics, intramurals, the kinesiology department, classrooms, and offices and is the site for leisure sports, concerts, and other events. Three blocks to the west are the university's other athletic facilities, including football, track, baseball, softball, soccer, outdoor tennis, and practice fields.

In the heart of the campus, close to East College, is the Memorial Student Union Building, opened in 1951 and renovated with an addition in 1998. It has university offices, student services, a bookstore, meeting rooms, recreational areas, and the Hub food court.

On the perimeter of the campus are handsome fraternity and sorority houses as well as other university buildings. In all, there are thirty-six major structures on the 655-acre campus, including a new 400-acre nature park with trails.

GETTING THERE: On U.S. 231 in Greencastle, turn west on Hanna Street, which takes you directly to the Memorial Student Union Building at the intersection of Hanna and Locust streets.

INFORMATION: A DePauw University guide may be picked up on campus. Also go to the Web site at http://www.depauw.edu/visitors/ or call (800) 447–2495. The Web site has a virtual tour of campus and other information.

FEES: None to tour.

ON DOWN THE CREEK. The point where water from Cagles Mill Lake goes through the tunnel under the dam and flows into Mill Creek is in the upper right center of the photo.

WATERSLIDE, TOO. This modern swimming pool at Lieber State Recreation Area is complete with a waterslide, as well as sheltered relaxing and eating areas.

Lieber State Recreational Area/ Cagles Mill Lake/Cataract Falls State Recreational Area, Cloverdale

CLOVERDALE—My advice when you're in western Indiana going to Lieber State Recreation Area of the Lieber SRA/ Cagles Mill Lake/Cataract Falls SRA complex would be to not take the first marked exit off Interstate 70 at U.S. 231. The exit would work if you were first going to Cataract Falls, but not the recreation area.

Maybe some other driver would do a better job than I did, but I found myself winding around county roads, trying to head in the general direction of the Lieber recreation area and the lake. Yes, I eventually did end up at the recreation area, and, yes, I did find the lake and its dam, but don't ask me how.

When I drove back toward Interstate 70 for my return trip, I followed Indiana 243 north to the interstate. That interchange would be the second exit to the lake and state recreation area if you are going west on I-70. That's the way to do it. Just turn south on Indiana 243 and you're there—approximately two and a half miles.

First, you will come to the Lieber State Recreation Area—more than eight thousand acres with a visitor center, 120 class A and 96 class B camping sites, a basketball court, playground, picnic tables, shelter houses, and swimming.

The swimming pool is worth a special note. It must be one of the nicest in any of Indiana's state parks. Plus, it has a waterslide that is a big favorite of children. In the summer the pool also is the site of daily "pool games" sponsored by the interpretive and recreation program staff.

The visitor center is the place to sign up—a fee is charged—for boat tours of the lake and dam. You need to make reservations. Most days there are two tours, with Tuesday and Thursday set aside for special tours.

The 1,400-acre Cagles Mill Lake is one of Indiana's smaller reservoir-created lakes, especially compared to the 10,750-acre Monroe Lake near Bloomington and the 8,800-acre Patoka Lake in southern Indiana. However, since it is one of only two such lakes in western Indiana—Cecil M. Harden Lake near Rockville being the other—water enthusiasts give it good use.

Naturally, fishing is the major sport. There's a fishing pier at Lieber, along with rental of boats and pontoons from the concessionaire.

The lake is sometimes called Cataract Lake by the local residents because of its near proximity to the upper and lower Cataract Falls on Mill Creek and the community of Cataract. It spreads across Putnam and Owen counties.

VIEW FROM THE TOP. Looking out onto Cagles Mill Lake from the road going over the dam. A tour boat is in the water near the trash boom, constructed to stop large objects from entering the tunnel under the dam.

The dam, which creates the lake, lies 2.8 miles above the mouth of Mill Creek. You can hike down to the falls, the upper having a drop of forty-five feet, supposedly the largest in width in Indiana.

The dam, built and maintained by the U.S. Army Corps of Engineers, was completed in 1953. It is the oldest lake project in the Corps's Louisville district. While other Corps projects have a formed concrete basin below the dam, Cagles Mill's dam uses a tunnel bored through solid rock. The water passes through the tunnel and comes out directly into Mill Creek's natural basin.

That's one of the things you can find out if you drive across the dam and up to the Corps's office at the end of the road and talk to the engineers on duty there. They're not necessarily looking for company but seem quite ready to answer questions and give directions.

You might be even better received in the dead of winter when, they say, "only the mailman" gets through.

The dam's maximum height is 150 feet and measures 900 feet in length. The drainage area above the dam is 295 square miles. You can gain a panoramic and picturesque view from the overlook on the north side of the dam.

The name, Cagles Mill, comes from an old gristmill downstream from the lake. It burned and was rebuilt several times before the last fire in 1975. That time it wasn't rebuilt. The recreation area is named for Richard Lieber, considered the founder of the Indiana state park system.

GETTING THERE: Take exit 37 off Interstate 70 to Indiana 243 and go south to the entrance of Lieber State Recreation Area. For Cataract Falls State Recreational Area, take U.S. 231 south off Interstate 70; go approximately twelve miles and follow the signs.

INFORMATION: Call Lieber State Recreation Area at (765) 795–4576 or the marina at (765) 795–6135.

FEES: Fees for camp sites.

MOSTLY FROZEN FALLS. Ice forms on the falls of McCormick's Creek during wintertime in the southern Indiana state park. The creek empties into the west branch of the White River.

THE UNVEILING. This statue, dedicated to Dick Viquesney's wife, marks the Viquesney family graves in Spencer's Riverside Cemetery. Viquesney is best known for his *The Spirit of the American Doughboy* statue, which stands, mostly at courthouses, in thirty-five states.

McCormick's Creek State Park and Spencer

SPENCER—If you were looking for lots of activity, then McCormick's Creek State Park wasn't the place to go when I was there. Remodeling of the inn was under way. Plus, it was wintertime, so the park's summertime outdoor activities were shut down.

What if, however, you'd like a peaceful place to get away from it all, where you could just be left alone with not too many people around. That's what I found when I stayed overnight at McCormick's Creek.

Actually, that's what Frederick Denkewalter envisioned when he opened his sanitarium on the Canyon Inn site in 1888—a place to get away and rest. That's how it remained until the state bought the land in 1916 and dedicated the first state park here on July 4 of that year.

Even with all this tranquility, though, on my one evening at the inn, a couple beat me to the two rocking chairs in front of the gas-log fireplace. So I went for a walk, ate dinner, and worked at my word processor in my room. More than three hours later, when I checked, the couple was still there, rocking away and swapping stories with another couple sitting in straight-back chairs.

Come springtime, activity at the park and the inn would be a different story, of course, when all the park's activities would be in full swing: camping, hiking, picnicking, horseback riding, swimming, tennis and other games, and programs at the interpretive center.

On my visit, though, it was so quiet at night you could hear the proverbial pin drop. It reminded me somewhat of the Trappist retreat house I visited in Kentucky many years ago—slow paced, restful, and very quiet. (Trappist monks normally don't talk.)

Close to the state park, I found an even quieter place.

Of course, that would be a cemetery—Riverside Cemetery in Spencer, the Owen County seat, just two miles west of the park.

I was especially drawn there to see the grave sites of two persons—Byron Bancroft Johnson and Ernest Moore "Dick" Viquesney—after reading about the cemetery in *Indiana: A New Historical Guide*.

Ban Johnson is considered the father of professional baseball's American League. He was its president from 1893, when it was called the Western League, until his retirement in 1927. His is the easiest one to find in the cemetery—a flat, three-tiered, marble-covered grave.

Viquesney is the sculptor who created *The Spirit of the American Doughboy* statue found on courthouse lawns in thirty-five states, including at least Randolph, Owen, and Kosciusko counties in Indiana, as well as at the Henry County Memorial Park in New Castle.

CANYON INN. The remodeling of McCormick's Creek State Park's Canyon Inn and its dining area has returned the family-oriented facility to full use.

IF YOU GO

GETTING THERE: McCormick's Creek State Park is located off Indiana 46, northwest of Bloomington. In Spencer, turn on Main Street to Riverside Cemetery.

INFORMATION: Canyon Inn's toll-free telephone number is (877) 922–6966. The McCormick's Creek State Park office number is (812) 829–2235.

FEES: Admission charged. Call the inn for room rates.

Viquesney's family graves also are easily found. They are marked by a tall, sculpted headstone monument dedicated to his wife, titled *The Unveiling.* His own small grave marker today is almost overgrown with grass.

Also, old-timers will recall Hickam Field in the Hawaiian Islands, which Japanese planes targeted in the December 7, 1941, attack that drew the United States into World War II. It's named for Lieutenant Colonel Horace Hickam, another Spencer native.

A final note about those two rocking chairs near the fireplace at the state park's Canyon Inn. Early the next morning, one of the four persons from the previous night still occupied one of them. It did occur to me to ask if he had gone to bed or spent the night there. No matter. I commandeered the other, possession being nine-tenths of the law.

JOHN PURDUE IS BURIED HERE.
Or at least he is supposed to be.
Rumor has it that his bones have
been dug up many times and dis-
tributed elsewhere. But that's apparently all they are—rumors. The site
was rededicated in 1997 by the Class
of 1946.

ACADEMY PARK TABLET. It reminds
viewers that Plato founded the Athens academy in 387 BC as a place
where Greek philosophers taught.
"The same academic tradition" holds
true at Purdue, the tablet declares.

Purdue University, West Lafayette

WEST LAFAYETTE—Visiting any university campus can be intimidat-
ing, even more so if it is a large campus. While Purdue University certainly is big, following *A Walking Tour of Historic Purdue* makes your visit
less daunting, especially if you follow one word of advice: Take your trip
on a weekend or during the summer.

The reason? Parking. It's always a problem on any campus, but, generally speaking, if you show up when most of the students are gone,
then your tour gets simpler.

The best solution at Purdue is to park in the campus Grant Street
parking garage as you start your tour. You might be lucky, as I was one
Sunday, to find a parking place on the street, but the Grant Street
garage is easy to find and it's free on the weekends, on holidays, and
after 5 p.m. Also, it's directly across from the Purdue Memorial Union,
where you will find the campus walking-tour guide in publications
racks. Plus, you're near the center of the campus and the beginning of
your walking tour.

The Memorial Union is the place to start. Built in the Tudor Revival
style, it originally honored the 4,013 Purdue students who served in
World War I. Since its construction in 1924, the building has had six
additions, the last in 1987. The structure seems to go on forever with
meeting rooms, dining facilities, lodging, and recreational facilities. Its
stained-glass windows are a highlight.

When you leave Memorial Union, walking to the west, you go by
the university's first library, which now houses special collections. Like
many universities, today Purdue has numerous libraries.

The main undergraduate library, to the south and named for former university administrator John W. Hicks, doesn't look very large.
That's because it's mostly underground. (That's one way to solve the
space problem.)

As you walk north by classroom buildings and laboratories, you
can't miss the Bell Tower. Constructed in 1955 with a gift from the
Class of 1948, four of its bells in the belfry were taken from razed
Heavilon Hall.

Going to the south past other academic buildings, you pass University Hall, the oldest building on campus, built in 1877. It was modern-
ized in 1960, and the outside has been under renovation recently. If
any spot on campus might be called its heart, you're there.

Nearby is the grave site of John Purdue. One of the early settlers
of Lafayette, Purdue offered the state of Indiana $150,000 if the pro-
posed agricultural school—to be established under the Morrill Act—

BELL TOWER. Southeast of the Elliott Hall of Music is Purdue's Bell Tower, rising 163 feet above the campus. It's between Memorial Mall to the south and Purdue Mall to the north.

would be built in Tippecanoe County. When he died in 1876, he was buried on campus.

Nearby is Loeb Fountain. Donated in 1959 to honor Solomon Loeb, another Purdue benefactor, the fountain was moved to its present location, called Founders Park, from its previous site on the Purdue Mall.

The mall is another place you'll want to see. It's a few buildings to the north and faces Northwestern Avenue. Directly across the avenue from the mall is the visitor center.

Facing the mall are Hovde Hall, the central university administration building, named in honor of a former Purdue president Frederick L. Hovde, and, behind it, the Elliott Hall of Music, one of the world's largest theaters with six thousand seats. It was completed in 1940.

Keep going a few more blocks on Northwestern Avenue and, as all Boilermaker fans know, you'll come first to Mackey Arena and then, to the west, Ross-Ade Stadium, home of the football Boilermakers.

For sports fans, that's probably the real heart of the campus.

GETTING THERE: After crossing the Wabash River into West Lafayette on Indiana 26, turn right on Grant Street and the parking garage will be on your right.

INFORMATION: The Purdue Visitor Information Center is located at 504 Northwestern Avenue, about four blocks north of the Grant Street parking garage and across from the Purdue Mall and the Materials Science and Electrical Engineering Building. It's open 8 a.m. to 5 p.m. Monday through Friday and 8 a.m. to 4 p.m. Saturday. The telephone number is (765) 494–4636. A calendar of events can be found on the Web site at http://www.purdue.edu/calendar/. Athletic information is available at http://www.purdue.sports.com/ or by calling (800) 497–7678. Copies of the walking-tour guide can be obtained at the visitor center or in racks at the Memorial Union.

FEES: None to tour the campus.

IT'S MY TURN. Children clamor to sit in the driver's seat of the 1928 fire truck that's part of Imagination Station in downtown Lafayette. While hardly high tech, it's a favorite of young visitors.

REFLECTION OF A REFLECTION. With a mirror on each side of a hallway at Imagination Station, the writer's image is reflected back, creating yet another image which then is reflected back again, and—well, you get the idea.

Tippecanoe County Courthouse and Imagination Station, Lafayette

LAFAYETTE—The Tippecanoe County Courthouse may be the grandest in Indiana.

Completed in 1884, it cost $500,000—a hefty sum for the day. Several additions over the years enhanced the building and grounds, but the major upgrading occurred in 1991–93—a $15 million restoration.

Actually, the restoration made the courthouse more functional than before. For example, the fifth floor held only storage over recent years. Now it's the most modern of the floors, with the prosecutor's office plus additional space for expansion. Skylights have been restored to provide more natural light as well as providing a view of the building's dome.

The shape of the building is in the form of a Greek cross—two sections meeting at right angles in the middle. Indiana limestone and brick, cast-iron beams, and Indiana woods—oak, ash, and walnut—were used in the construction.

A fourteen-foot statue made of sheet metal sits atop the courthouse dome. According to records, the statue is described as the Goddess of Liberty, but some argue she really is the Statue of Justice. The statue now holds the scales of justice, found in the clock tower during the restoration.

A self-guided walking tour for the courthouse is available. Arrangements for guided tours of the courthouse also can be made for groups of ten or more through the Lafayette/West Lafayette Convention and Visitors Bureau.

Every floor has something to see. On the first is a restored staircase, the original long since removed. The second floor has hallways painted to look like granite, uncovered original skylights, a forty-eight-foot mural of the Battle of Tippecanoe moved to the courthouse from the old Fowler Hotel, and busts in the rotunda of General William Henry Harrison, Battle of Tippecanoe hero and later U.S. president, William Digby, founder of Lafayette, John Purdue, for whom the university is named, and Tecumseh, famed Shawnee warrior.

In some places on the third floor, thirteen coats of paint were removed to get down to hand-painted stencil patterns dating back to 1885. The large wooden doors to Superior Court I are original.

On the fourth floor is perhaps the best example of the restoration efforts to make certain new work can be distinguished from old. The flooring in Superior Court II is new and is separated from the walls by a six-inch strip of glass where the old part of the building is visible.

RESTORED GRAND OLD BUILDING. A $15 million restoration of the 1884 Tippe-canoe County Courthouse in the early 1990s made the structure ready for service into the twenty-first century. Among the courthouse's features are its one hundred columns.

The courthouse can occupy some time for persons interested in architecture and history. But what about children? Five blocks away, they'll have their reward at Imagination Station.

"Imagination is more important than knowledge" is the Albert Ein-stein quote on the wall just inside the former gas company service building. Its two floors have been converted into a hands-on, interac-tive museum, "where children and their families explore the world of space, science, engineering, and technology."

The center opened in 1994 and features a T-38 flight simulator, where children can sit in the cockpit (think eight years old and you're imagining taking off into the wild blue yonder), jet engine cutaways, a computer room, and—tried, true, and still a great favorite—a 1928 fire engine where they can sit in the driver's seat and ring the bell.

It depends heavily on volunteers. The day this writer was there, one volunteer was solving a computer problem in the second-floor lab. "Yeah, they get a real workout with the kids," he observed.

But that's the idea—encouraging imagination and excitement.

Since the courthouse is open Monday through Friday and Imagination Station on the weekends, they're both open together only on Friday.

IF YOU GO

GETTING THERE: Indiana 26 becomes a one-way street (Columbia) near downtown Lafayette. The court-house is bounded by Columbia Street on the south and Main Street on the north between Third and Fourth streets. Imagination Station is north five blocks on Fourth Street, a one-way street going north.

INFORMATION: The courthouse self-guided walking-tour booklet is available from the Lafayette/West Lafayette Convention and Visitors Bureau, 301 Frontage Road, (800) 872–6648, as well as at the court-house. Frontage Road goes off Indiana 26 east of Interstate 65. The e-mail address is info@homeofpurdue .com/, and its Web site is http://www .homeofpurdue.com/. Guided tours of ten or more also can be arranged by contacting the bureau. Imagination Station is open Friday through Sunday 1 p.m. to 5 p.m. and weekdays for groups. Its address is 600 N. Fourth Street, telephone (765) 420–7780, and Web site, http://www.imagination -station.org/.

FEES: No admission for the court-house walking tour. Imagination Sta-tion charges admission fees, but none for those under three and over ninety. (Yes, that's right.)

BATTLE'S HERO. William Henry Harrison became an American hero in the Battle of Tippecanoe, fought near Lafayette at Battle Ground in 1811.

AT THIS PLACE. Monument commemorates the Battle of Tippecanoe, fought November 7, 1811. It was dedicated in 1908, ninety-seven years after the battle.

Tippecanoe Battlefield Park, Battle Ground

BATTLE GROUND—A cold, light drizzle was falling on the American army's encampment on Burnett's Creek, about two miles from Prophetstown on the Wabash River north of Lafayette.

Indiana territorial governor William Henry Harrison was already up at a quarter after four in the morning, November 7, 1811. He was within minutes of giving the order for "calling out" the nine hundred men under his command who had spent the night sleeping on their weapons in an irregular quadrangle battle formation—just in case.

Then the Indians attacked. It would be known as the Battle of Tippecanoe.

No one really is certain how many Indians charged Harrison's army. An account in Ross Lockridge's *The Story of Indiana* estimates the number at around seven hundred.

For two hours, the battle raged. The American army—made up of regulars, militia, and volunteers—gave way at some points but essentially held their positions. Finally, the Indians retreated into the marshes.

The American losses were 37 dead, 25 dying later, and another 126 injured. Indian dead left on the battlefield numbered 38. Historian Lockridge wrote that the Indian losses undoubtedly were many more, as the Indians rarely left behind those who were killed on the field.

The battle was significant for many reasons, most notably two—one about the Indians and the other, Harrison. His army then marched on and destroyed the Indian headquarters at Prophetstown, effectively ending an attempt to build an Indian confederacy. Also, the Indian leader, the Prophet, apparently told his warriors he had cast a spell on the American force and their bullets would be ineffective. He was discredited, and his future as a leader was ended.

As for Harrison, in later years he went on to campaign for—and win—the U.S. presidency under the slogan "Tippecanoe and Tyler, too"—the latter, a reference to his vice presidential running mate.

The story of preserving the battlefield as a monument is of considerable interest.

John Tipton, a powerful figure in Indiana history, had been a young officer in Harrison's army. When he visited the area in 1829, he found "eight graves seemed to have been opened, bones of men and horses found bleaching together," whether "our men or Indians" being unknown.

Tipton bought the two hundred-acre tract, and the state purchased it from him in 1836. But then Tipton died in 1839, Harrison in 1841, and Governor Noah Noble, who helped push for a state monument, in 1844.

NOVEMBER 7, 1811, BATTLE. This plaque at the Battle of Tippecanoe battlefield cites the details of the struggle, won by the American troops under the command of William Henry Harrison.

Slowly, however, the state began to act. The legislature passed a resolution to enclose the battlefield in 1850, a wooden fence was replaced by an iron one in 1873, the Tippecanoe Monument Association was formed in 1892, and a contract was let to build a monument in 1908.

The monument was dedicated November 7, 1908—the ninety-seventh anniversary of the battle, and a reenactment took place in 1911 on the battle's one hundredth anniversary.

Today, Tippecanoe Battlefield Park's 104 acres are maintained by the Tippecanoe County Park and Recreation Department. The Tippecanoe County Historical Association operates a nearby historical museum with excellent exhibits and a gift shop. Also on the grounds are a nature center, swimming pool, picnic shelter, and an environmental education center. The Burnett's Creek section of the Wabash Heritage Trail also begins at the battlefield park.

When I visited the battlefield on a quiet, late autumn evening, I had the same feeling as when I earlier went to the Battle of the Mississinewa grounds near Marion. Could it be that in the silence the two forces were gathering, that the battle was imminent, that the spirit of these men from nearly two hundred years ago still was evident in some strange way?

IF YOU GO

GETTING THERE: From the south, take exit 178 off Interstate 65. Turn south on Indiana 43 to Burnett's Road. Follow it to Ninth Street. Turn north toward Battle Ground.

INFORMATION: The museum usually is open noon to 5 p.m., Tuesday through Sunday, October through April, and 10 a.m. to 5 p.m., Monday through Sunday, May through September. Hours are subject to change. For more information, call (765) 567–2147.

FEES: Museum admission charged.

CENTER FACADE. Constructed to resemble old downtown Delphi buildings, the interpretive and conference center includes a balcony where visitors can look out over the canal.

REED CASE HOUSE. Moved from downtown Delphi, this house was built by Reed Case in 1843–44. He was the canal construction superintendent and later a prominent entrepreneur. After he became more prosperous, Case moved his family into a newer brick house and used this building as a tavern and inn.

CANAL PARK. Other buildings at Delphi's Canal Park include these structures. In the center is the Speece shelter house, partially constructed from timbers taken from the land of a canal businessman, William Speece.

Wabash and Erie Canal Interpretive Center, Delphi

DELPHI—July 4 and 5, 2003, were great days in Delphi. That's when the thirty-year dream of the Carroll County Wabash and Erie Canal Association came true with the official opening of the Wabash and Erie Canal Interpretive Center.

Every last thing at the center wasn't complete when the doors first opened during Delphi's Canal Days Festival, says Dan McCain, president of the organization. No matter. It was close to finished, and besides, the totally volunteer group that made it happen simply couldn't wait any longer to show off their twelve thousand-square-foot center. Today, it is complete.

The 3,100 square feet in the exhibit space includes a functioning water model of the canal, a reproduction of a canal lock that shows how it was possible for boats to go both directions by raising and lowering the water level, a depiction of life in 1850s Delphi, a full-scale mock-up of a section of a canal boat's interior cabin, other exhibits, and graphics about the history of the canal.

The section of a canal boat's cabin is bordered by authentic walls so that visitors inside the cabin look out at rough-sawn timbers, giving the illusion of a boat passing through a canal lock—the cabin itself rocking gently as if on water.

The exterior of the building in Canal Park, based on historic photographs, represents commercial buildings of the mid-1800s in Delphi's downtown square. From the balcony of the Buford House, visitors look out on the canal and the site of the canal boat landing. To the right, the building facade appears as the former George Pigman Building, which stood at the downtown corner of Main and Washington streets.

The center's volunteer staff in those last days before the grand opening scheduled Saturday morning work days to plant trees and flowers, develop a new trail, pick up winter debris, and provide landscaping.

A training session for volunteers followed. The list of persons needed was a long one, ranging from construction and maintenance to gardening to staffing the gift shop to hosts and guides. That volunteer spirit continues today.

The center as now completed cost about $2 million. Exhibits, galleries, and rooms inside, as well as facades outside, are still available for naming rights. Membership in the canal association has been another source of funding.

Impressive as the new interpretive center appears, it isn't the only attraction at Canal Park. First, there's a two-and-a-half-mile section of the canal itself. The restoration process began in 1996, with water for

WABASH AND ERIE CANAL. A restored section of the Wabash and Erie Canal passes near the new interpretive center at Delphi.

the canal coming from a nearby limestone quarry. The Wabash and Erie Canal generally was about forty feet wide and four feet deep.

Most prominent among other buildings on the grounds of the Canal Park Village is the Reed Case house, constructed in 1844 on West Front Street by the superintendent of canal construction and later a banker and grain dealer. Rooms were added to the original four rooms, two down and two up. It also became a tavern and inn for canal travelers. Visitors can follow a self-guided tour.

Other buildings include a blacksmith's shop, fur trapper's cabin, smokehouse, two cabins moved to the site, and a shelter.

Also considered part of the park is the Washington Street stone-arch bridge, used to approach the park from the south and constructed in 1901. The original wooden bridge, built in 1840, collapsed into the canal in 1874 at a time when the canal's usefulness was near an end. This light-duty bridge was replaced by a bowstring arch iron bridge that looked like the restored, relocated Paint Creek bridge, now crossing the canal a thousand feet to the north.

IF YOU GO

GETTING THERE: Where Indiana 39 turns at the courthouse in downtown Delphi, proceed north on Washington Street a dozen blocks to the Canal Park entrance.

INFORMATION: Write Carroll County Wabash and Erie Canal, 1030 N. Washington Street, Delphi, Indiana 46923, go to its Web site at http://www.wabashanderiecanal.org/, or call (765) 564–6572. Open Friday, 1 p.m. to 4 p.m. during summer months; Saturday, 10 a.m. to 4 p.m.; Sunday, 1 p.m. to 4 p.m.; or by appointment.

FEES: No charge, but donations accepted.

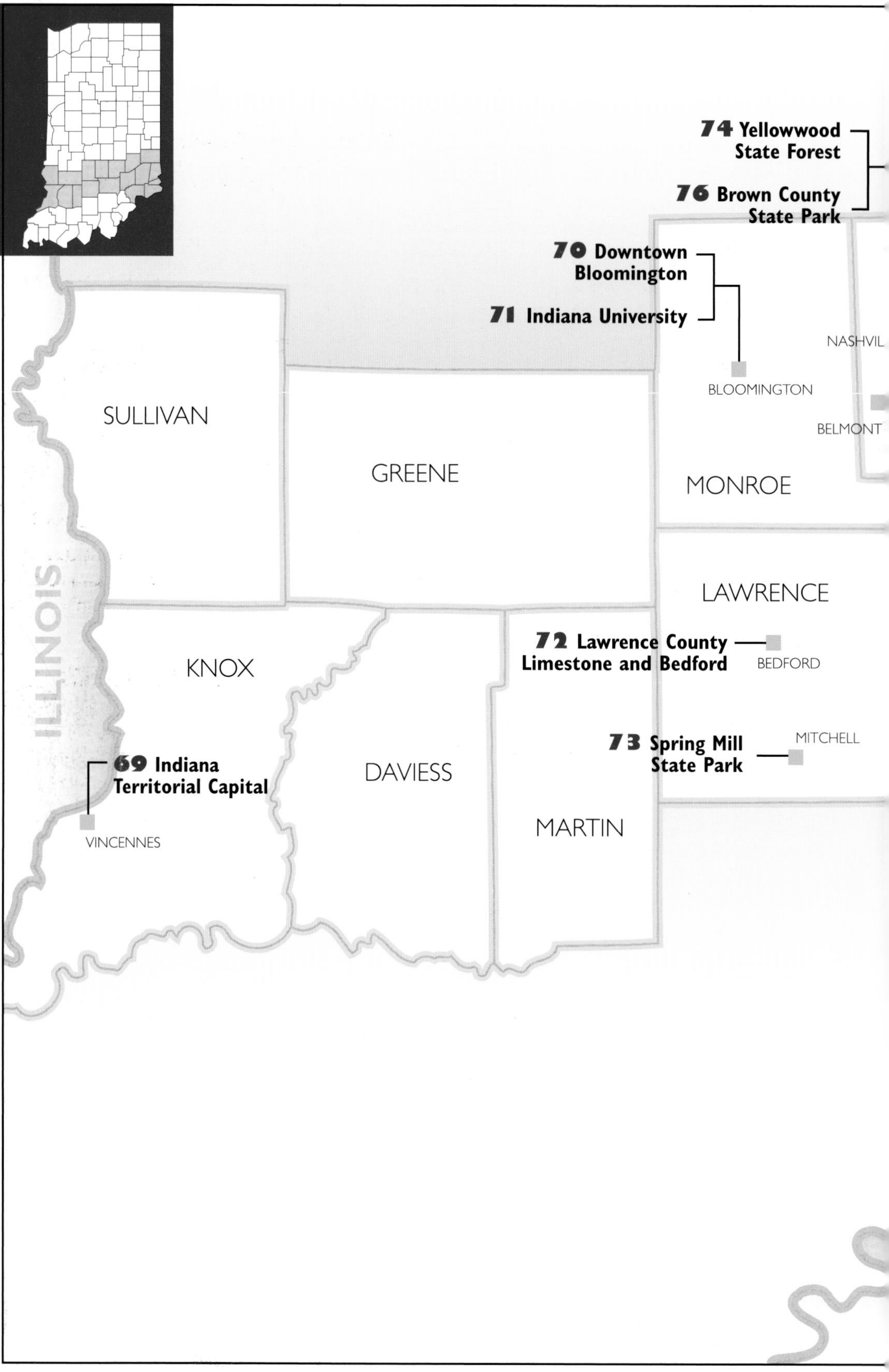

74 Yellowwood
State Forest

76 Brown County
State Park

70 Downtown
Bloomington

71 Indiana University

NASHVIL

BLOOMINGTON

BELMONT

SULLIVAN

GREENE

MONROE

ILLINOIS

LAWRENCE

KNOX

72 Lawrence County
Limestone and Bedford

BEDFORD

MITCHELL

73 Spring Mill
State Park

DAVIESS

69 Indiana
Territorial Capital

MARTIN

VINCENNES

FRANKLIN

82 Whitewater Memorial
State Park and ──■
Brookville Lake   BROOKVILLE

WN

DECATUR

77 Columbus
Architecture

COLUMBUS ■

BARTHOLOMEW

81 Milan and ─┐
Moores Hill

DEARBORN

84 Hillforest ─┐
and Veraestau

MILAN ■

5 T. C. Steele's
ouse of the
nging Winds

80 Versailles State Park ──■

VERSAILLES

AURORA ■

JENNINGS

RIPLEY

OHIO

RISING SUN ■

SEYMOUR ■

78 The Reno Gang

83 Ohio County ─┐
Courthouse

JACKSON

JEFFERSON

SWITZERLAND

MADISON ■

79 James F. D. Lanier Mansion
and Historic Madison

N

KENTUCKY

WHERE THE HOUSE ASSEMBLED. Inside the first floor of the territorial capitol, where the nine members of the House of Representatives met.

Indiana Territorial Capital, Vincennes

TERRITORIAL CAPITOL. This is the former business building that was converted into the Indiana territorial capitol. It was moved for the last time in 1949 to Harrison Street in Vincennes to become part of a historical building complex.

STOUT'S PRINT SHOP REPLICA. To the right is an original wooden Ramage printing press, similar to the one Elihu Stout used at his print shop in Vincennes in the early 1800s.

VINCENNES—"Where Indiana began" is Vincennes's motto. The city has a good case for its claim's accuracy.

When Governor William Henry Harrison was negotiating treaties with the Native Americans—five of them between 1803 and 1809—he also had the responsibility to govern the Indiana Territory. Remember, this land was a territory before it was a state.

Until Michigan was split off in 1805 and Illinois in 1809, that territory consisted of 291,602 square miles. (That's "miles" not "acres." The territory included today's states of Illinois, Indiana, Michigan, Wisconsin, and part of Minnesota.) Actually, for nine months in 1804 and 1805, most of the Louisiana Territory was attached to the Indiana Territory for administrative purposes. More land was governed from Vincennes during that period than any other place in the United States, with the exception of Washington, D.C.

One of the buildings from which the Indiana Territory was governed was the territorial capitol. When you visit that "capitol" today, however, don't expect to find something like the halls of the U.S. Congress. Rather, expect to find a structure about the size of a modern family room with two floors.

The General Assembly of the Indiana Territory didn't need a lot of room, however. The House of Representatives, meeting on the first floor, had nine members, elected by the free, white, male inhabitants. Upstairs, the Legislative Council—the equivalent of the Senate—consisted of five men, named first by the U.S. president and later elected.

The capitol, originally located in Vincennes on Main Street, has been moved several times, the latest in 1949 to First and Harrison streets, where it has been joined by three other structures to represent life on the Indiana frontier. They are but a few feet from Harrison's home, Grouseland, making a visit to all of them possible within a couple of hours.

The capitol is called the oldest major state government building in the Midwest and rightly is the best known of the buildings. The others have their own stories, however.

Perhaps the next best known is the replica of Elihu Stout's print shop. As the first printer in the Indiana Territory, he published the *Indiana Gazette*, beginning in 1804, although two years later a fire temporarily put him out of business. He restarted in 1807 with the *Western Sun*.

Again, this is no elaborate operation—just one fairly large room with a lean-to at the side. The centerpiece of the print shop is an original wooden Ramage printing press, built around 1800 and similar to the one Stout used.

MAIN STREET. Hostess Terri Talarek King awaits guests at Vincennes's depiction of a frontier Indiana main street. She is in front of the visitor center, built in part from the logs of a 160-year-old barn. Next is Elihu Stout's print shop, then the Indiana territorial capitol, and, finally, the birthplace of author Maurice Thompson.

Like many other printers of the time, the newspaper wasn't how Stout made his money. Only a few copies could be printed, no real distribution system existed, and many of the folks weren't literate anyway. The money came from printing official documents for the government, including laws enacted by the legislature.

The residence in the group of four buildings was where Maurice Thompson was born in 1840. It's called a "home ahead of its time." It's a frame construction house instead of being built of logs and has a cast-iron stove instead of the usual fireplace.

But, who, one might ask, was Maurice Thompson? His claim to fame was that he wrote *Alice of Old Vincennes*, a romantic tale set during the time of the American Revolution. It became the best-selling novel of 1900.

The first building you come to when you reach the complex is the visitor center, built in part using logs from a 160-year-old barn. Next to it is a replica of the Jefferson Academy, established here in 1801 as the predecessor of today's Vincennes University. That makes Vincennes University the oldest institution of higher education in the state.

In front of them all—visitor center, print shop, capitol, and Thompson house—is the re-creation of what a city street might have been like in the early 1800s. Doors of the houses open directly onto the street.

Just like today, however, things changed in Vincennes.

When the War of 1812 began, Harrison took command of American military forces, ultimately defeating a combined British and Native American force at the Battle of the Thames in Canada, where Tecumseh was killed. Thomas Posey became Indiana territorial governor on March 3, 1813, and eight days later the state capital was moved to Corydon.

Three years later, Indiana became the nineteenth state.

IF YOU GO

GETTING THERE: Use the Sixth Street exit into Vincennes off U.S. 41 and turn right on Harrison Street six blocks to the historic buildings.

INFORMATION: Open Tuesday through Saturday 9 a.m. to 5 p.m. and Sunday 1 p.m. to 5 p.m., April through mid-November. The Web site is http://www.state.in.us/ism/ or call (812) 882-7422. Tours begin at the log cabin visitor center.

FEES: Donations are requested.

THE COPPER FISH WEATHER-VANE. Saved when the old court-house was demolished in 1906, this weathervane sits atop the court-house and is considered a local landmark.

LOOKING UP AT STAINED-GLASS DOME. This is the view the visitor sees from the first floor of the court-house, looking up into the rotunda. The stained glass had been covered over during a previous remodeling.

Downtown Bloomington

BLOOMINGTON—The downtown of this southern Indiana city may be the envy of almost every town's government in the state. Shops and restaurants fill the storefronts surrounding the traditional court-house square. Not only are these businesses there, but on a cold winter weekday morning when I visited, the streets were lined with cars while people moved briskly along the sidewalks going about their errands.

It looked very much like the courthouse square scenes that those persons from my generation would remember from fifty years ago.

My visit to downtown Bloomington was not to observe urban planning or for sociological or nostalgic purposes, however. Rather, I was fascinated by the walking tours of historic districts in the city, organized by Bloomington Restorations Inc.

Notice, "walking tours"—plural. Not one tour, but eight, each one laid out in its own attractive brochure. Perhaps some other city has produced its equal, but I'm not aware of it.

The walking tours include West Side, North Washington, Prospect Hill, Vinegar Hill Limestone, Cottage Grove, North Indiana Avenue, University Courts, and, the one that I found especially intriguing, the Courthouse Square.

Its centerpiece, of course, is the 1907 limestone courthouse with its stained-glass ceiling rotunda topped by a copper fish weathervane, saved from the first brick and stone courthouse. According to *Indiana: A New Historical Guide*, the five-foot fish may have been designed to represent the reigning Jeffersonian Republican Party of the day, forerunner of today's Democratic Party. Now, it is considered a local landmark.

The courthouse has been meticulously restored. At least on the day I was there, it was as clean as a pin, as the saying goes. It's the stained-glass dome that particularly catches the eye of the visitor. Seen from the first floor of the rotunda, it is as striking as any public building view I've found anywhere in the state.

I wasn't surprised to learn at one time the stained glass in the dome had been covered over in one of the courthouse's past remodelings. Thankfully, it was not destroyed and was found later.

The courthouse's architects were Marshall and Guy Mahurin of Fort Wayne. Among Marshall Mahurin's other commissions early in the twentieth century were the Edmund B. and Bertha Ball home on Minnetrista Drive in Muncie, now the Center for University and Community Programs at Ball State University, and numerous homes and buildings in Fort Wayne.

HISTORIC COURTHOUSE. Almost a hundred years old—constructed in 1907—the Monroe County Courthouse today is in tip-top condition.

Another key feature of the lively courthouse square is the Fountain Square Mall, across West Kirkwood Avenue from the courthouse. This mall by the Bill Cook Group is in renovated space that formerly housed, among other establishments, the Old Opera House.

Built in 1868, the building's second floor was where James Whitcomb Riley held poetry readings in 1885. At the time, it was called Mendelssohn Hall before it later was used as an opera house. The building became part of the mall expansion through a renovation project in 1988.

The best way to tour this historic district, or to take any of the other tours, is with tour guide in hand. The guides' descriptions include addresses, photographs, and maps. Following more than one tour is a project that obviously would take several trips to Bloomington to complete.

The entire Courthouse Square Historic District was listed on the National Register of Historic Places in 1990.

GETTING THERE: Follow the Walnut Street and College Avenue exit off Indiana 37 south into Bloomington. It goes by the Bloomington Convention and Visitors Bureau on the city's north side, which has a wealth of information about the city and area, including the tour guides.

INFORMATION: Stop at the bureau at 2855 N. Walnut Street or call toll-free at (800) 800–0037. The Web site is http://www.visitbloomington .com/, and the fax number is (812) 334–2344. The Monroe County Courthouse is open during business hours from 8 a.m. to 4 p.m. Monday through Friday.

FEES: All information at the convention and visitors bureau is free, including the tour guides.

IU AUDITORIUM. The 3,760-seat IU Auditorium was constructed on the Bloomington campus in 1941. It has twenty of Thomas Hart Benton's murals showing the social history of Indiana.

THE CEMETERY. In the foreground is Dunn Cemetery, located immediately east of Memorial Union on the Bloomington campus. Next to the cemetery is the small Beck Chapel. In the background is a large academic building, Ballantine Hall.

PRESIDENT'S HOME. Home of IU presidents since 1924 is the William Lowe Bryan house. Bryan served as IU's president for thirty-five years.

Indiana University, Bloomington

BLOOMINGTON—There's good news and there's bad news about visiting a university campus when the students are on vacation.

The good news, of course, is that you can find a place to park. The bad news is that some of the places you might like to see may be locked. Both were true when I took a walking tour of the Indiana University campus during a recent Christmas break.

I first stopped at the Bloomington Convention and Visitors Bureau. It's easy to find as you drive into the city from the north, taking the Walnut Street and College Avenue exit. It's filled with useful information about both the campus and the Bloomington area. That's where I picked up a copy of "A Self-Guided Walking Tour of the Indiana University Bloomington Campus."

Since I was somewhat familiar with Indiana University, I drove right to a prime parking place—next to the Indiana Memorial Union off Seventh Street, in the very heart of the campus.

Located east of downtown Bloomington, the IU campus long has been considered one of America's most beautiful—rolling hillsides; large, impressive limestone buildings; meadows; creeks; nearby sports facilities; and even a cemetery.

The cemetery—nestled next to the Union building and the small Beck Chapel, near a meandering creek with a huge academic building, Ballantine Hall, nearby—was donated by George P. Dunn for perpetual use as a cemetery. Not far away is Dunn Meadow, sometimes the scene of campus demonstrations, and Dunn's Woods, a twenty-acre site surrounded by older campus buildings—now referred to as the Old Crescent Historic District of campus structures, built between 1884 and 1908.

It's the Memorial Union that dominates all other sites along Seventh Street. It's reputed to be the largest student union in the world. It includes a 186-room hotel, conference and banquet facilities, a three-floor bookstore, post office, restaurants, bowling alleys, game rooms, an auditorium, lounges, offices, and an art collection along its hallways and in rooms.

Under its shadow is Ernie Pyle Hall, named after the famed Hoosier World War II war correspondent and the home of the IU School of Journalism.

The Union actually is surrounded by academic buildings, usually set off by grassy spaces. Nearby are the IU Art Museum, Woodburn Hall, and Lilly Library, IU's home for rare books. They range from the New Testament of Gutenberg's Bible to a Shakespearean folio to American works.

In all, the library holds more than 400,000 books, seven million manuscripts, and 130,000 pieces of sheet music. It is a research library whose

LILLY LIBRARY. The Lilly Library is home to rare books numbering in the thousands.

IF YOU GO

exhibitions also attract the general public. The newest attraction at the time I visited was Jack Kerouac's original manuscript of *On the Road*, purchased by Indianapolis Colts' owner James Irsay for $2.43 million.

The Lilly holdings number, however, pales compared to the Main Library at the corner of Tenth Street and Jordan Avenue. It has more than 3.5 million books and journals and 12 million other materials. Between it and Seventh Street, where IU's old Memorial Stadium once stood, is the Arboretum with trees, shrubs, and hundreds of plants.

Even farther to the north, and not part of the main campus walking tour, are the university's athletic facilities, including the 17,500-seat Assembly Hall, home of the basketball Hoosiers; the 52,000-seat football Memorial Stadium; the 100,000-square-feet John Mellencamp Pavilion; the Bill Armstrong soccer stadium; and the $22.5 million student recreational sports center.

Back on the main campus are the music buildings; the law school; the William Lowe Bryan house, which has been the home of IU's presidents since 1924; and other academic buildings and student residence halls. It takes a bit of walking to see even most of them.

When I returned to my car, I had spent about three hours on my tour. The parking lot still had plenty of spots available, and I had no fees to pay.

As to finding a place to park if you go when the students are there, you're on your own.

GETTING THERE: At Bloomington on Indiana 37, take the Walnut Street and College Avenue exit south into the city. The bureau is north of the city and well marked. Continue south to Seventh Street and turn left toward the campus.

INFORMATION: For the Bloomington Convention and Visitors Bureau, go to its Web site at http://www.visitbloomington.com/, call (800) 800–0037, or go to the office at 2855 N. Walnut Street. (In the city, it's College Avenue one way going south and Walnut Street one way going north.) For the IU Visitor Information Center, go to its Web site at http://www.indiana.edu/~iuvis/, call (812) 856–4648, or stop at the center at 530 E. Kirkwood Avenue, located in the Carmichael Center at the corner of Kirkwood and Indiana avenues. Another parking solution is a one-day parking pass that can be purchased at the Bloomington visitor bureau.

FEES: None for tours.

FAMOUS SKYSCRAPER. New York City's Empire State Building is one of the most famous buildings in the world and perhaps the most outstanding example of the use of Indiana limestone. The photograph was taken shortly after its completion in 1930.

HEADSTONE. This limestone headstone depicts the workbench of a young stone carver, Lewis Baker. His fellow stone workers carved it as it appeared on the day he suddenly died. It shows the tools he was using to carve a cornice. The headstone is in the Greenhill Cemetery in Bedford.

THE CHAMPION. A Joe Palooka statue stands in Oolitic, heart of the Indiana limestone industry. Palooka, depicted to be the world's heavyweight boxing champion, was a popular cartoon figure of the mid-twentieth century.

Lawrence County Limestone and Bedford

BEDFORD—The Empire State Building, Washington National Cathedral, Grand Central Station, Rockefeller Center, U.S. National Archives, Chicago Tribune Tower, Waldorf Astoria Hotel, and Chicago Museum of Science and Industry. They're some of America's great historic buildings, and all have one thing in common: They were built of Indiana limestone.

Most of the stone came from Lawrence and Monroe counties in southern Indiana. At one point in the late 1800s, more than a hundred stone quarries and mills were in operation in these two counties. Even today, the limestone industry is the third largest employer in Lawrence County.

You can go visit these great buildings and marvel at what Indiana stonemasons accomplished. Many pieces weighed tons and, if they required design or special carving, took months to complete.

But there's an easier way to understand and see the story of Indiana limestone. That's to take a trip to Bedford.

Since 1994 Land of Limestone: An Indiana Heritage Exhibition has been housed on the Bedford campus of Oakland City University. The exhibit is in the Indiana Limestone Company building, the former headquarters of this limestone firm. Along the walls on the ground and second floors is an accounting of the industry's history—more than two hundred photographs, news accounts, official documents, records, and artifacts.

It's an unpretentious exhibit of more than five hundred running feet. You just walk in the front door of the building and start looking. Oakland City University personnel in the building try to be helpful but make no pretense of being limestone experts; you do it yourself with the assistance of informative narratives.

The exhibit, however, is only part of the reason for a Bedford limestone visit. The Lawrence County Tourism Commission offers three tours of county places to see, labeled blue, red, and green. Since each takes three to four hours, however, a choice probably must be made. Each begins when the visitor picks up an audiotape and printed guide at the commission's office on Main Street in Mitchell, just south of Bedford. Copies of the printed guides also are available at the commission's Web site.

The blue tour, for example, goes north to Needmore and then drops down to the Hopkins Cemetery. At the southern edge of the cemetery, you can look down into the Empire Quarry, from which stone for the Empire State Building was mined. The tour also goes

EMPIRE STATE BUILDING QUARRY. The Empire State Building limestone came from this quarry in Lawrence County. It's even called the Empire Quarry. Stone was sent in recent years for repairs at the New York City landmark.

IF YOU GO

through Heltonsville, home of IU's Damon Bailey, who was the nation's outstanding basketball player of 1990.

Actually, all three tours cover much more than the limestone industry, taking you through Lawrence County history. For instance, the green tour goes through Bono, Indiana. You remember Bono. Because of its location on the White River, it was another one of those towns considered as a possible capital of Indiana.

In Bedford, four walking tours display limestone as the dominant building material for buildings in different architectural styles, in cemeteries, and, to a lesser degree, in Hillcrest Circle, one of the first planned residential communities in the area built from the 1920s through the 1970s.

The cemetery tours feature two variations of stone carving. One is representative tree trunks carved from stone that serve as headstones. The Maddoxes' headstone, for example, has two tree trunks intertwined. Another has an open book lying on a broken limb of a tree stump, marking the graves of three family members.

The second cemetery walking tour shows other creative uses of stone carving. In numerous cases, the stoneworks are headstones for limestone carvers and their families. Several show children watching over the graves of youngsters. Others are monumental in design. Both cemetery tours are about one-fifth mile in length.

GETTING THERE: In Bedford, turn on Indiana 58 and go to I Street. Make a left and go a block to the Bedford campus building of Oakland City College. Go to the visitor center at 533 W. Main Street in Mitchell to pick up a map and audiotape.

INFORMATION: Call the Lawrence County Tourism Commission office at (800) 798–0769. The Web site is http://www.lime stonecountry.com/. Exhibit hours of the Bedford exhibit are 8:30 a.m. to 4:30 p.m. Monday through Friday. It is closed on Saturday, Sunday, and holidays.

FEES: Admission to the exhibit is free. You pay a fee for a tour audiotape but that's returned when you take back the tape. The audiotapes also are available at Spring Mill State Park and the Bedford Area Chamber of Commerce.

THE REAL THING. Mitchell native Gus Grissom's *Gemini 3* capsule can be seen at his memorial just inside the gatehouse of Spring Mill State Park. Other space exhibits also are housed here.

HE JUST GROUND IT. Cornmeal is for sale at the gristmill in the Pioneer Village of Spring Mill State Park. Several times a day through the spring, summer, and autumn months, this "pioneer" operates the mill to produce the meal from corn.

Spring Mill State Park, Mitchell

MITCHELL—Hoosiers often tend to think about their state parks in terms of only the summer months. While some of the state's twenty-five parks do go on reduced programming during the winter, other parks because of location and facilities attract visitors year-round.

That's true of Spring Mill State Park, a place for all seasons.

Located three miles east of Mitchell on Indiana 60, Spring Mill is far enough south to escape at least some of the bitter winter weather that can sweep across the state. Plus its inn with full-service dining room, game room, and conference rooms makes it a favorite for weekend get-aways and groups wanting a meeting place away from big-city hustle.

The cozy lobby makes a tempting resting place to take the chill off an early morning walk or a late afternoon return from visiting other Lawrence County points, such as limestone industry places of interest. The inn was built in 1939 but has been more recently renovated with modern air-conditioning, private baths, telephones, and television. In 1976 a twenty-nine-room wing was added plus a conference room.

But Spring Mill has even more going for it.

For one, it's the home of the Virgil I. "Gus" Grissom Memorial. Located just inside the main gate to the park, the memorial honors the Mitchell, Indiana, native who graduated from Purdue University, joined the air force, and became the second American in space on July 21, 1961. Four years later he commanded the first Gemini flight on March 23, 1965. Then on January 27, 1967, Grissom was involved in a test of the command module at Cape Kennedy with two crew members for the *Apollo I* flight when a cockpit fire broke out. All three of the crew were suffocated and died.

The memorial holds some of Grissom's effects related to space travel as well as the *Gemini 3* capsule—"the unsinkable Molly Brown"—in which he orbited the earth. The memorial building doesn't have the grandeur of the Air and Space Museum at the Smithsonian, of course, but, in its quiet and understated way, it certainly honors the Hoosier space pioneer.

For many park visitors, a highlight is the Pioneer Village. This reconstructed area is meant to look as much as possible as it was in 1863 during the Civil War and when the village was somewhat in decline, in part because its young men had gone off to the war.

You can watch Hoosiers operating looms, woodworking equipment, a sawmill, and—a favorite—the gristmill, where you can buy cornmeal for making cornbread. These workers operate their equipment hourly, so you can almost always catch them as you walk around the village look-

THE PLACE FOR ALL SEASONS. Spring Mill State Park Inn, built more than sixty-five years ago, is open year-round.

ing at the twenty pioneer buildings—blacksmith, apothecary, carpenter, shoemaker, distillery, tavern, and post office in addition to the gristmill.

Much of the repair and reconstruction of the village was done during the depths of the Depression by the Civilian Conservation Corps. The CCC, mostly made up of young men eager for work and a paycheck during one of the country's bleakest economic periods, also built the park's shelters, camping areas, roads, and trails from 1933 to 1942. The state park camping area has class A and primitive campsites.

Eight trails wind through the 1,360-acre park, ranging from easy to rugged. Some of them go through the Donaldson Woods Nature Preserve, where old-growth timber remains. (George Donaldson came here from Scotland in 1865 and did not allow cutting of timber or hunting on his property.) Two of the trails also go near caves in the park, including the best-known Donaldson Cave with its northern blind cave fish, an endangered species.

It's a good idea to stay on the marked trails. Numerous sinkholes are part of the Lawrence County terrain.

Camping, fishing, hiking, interpretive naturalist service, and picnicking go on year-round. During summer months the park also offers a camp store and swimming in an Olympic-sized outdoor pool.

While you're in Pioneer Village, see if you catch the spelling error in the plaque honoring the CCC builders.

GETTING THERE: At Mitchell, go east three miles on Indiana 60.

INFORMATION: Call the park office at (812) 849–4129 for information. The inn's telephone number is (812) 849–4081. The park is closed between 11 p.m. and 7 a.m. except for campers and inn guests. The Grissom Memorial is open daily, 8:30 a.m. to 4 p.m. Closed Thanksgiving Day, Christmas Day, and New Year's Day.

FEES: Admission charged. Call the inn for room rates.

DONE ANYTHING INCRIMINAT-ING? When asked if it were okay to take their photo, these Yellowwood State Forest campers agreed. "We haven't done anything incriminating," they said, telling the photographer to shoot. They were from Fort Wayne and Illinois and said they have been coming to the forest "for a number of years."

Yellowwood State Forest, Nashville

NASHVILLE—Almost everybody in Indiana has heard of Brown County State Park—probably even been there. They know the beauty and facilities of the park, and they certainly know about neighboring Nashville and its antique and craft shops.

But see what response you get when you bring up another Brown County landmark—Yellowwood State Forest. Probably a head shake and a "never heard of it."

There's a reason. Unless you like to fish or hunt, take your horse for a trot, run your dog, or go off-road into some hilly territory, you probably haven't been to this state forest.

Well, there might be one more reason why you've been there.

If some pleasant day you just want to hang out, get away from the frantic pace of life, and return, even briefly, to land where the loudest sound may be the call of a bird or some low conversation around a fire at a primitive campsite, then Yellowwood State Forest may be that place.

Actually, it's several places. Yellowwood State Forest is contained within Brown County, but it's made up of seventeen different parcels of land—23,326 acres in all. The largest section is west of Nashville and north of Indiana 46 as the highway makes its way to Bloomington, ten miles away. If you continue west, just across the county line is a similar state forest, Morgan-Monroe, which occupies much of the eastern part of those two counties.

The forest is named for a tree rarely found this far north. The tree flowers every three to five years. Only about two hundred of the forest's acres support the tree on the north-facing slopes and deeper ravines near Crooked Creek Lake, according to the Department of Natural Resources. A specimen has been planted at the forest office on Yellowwood Lake.

Yellowwood, as other state forests, has multiple uses—recreation, forest products, watershed protection, wildlife habitat, and maintenance of natural beauty.

Five trails cross through the main part of the forest. The longest circles around Yellowwood Lake and uses parts of other trails, some of them fire trails, so you have to carefully watch for trail markers. In addition, the forty-two-mile Tecumseh Trail runs through Yellowwood and ends at the Morgan-Monroe State Forest office. You're also advised to wear hunter orange or other bright clothing during hunting season.

Horse riders get the same advice for their trails, also five of them. An annual horse-use permit is required.

GOOD FISHING SPOT. This spillway, just beyond the dam that forms Yellowwood Lake, seemed to be the fishing spot of choice one recent afternoon.

The forest office can be contacted for year-round boat rentals on Yellowwood Lake, one of three lakes in the forest and the largest at 130 acres. Boat motors are limited to electric trolling motors. On summer weekends, boats can be rented at the camp store.

Hunting is permitted during season, but guns cannot be fired in safety zones—within two hundred feet of trails—or for target practice.

Camping offers eighty primitive sites, with another eleven primitive sites at the horseman's camp at the south end of the lake. Primitive means a picnic table, fire ring, parking, and drinking water in the area, but no showers or restrooms. No reservations for camping—first come, first served. Yellowwood also has a tent area for youth groups at the north end of the lake.

Don't go into this state forest with a just-washed car. It's usually dusty on those gravel roads. Be sure to stay well to the right because most of the roads are quite narrow. In addition, you can expect to ford a creek or so. The area hadn't had much rain when I was there, but in one stretch of about a mile I still crossed three small creeks.

Yellowwood State Forest probably never will be the "in" place to go. My guess is that's just fine with those who like it the way it is.

GETTING THERE: Turn north off Indiana 46 west of Nashville and follow the signs about three miles to the forest entrance.

INFORMATION: Call (812) 988–7945. E-mail is yelstfor@dnr.in.gov. Mailing address is 772 S. Yellowwood Road, Nashville, Indiana 47448.

FEES: No cost to enter the state forest. Picnic shelter can be reserved.

READY FOR THE ARTIST. A number of Steele's paintings are in the collection at the Large Studio to the north of the residence. His working materials face the large northern windows of the studio.

STEELE'S STUDIO. The Large Studio, with its enormous north window, is part of the House of the Singing Winds of Hoosier artist T. C. Steele, now a state historic site.

T. C. Steele's House of the Singing Winds, Belmont

BELMONT—The dateline also might read "Bloomington" or "Nashville," since the turnoff to T. C. Steele's House of the Singing Winds lies almost equidistant—nine miles from Nashville in Brown County and ten miles from Bloomington in Monroe County.

Both towns, in addition to tiny Belmont, have a claim on the famed artist who typifies the Hoosier Group that was famous early in the late nineteenth and early twentieth centuries for their outdoor painting in southern Indiana. Steele, whose full name was Theodore Clement Steele, was the most famous of the group that achieved, at the very least, a strong regional reputation.

Nashville gets most of the credit as the Hoosier Group's hometown, largely because Nashville and Brown County are so strongly associated with painting even to this day with what became the Brown County Art Colony. Steele also had an Indianapolis winter home and was artist in residence in the 1920s in Bloomington at Indiana University, which provided him with a studio and housing.

It was to their Brown County home, however, that Steele and his second wife, Selma, returned each spring, along with artists from throughout the Midwest, to paint outdoors. Even now, about eighty artists have taken up residence in and around Nashville, while others arrive during the summer months to paint.

No matter which town you favor, you should turn off Indiana 46 at Belmont and go south about a mile and a half to where Steele and Selma built their House of the Singing Winds in 1907. They lived there until Steele's death in 1926. The house and grounds, which lie up a short incline to the right, today are a state historic site.

That happened in 1945 when Selma donated the property to the state. The agreement was that the estate would be preserved for art and nature purposes. It includes the house, Steele's large studio, the Dewar log cabin, the Selma N. Steele Nature Preserve, and the several acres of gardens created by Selma.

The views from the porches of the house are typical of Brown County—rolling land, trees—forests really—hillsides, and, everywhere, the colors of the season. The house obviously was constructed to offer the best possible views of the surrounding countryside.

Steele's studio, no doubt, would be the envy of many an artist. Spacious, with large windows opening to the north, it houses some of his work, the site's gift shop, and, over in the northwest corner, the artist's working materials. You ring the bell for admission unless some special event is under way.

HOUSE OF THE SINGING WINDS. View of the Steeles' Brown County home. The house was built in 1907.

IF YOU GO

The house itself looks as if the artist and his wife might be returning later in the day. Unlike many historic sites that have had other owners between the period for which they were well known and when the historic site group took over, this property passed directly from Selma to the state.

Her influence is also prominent on the grounds. From what is known, Steele had little to do with establishing or maintaining the gardens and the remainder of the estate. That, Selma took as her assignment.

The 211-acre site has five hiking trails, one of which is wheelchair accessible. The ninety-two-acre nature preserve, as well as the studio, are also wheelchair accessible.

The artist's surroundings—house and panoramic views of the southern Indiana countryside—are similar to where Steele lived with his first wife at The Hermitage near Brookville, some ninety miles to the east. It, too, is set high with views of sweeping hillsides and trees overlooking the Whitewater River, and, to the north, the town of Brookville. He shared the house with J. Ottis Adams after they moved there from earlier painting around Metamora.

GETTING THERE: Follow Indiana 46 to Belmont between Nashville and Bloomington. Turn south on T. C. Steele Road for one and one-half miles.

INFORMATION: Call (812) 988–2785 for the historic site; e-mail tcsteele@bloomington .in.us; or fax (812) 988–8457. Hours are 9 a.m. to 5 p.m. Tuesday through Saturday and 1 p.m. to 5 p.m. Sunday. Closed Monday and most major holidays. Closed during the winter months; exact dates vary, so call for information.

FEES: Free admission.

PARK'S NORTH ENTRANCE. You enter Brown County State Park through this 1838 covered bridge, built by the Wolf family.

Brown County State Park, Nashville

NASHVILLE—With its gorgeous autumn colors in the trees and across the landscape, why would anyone choose to go to Brown County State Park in the spring? Well, what about:

The beauty of spring itself, with as many variations of green as Mother Nature can provide.

And—perhaps as important as any other reason—you won't be in solid lines of cars and people so you can more easily do and see what you want.

A Sunday afternoon trip in late spring to the park was an example.

Abe Martin Lodge, somewhat crowded to be sure, wasn't packed. You could get into the small gift shop. Outside, the trails only had a few hikers. The roads were open. Playgrounds had room for more children. Even at noon, picnic tables were available.

Of course, Brown County State Park is one of Indiana's treasures during any season. It's Indiana's largest state park at 15,696 acres. Established in 1929, it has one of the state's first park lodges—Abe Martin—now with eighty-four rooms in the main inn and the adjacent lodge. It's also a popular conference spot, with two large meeting rooms, six breakout rooms, a dining room, and banquet seating for 250. Twenty-four sleeping cabins have a total of fifty-six bedrooms, along with twenty family housekeeping cabins, completely furnished. Reservations are just about a must.

If you're into camping, the park has 401 class A sites—electrical hookup, fire ring, picnic table with available restrooms and showers— and twenty-eight class B with the same but no electrical connections. Over in the horseman's camp, another 118 class A and eighty-six class C sites—primitive with no restrooms or showers—are available, plus seventy miles of bridle trails for those who bring their own horses. A camp store has supplies.

Didn't bring your own horse? The park has a saddle barn and horses for its guided trail rides of 2.2 and 3.3 miles.

It's what the outdoors offers, especially during the warmer months, that's the park's biggest draw. You can almost pick your spot while driving along the nearly twenty miles of roads for a grand vista of southern Indiana's rolling hills and meadows. On foot, the park's nearly eighteen miles follow ten trails. Eight of the trails are rated moderate, ranging from 1.25 to 3.5 miles in length. There's an easy .9-mile trail as well as a short paved trail for those with limited mobility. One is termed rugged, a .75-mile self-guided trail that goes through the Ogle Hollow Nature Preserve.

ABE MARTIN LODGE. The historic lodge was the center of park activity on a warm Sunday afternoon.

A year-round nature center contains a snake exhibit, bird-watching room, and other displays. Naturalist services are also on site every season. Wildlife abounds, including deer, raccoons, squirrels, birds, and wild turkeys.

The swimming pool is open Memorial Day through Labor Day, and fishing on two park lakes—Ogle and Strahl—attracts anglers. You can put a rowboat into Ogle Lake. Of course, you need a state fishing license, available at the park office.

The state park is another of those facilities that benefited from the 1930s labor of the Civilian Conservation Corps, the Depression-era federal program to put unemployed Americans to work. They planted trees and built shelters, roads, buildings, lookout towers, picnic tables, and ovens. What they produced still serves Hoosiers seventy years later.

In a word, Brown County is the complete state park. Naturally, it's an artist's delight, too. The early 1900s Hoosier Group of well-known painters made the park, Nashville, and the rest of Brown County their headquarters. The county still has a large colony of painters, with galleries lining the Nashville streets.

Of all the state parks, Brown County probably is the best known. There's a reason.

IF YOU GO

GETTING THERE: East and south of Nashville with two entrances off Indiana 46. Horseman's campground entrance is off Indiana 135 South.

INFORMATION: Room reservations are a must. Call the lodge at (812) 988–4418, toll-free at (877) 265–6343, or fax (812) 988–7334. You also can register online at http://www.indianainns.com/. The park office telephone is (812) 988–6406. Lodge mailing address is Box 547, Nashville, Indiana 47448 and the park, 1405 State Road 46 West, Nashville, Indiana 47448.

FEES: Admission required. Rates vary for lodge rooms and housekeeping cabins.

A MODERN RESORT, PERHAPS? No, this is the entrance to the Columbus Regional Hospital, renovated under a new master plan in 1992 by architect Robert A. M. Stern.

IT WAS THE FIRST. Eliel Saarinen was the first major architect to design a Columbus building, the First Christian Church, in 1942.

Columbus Architecture, Columbus

COLUMBUS—Tour guide Lynn Bigley settles in her seat and begins her comments about Columbus architecture as the visitors center's bus, with its dozen or so passengers, starts a two-hour trip around the city. Despite the fact that she has a group of University of Maryland architecture students and two of their professors listening to her every word, it doesn't seem to bother her one bit.

After all, Columbus is accustomed to architects—and many other visitors, too—from around the world visiting this Indiana city, long recognized as an architectural mecca.

"As groups of buildings by distinguished architects go, there is no place in the United States like Columbus, Indiana," says Paul Goldberger, the *New York Times* architectural writer. The American Institute of Architects' ranking of cities for innovation and design of architecture? In this order—Chicago, New York, San Francisco, Boston, Washington, D.C., and Columbus.

The basics of the Columbus architectural story are well known by now.

In 1942 the downtown First Christian Church hired famed architect Eliel Saarinen to design its new building. The church, with its monumental bell tower and its west wing affectionately known as the "bridge," is said to have been one of the first contemporary church designs in the nation.

The catalyst to what followed was the Cummins Engine Company, a world leader in diesel engine production, through funds available from its foundation. Under the leadership of J. Irwin Miller, the foundation agreed to pay the architectural fees, first for schools and later for other public buildings, if the architects would be selected from an approved list of the nation's very best. Those in charge of the building could select any architect they wished, so long as the name came from the list.

To date, more than thirty-five major Columbus buildings have been constructed based on these architectural standards. In addition, older downtown buildings have been restored, not the least of which is the 1874 Bartholomew County Courthouse, renovated in 1969 and 1998. The courthouse is listed on the National Register of Historic Places.

An architectural driving tour, for which a map is available, actually has seventy-one stops throughout Bartholomew County, showing the work of prominent architects and other artists. The map is excellent. It not only shows all the stops and suggests directions for the tour, but

MORE THAN A HUNDRED YEARS APART. It's difficult to tell where the 1864 Victorian house stops and the 1995 addition designed by Kevin Roche begins. The building now houses the visitors center in downtown Columbus.

it also has photographs and brief annotations about the buildings and, in a few cases, sculptures.

You can take either a two-and-a-half hour driving tour or one that lasts five-and-a-half hours. If you know enough about architecture so you don't need any other explanation, that's okay, too.

But that's not quite the same as a real pro like Bigley adding more detail and helping the visitor see what might otherwise be missed. For example, before you even leave the visitors center, she shows you the Dale Chihuly handblown glass chandelier hanging in the center's front window, pointing out its nine hundred pieces, individually hung with a fifty-foot neon tube down the center.

She also notes the seamless addition to the 1864 Victorian home, now serving as the visitors center. The addition was designed by 1982 Pritzker Prize winner Kevin Roche.

The visitors center bus tours—one or two hours—are at 10 a.m., Monday through Friday, 10 a.m. and 2 p.m. Saturday and 11 a.m. Sunday. Reservations are recommended.

It's also a good idea to take the few minutes to see the center's video before you start your tour. It offers an excellent introduction to what you will see, so get there thirty minutes before the bus tour begins. The video tells you the idea behind architectural excellence when an architect is quoted as saying about Columbus and its buildings: "[They] are not monuments to the architect but service to the community."

IF YOU GO

GETTING THERE: The Columbus Area Visitors Center is on the northeast corner of Fifth and Franklin streets, 506 Fifth Street, in downtown Columbus.

INFORMATION: Call the visitors center (800) 468–6564 for more information about the tours or other Columbus activities. The Web site is http://www.columbus.in.us/. The center is open 9 a.m. to 5 p.m. Monday through Saturday and, March through November, on Sunday from 10 a.m. to 4 p.m.

FEES: Charges for tours and maps.

1868 HANGING. Not Hangman's Tree, which since has been cut down, but close to the spot west of Seymour, where members of the Reno gang were hanged by vigilantes in 1868.

MARKER. Train robbery marker in Seymour describes the "world's first train robbery" carried out there by the Reno gang in October 1866.

ROBBERY SITE. Two Seymour visitors, Charles Johnson of Anderson and Earl Muterspaugh of Muncie, stand on the railroad tracks where it is believed Reno gang members committed the first train robbery in the United States. Ironically, the site is not far from an Indiana State Police post.

The Reno Gang, Seymour

SEYMOUR—Was it the "world's first train robbery," as the plaque at the corner of Saint Louis and Chestnut streets states? Probably not—find out why at the end of the column—but it appears the Reno gang's theft of more than $10,000 in a train robbery just east of downtown Seymour on October 6, 1866, was the first in the United States.

Not much remains today about the robbery, except for the plaque on the grounds of the Chamber of Commerce building and the City Cemetery graves of three Reno brothers who were members of the gang.

While some of the facts of the robbery still are in dispute—were there two, three, or four robbers, and how much did they get?—others seem well documented.

First, some background. Wilkinson Reno had moved to Jackson County from Kentucky in the early 1800s. Five sons and a daughter were born into the family, according to local historian John M. Lewis III's account of the gang in his booklet, *The Reno Story*. Over time, the family acquired considerable land. Sons Frank, the oldest, and John went off to fight in the Civil War.

Seymour in the mid-1860s was gaining a reputation for lawlessness. According to Lewis, the local newspaper already had reported sixteen recent murders in town and thirty-five "major robberies."

Then on October 6, 1866, as the O & M Railroad train left the Seymour station, two men jumped into the express car. The robbers forced open one safe and heaved a "through" safe, for which there was no key, out the railcar door. They pulled the rope signaling the train to slow down and jumped. Other gang members were believed to be nearby, holding horses. The thieves stole somewhere between $10,000 and $12,000 from one safe but never could open the other, which contained a supposed $30,000 in gold. Suspicion quickly settled on the Reno gang, especially after the Reno boys were seen displaying large sums of money.

Within two years, three other attempted train robberies followed. The first again by men boarding a train as it left the Seymour station, the robbers getting $10,000; the second near Marshfield, south of Seymour, where the robbers disconnected the engine and express car and took $96,000; and an aborted third robbery at Brownstown, thwarted by forewarned Pinkerton agents who engaged gang members in a gun battle.

The robberies are part of the Reno gang legend. The vigilantes' hangings of gang members is the rest.

West of Seymour is a spot called Hangman's Crossing. It was near here on July 20, 1868, where several hundred masked men stopped

RENO GRAVES. Three Reno gang leaders—Frank, William, and Simeon—are buried in this plot at Seymour. They were taken from their jail cells in New Albany by vigilantes and hanged in December 1868.

a train carrying three members of the gang on their way to jail in Brownstown. They were hanged from a large beech tree. Five days later, a Pinkerton wagon with three more gang members was stopped near the same place and the prisoners were also hanged from the same tree, since cut down.

Finally, on December 12, a train carried perhaps a hundred masked men from Seymour to New Albany, where Frank, William, and Simeon Reno and a fourth gang member were held. They were taken from their cells and hanged.

Interestingly, John Reno, thought to be a key figure in the gang and almost certainly involved in the first robbery, had been jailed in Missouri for robberies there. He was released ten years later and returned to Seymour, where the old robbery charges were dismissed. He married, went to jail briefly in 1885 for counterfeiting, and died a peaceful death in 1895.

A fifth brother, "Honest Clint," was believed never to have been involved with the gang.

The world's first train robbery? That likely occurred in England in 1855 when thieves with stolen keys unlocked strongboxes loaded with millions of dollars in gold bars being sent to pay British troops fighting in the Crimea. It became the basis for the Michael Crichton book and movie, *The First Great Train Robbery*.

IF YOU GO

GETTING THERE: Take U.S. 50 into Seymour. The plaque at the chamber office is one block north on Chestnut Street. The cemetery is another one-half mile north on Indiana 11 at Ninth Street.

INFORMATION: Visit the Jackson County Visitor Center's Web site at http://www.jacksoncountyin.com/ or call toll-free (888) 524-1914.

FEES: None.

MADISON CENTERPIECE. The James F. D. Lanier mansion, its south side facing down to the Ohio River, is the principal mid-nineteenth-century building open to the public in Madison. Formal gardens are between the mansion and the river.

DOWN THE OHIO. This view looks west down the Ohio River from Madison. The Clifty Creek Power Plant, where electrical power is produced for a conglomerate of companies, can be seen in the distance.

James F. D. Lanier Mansion and Historic Madison

MADISON—It's a warm, late autumn Saturday evening in Madison. Most of the businesses along Main Street—antique shops, small restaurants, crafts stores—have closed. Still, the town is bustling because it's the annual "Nights before Christmas" tour of historic homes. Madison residents and out-of-towners move mostly by foot along the nine stops of the tour—with everyone certain to visit the James F. D. Lanier mansion overlooking the Ohio River.

As a matter of fact, something often is going on in Madison to attract visitors to this historic river city—festivals, chautauquas, regattas, garden tours.

Founded in 1809 shortly before Indiana became a state, Madison was one of several river towns that drew eastern entrepreneurs to make fortunes "out west." It was one of the important gateways to the Northwest Territory and had the first railroad west of the Allegheny Mountains, from Madison to Indianapolis.

One of the young men "gone west" to make his fortune was James F. D. Lanier, who moved with his parents from North Carolina, first to Ohio and then to Madison. (Other North Carolinian Lanier descendants of note included the poet Sidney Lanier and Thomas Lanier "Tennessee" Williams.)

In his early thirties, Lanier went into banking and, indeed, did make his fortune, both here and later in New York. No less than three times it's said he helped save the state and the Union—first in 1837 after a financial panic struck by carrying gold bullion overland in a hazardous journey from Indiana to Washington, and later by loaning the state more than a million dollars during the Civil War to outfit Indiana troops and to avoid state bankruptcy when the state was unable to meet its debts.

In the meantime, Lanier had the well-known architect Francis Costigan design his Greek Revival mansion that overlooks gently sloping hillside gardens down to the Ohio River. (The classical style mandates balance in everything, so that a door to the left must be accompanied by a door to the right—even if that door opens only onto a wall as it does at the Lanier mansion!) In the mid-1800s, the Lanier mansion was considered one of the finest houses on the Ohio.

Lanier lived here but seven years, through the death of his first wife in 1846 and his remarriage. Ten years after his move to New York City, his son, Alexander, resided here from 1861 to 1895.

A few of the present-day furnishings were owned by various members of the Lanier family or were part of the mansion when it was furnished. Numerous redecorations and restorations have taken place

MADISON'S MAIN STREET. Antique shops, restaurants, and small businesses occupy Main Street in Madison. Most historic buildings remain in good repair. This view is looking east.

in the past 150 years, with work in recent years attempting to uncover or replicate the original work on the mansion and its grounds in the most historically correct manner.

While the Lanier home, part of the Indiana State Museum and the Historic Sites Division of the Department of Natural Resources, is the focal point of historic sites in Madison, it is but one.

Other buildings open to the public as part of this Christmas candlelight tour included the Jeremiah Sullivan house, River Cottage and Phillips/Michl home, the former Indian-Kentuck Hotel, Schofield house, Madison Presbyterian Church, James Anderson home, and Jefferson County Historical Society—all located in the downtown area.

In addition, more than 130 blocks of Madison are part of a National Historic District. The visitor finds at almost every turn Federal, Italianate, and Gothic Revival structures, many of them carefully preserved by their present Madison owners. The Madison Area Convention and Visitors Bureau has two printed walking-tour guides—one for the eastern city blocks and one for the western—pointing out forty-nine places of special interest. One of them is the county courthouse, built in 1854–55, with the exterior unaltered to this day.

And to show those early Madison entrepreneurs were no slouches in the political arena, consider that they named the city after James Madison—president at the time—and the county after Thomas Jefferson. The two leaders of the anti-federalist party swept into power with the election of Jefferson to the presidency in 1800.

IF YOU GO

GETTING THERE: Madison is on the Ohio River at the Indiana southern end of U.S. 421.

INFORMATION: The Madison Area Convention and Visitors Bureau's telephone is (800) 559-2956. Call for specific information about sites, hotels, bed-and-breakfasts, tours, hours, etc. The Lanier mansion is open Tuesday through Saturday from 10 a.m. to 5 p.m., Sunday 1 p.m. to 5 p.m., and is closed on all state and federal holidays. Guided tours on the hour and half hour. Call (812) 265-3526 about winter hours.

FEES: Admission charged for mansion tours. Tickets vary for special events; call for prices.

LAUGHERY DAM. Built in 1954, this dam backs up the 230-acre Versailles Lake at the state park. Laughery Creek flows south into the Ohio River.

SADDLE 'EM UP. Horseback riding is a favorite pastime at Versailles State Park. These riders brought their horses to the Day Use Area and are ready for a bridle path jaunt.

Versailles State Park, Versailles

VERSAILLES—In the French language, the city where Louis XIV built his palace near Paris is pronounced "ver-sigh." The Hoosier pronunciation of the Ripley County seat and nearby state park is "ver-sales."

However you pronounce it, the park is one of southern Indiana's most scenic.

As farmland in the early 1900s, it was considered marginal. So there probably were few objections when the National Park Service bought nearly six thousand acres just to the east of the county seat and put the Civilian Conservation Corps to work. The corps, designed to give men jobs during the depths of the 1930s Depression, cleared brush, built roads, put together a "group camp," and, in general, turned basically unused land into a "recreational demonstration area." Later, in 1954, a private contractor constructed a dam on Laughery Creek to make possible a 230-acre lake.

In 1943 the project was deeded to the Indiana Department of Conservation—now the Department of Natural Resources—and the park's visitors today call its rolling hills, creeks, and wooded areas a haven of natural beauty.

The park combines many of the topographical features of southern Indiana. Laughery Creek runs through it and, dammed, creates Versailles Lake, which runs down the western park border. It's joined by Fallen Timber Creek, and they frequently have limestone outcroppings on their hillsides. Some of the drop-offs along the roads and trails are deep. In the middle of the park there are sinkholes. Many trees grow throughout the park, including oak, hickory, tulip poplar, beech, maple, and walnut.

Versailles does not have a lodge—six of Indiana's state parks do—or housekeeping cabins, as do eight others. But it does offer Camp Laughery, a group camp. Also built by the corps, these sleeping quarters can accommodate up to 120 people with cots or bunks—no linens. The camp also has a kitchen with appliances, dining hall, shower house, and a recreation hall. (You can almost sense the CCC worker resting up here after a hard day's physical toil in building the park. Seven state parks have these group camps, the largest housing 270 at Shakamak State Park, which is located south of Terre Haute.) Camping also is available with 226 class A sites—restrooms, electricity, and grills.

The park is very much an outdoor place. Fishing, hiking, and horseback riding are major activities. Boats can be rented or you can put your own into the water at the boat ramp. Swimming is not allowed

ARTISTS' FAVORITE. When this photo of the Busching covered bridge at Versailles State Park was taken, an Oregon artist was just out of camera range to the right. His painting was for his mother, a Versailles resident. Indiana's many covered bridges are great favorites of artists.

IF YOU GO

GETTING THERE: In Versailles, go east on U.S. 50 to the park entrance.

INFORMATION: Call the park office at (812) 689–6424. The address is Box 205, U.S 50, Versailles, Indiana 47042.

FEES: Admission charged.

in the lake, but the park has a twenty-five-meter pool with a hundred-foot waterslide. The park has six miles of easy to moderate trails. If you want horseback riding, you can either get a trail horse at the saddle barn or bring your own horse to ride the bridle paths. Shelters can be reserved for picnics.

What every visitor immediately notes upon entering the park is the Busching covered bridge that crosses Laughery Creek. Crossing the bridge road is another route into the city of Versailles. The bridge was built in 1885 and is one of two covered bridges in the county. It is a 176-foot Howe truss bridge that was restored in 1993. Although the bridge is within the boundaries of the state park, it is owned by the county.

As at other state parks, you'll find a nature center and camp store, both near the lake. The park's educational and interpretive programs begin Memorial Day and run through August.

Cyclists know the park because of the Hoosier Hills and Whitewater Valley bike routes. Hoosier Hills begins in Batesville, runs through Osgood, Versailles, and the state park—a twenty-seven-mile route. In Batesville, it hooks up with the Whitewater Valley route, which goes north for sixty-six miles, eventually terminating on the Earlham College campus in Richmond.

STILL THE MAN. Bobby Plump, who hit the shot to defeat Muncie Central in the 1954 state high school basketball finals, poses during the first fund-raiser for a Milan museum. Told the photographer lived in Muncie, he quipped, "I've got a lot of friends in Muncie—now."

TODAY'S MILAN. The present-day Milan Middle and High School is located on Indiana 101, just south of its intersection with Indiana 350. Inside the main entrance, at the left center of the photograph, is the Indiana high school state basketball championship trophy in a special showcase.

Milan and Moores Hill

MILAN—The day had not gone well. First, two of the places that I had intended to see on a swing through southeastern Indiana were closed. Next, in a hurry to change film in my camera, I had inadvertently exposed an entire roll that I had shot that day and during an earlier reporting trip through northwestern Indiana.

Then, my luck changed.

Coming back north through Moores Hill in Dearborn County, I found Carnegie Hall open on a late Saturday afternoon. It had been closed earlier that day when I passed through the community. I talked with a woman who was using the building for a class she was teaching. She gave me information about the structure that had been built in 1907–8 as part of a gift from Andrew Carnegie to establish a college at Moores Hill. Carnegie Hall is all that remains.

Two miles later I was at the northern edge of Milan. Why not check it out? It was dinnertime, so perhaps I could stop at a restaurant and find someone who wanted to talk about "the game" or even "the shot."

Turning south on Indiana 101, I saw the present-day Milan Middle and High School. The door at the main entrance was open, and a man was standing there, watching me as I pulled my car into the drive. I thought I might be onto something when I saw the school billboard: "Welcome, 1956 Team."

After a few pleasantries, the man, obviously a school official, said, "Yes, that's right. The 1956 reunion is coming up. But you ought to go downtown now. The 1954 team is there." Directions? "Cross the railroad tracks and turn right into town. You can't miss it." Before I left the building, though, he pointed out an old-time scoreboard mounted on an inside school wall. The score read 32–30. Most readers know why.

When I saw people gathered in a downtown area about one-half mile south and just a block off Indiana 101, I parked my car, got out, and turned a corner, walking into the midst of what obviously was a small outdoor picnic with people eating and talking under tents and a porch.

The first person I saw was Bobby Plump.

Even though it has been more than fifty years, most people in Indiana don't need to be told it was Plump in 1954 who hit the winning shot when little Milan, enrollment 162, won the Indiana high school basketball state championship, 32–30, over mighty Muncie Central. Plump's game-winning shot came with three seconds left in what still is considered the greatest game in the history of Indiana basketball.

It has been immortalized in the motion picture *Hoosiers* and several books. Indiana sportswriters called it the number-one sports story of

GAVE $15,000. Philanthropist Andrew Carnegie gave $15,000 to start a college at Moores Hill, near Milan. Carnegie Hall is all that remains. It was placed on the National Register of Historic Places in 1994.

all time. *Sports Illustrated* called the Milan team one of the top twenty stories of the past century.

Believe me, Plump still is the hero in Milan.

Plump was the center of attention wherever he went during the dinner. Small children came up to get his autograph on basketballs. (I succumbed, too, having him autograph a fortieth anniversary newspaper about the game—and I'm no kid.)

The outdoor picnic was the first of a series of proposed fundraisers for what local people hope will become a permanent Milan museum.

For now, items that would go into the museum are located in the Milan Station Antiques and Collectibles store, 113 W. Carr Street, next to the site of that first fund-raiser. Owner Roselyn McKittrick was showing her scrapbooks, which she constantly updates.

She was even getting cooperation from Muncie.

"Leon Agulanna, a friend of Bobby's, sent me a 16-by-20 photograph of the Muncie Central team, which I have had framed. I really appreciated that. You know you can't have a winner without an opponent," she said.

At this picnic fund-raiser, I couldn't pass up the hamburgers, coleslaw, iced tea, homemade cake, and ice cream. I hope I'll be forgiven in Muncie for putting $10 into the Milan museum project.

IF YOU GO

GETTING THERE: On Indiana 101, the school is north of the business district. Turn west on West Carr Street to Milan Station Antiques and Collectibles.

INFORMATION: Call Roselyn McKittrick at (812) 654–2772 or (812) 654–3626, or e-mail her at rvmckitt@seidata.com. Hours are Thursday, Friday, Saturday, 10 a.m. to 4 p.m., and Sunday, noon to 4 p.m.

FEES: None to visit.

Whitewater Memorial State Park and Brookville Lake, Brookville

IT STRADDLES TWO COUNTIES. Brookville Lake, lying above the earth-filled Brookville Dam, crosses Union and Franklin counties in the southern part of east-central Indiana. A part of the dam's structure is on the right.

WHO HAS THE BEST YARN? The Borderline Wood Burners from Indiana and Ohio swap stories as they sit in the shade in Whitewater Memorial State Park's camping area. They said it was one of the best campsites they had found.

BROOKVILLE—If you have some time and you just want to kick back and watch the world go by, then Whitewater Memorial State Park and Brookville Lake are the places for you.

Nestled in the rolling country of southeast central Indiana, the lake/reservoir and state park cover more than twenty-three thousand square acres, making them the third largest such area in the state.

Extending for about seventeen miles along Indiana 101, south of Liberty on down to Brookville, Whitewater Memorial State Park is termed a memorial park because it was established and dedicated in 1949 to the servicemen and women killed during World War II. Fayette, Franklin, Union, and Wayne counties joined to make the initial purchase as a gift to the state.

Perhaps it seems even larger than it is because of the layout of the facilities and because it often isn't that crowded—although the campgrounds fill almost every weekend in the summer. Campsites number 318—236 class A and forty-five class B—plus thirty-seven in the horseman's camp. Twenty modern housekeeping cabins also are available.

Mostly, folks just hang out. Bicycles and boats can be rented during the summer, and it has picnic areas, shelters, and lakefront swimming from Memorial Day to Labor Day. The park also has a saddle barn for guided tours, paddleboats, canoes, and other boats for rent. But most people seem to enjoy sitting around the campfire in the evening or in the shade during the day and swapping stories. Either that or fishing for bass, bluegill, and other small game fish.

Then there's walking. The park has more than eleven miles of hiking trails plus nine miles of bridle trails. The hiking trails include two classified as easy of about a mile, two moderate trails of about two miles, and two rugged trails—the longest at 3.25 miles.

Included within the park is the man-made two hundred-acre Whitewater Lake, with boat rentals and two launching ramps, swimming beach, and a fishing pier.

Just south of Whitewater, Brookville Lake is more of the same. Constructed by the U.S. Army Corps of Engineers, it opened in 1974. It, too, has camping—450 sites, 388 of them class A and sixty-two AA, nine launch ramps, picnicking and shelter houses, hiking, and swimming on two beaches. It has an archery range and shooting range and allows hunting and water skiing. Four marinas are located on the lake. A favorite winter pastime is ice fishing. You can access Brookville Lake from the Whitewater property at the Saddle Creek launch ramp.

WHERE THE LIVING IS EASY. Houseboats and other craft lie at anchor on a lazy autumn afternoon at the Sagamore Marina on the east side of Brookville Lake.

The hiking trail at the lake is different from most. It is one long loop that can be divided into ten sections, including easy, moderate, and rugged backcountry trails. A favorite is the short loop, which takes the visitor past a two thousand-year-old mound. (Wear safety orange during the hunting season.)

Within the lake's territory are two state recreational areas—Quakertown to the north and Mounds to the south. (The mounds, traces of which are found throughout the valley, have largely disappeared because of excavations, erosion, and cultivation.)

At the south end of the 5,260-acre lake is the earth-filled Brookville Dam—2,800 feet in length and 181 feet high with a drainage area above the dam of 379 square miles. It provides flood control and water supply as well as the recreational area. You can drive your car across the dam and look down on the tailwater area below the dam onto the small town of Brookville.

If you like life in the fast lane, Brookville and Whitewater aren't for you. But if it's a quiet day outside that you're looking for, this is your place.

GETTING THERE: Whitewater Memorial State Park is three miles south of Liberty on Indiana 101.

INFORMATION: Whitewater State Park (765) 458–5565. Brookville Lake (765) 647–2657.

FEES: Admission charged, with fees for ramps, saddle barn, boats, cabins, and campsites.

WHITLOCK INVENTION. At the nearby Ohio County Museum is one of local entrepreneur J. W. Whitlock's better-known inventions. Whitlock, a Rising Sun inventor and manufacturer, created his Autoharp, forerunner to the jukebox. He sold it to Wurlitzer. Mostly though, Whitlock produced chairs, one of which is at the left of the Autoharp.

Ohio County Courthouse, Rising Sun

RISING SUN—The young woman in the county clerk's office says to go down the hallway to the assessor's office. The assessor "knows everything there is to know about this building and Ohio County," she declares.

I walk down the immaculately clean hallway to the assessor's office. I am amazed at the condition of the courthouse. After all, at 155 years, it is the oldest courthouse in continuous use in Indiana.

The man at the assessor's desk turns from his work on this late Saturday morning to ask if he can help.

My "I'm told you know everything about this place" brings a smile and a "Well, let me try" from Bobby Joe Keith.

Commenting on the building's condition, he says a major renovation took place in 1989 at a cost of more than $700,000.

"To go from one office to another on the ground floor, you had to go outside and come back in. So we lost a little office space by putting in the inside hallways, but we think it was worth it," he tells me.

A seamless addition was added to the south to provide needed space. A drawing has been prepared and is on display at the courthouse, showing another proposed addition to the west. "That's not definite, though," Keith adds.

Modern restrooms have replaced the older restrooms out in back, he says.

The land for the courthouse was donated to the county in the mid-1840s by Colonel Abel C. Pepper. The Greek Revival-style courthouse, according to *Indiana: A New Historical Guide*, sits on the highest ground in the city. The courthouse serves the smallest county in Indiana by land size, only eighty-seven square miles.

The *Guide* reports that during World War II an effort was made to change the name of the town, Rising Sun, because its name also was used as a reference to Japan, part of the Axis powers fought by the United States. The movement failed.

The name Rising Sun reportedly comes from the brilliance of the sun coming up in the morning over the Kentucky hills across the Ohio River.

For a number of years in its early history, Rising Sun flourished as a river town. The first official white settler was John Fulton, uncle of famed steamboat inventor Robert Fulton. Then, like some other riverboat towns with hilly terrain to the north and the river to the south, it was bypassed as railroads were built more to the north, supplanting the riverboats as the main form of transportation.

INDIANA'S OLDEST. Built in 1845, the Ohio County Courthouse in Rising Sun is the oldest in the state in continuous use. An addition was added at the back during a recent renovation that also added an interior hallway. Before that, patrons had to walk outside to go from one office to another.

Whatever business existed largely disappeared, so that today Ohio County mostly is rural. The significant exception, of course, is the Grand Victoria Casino and Resort at Rising Sun. On the Saturday morning I was in town, a steady stream of automobiles was headed toward the casino.

Historic Downtown Rising Sun Inc. has put together a walking-tour booklet that offers two routes for walks through its historic downtown. Building styles include log cabins, Greek revival homes from the 1840s, federal style from the mid-1800s, Italianate from the 1870s, and neoclassical from the early 1900s. The oldest building in the downtown is the former First Presbyterian Church, built in 1832.

As I left the courthouse to start my tour, it turns out Keith has indeed answered every question put to him. He only pauses on the last one: "How long have you been the assessor?" He takes just a moment, as if figuring: "Going on forty years."

IF YOU GO

GETTING THERE: Indiana 56, following the Ohio River, goes through Rising Sun in southeastern Indiana. Indiana 262 comes into the town from the north.

INFORMATION: The toll-free telephone number of the Ohio County Convention and Tourism Bureau is (888) 776–4786. The Web site is http://www.enjoy risingsun.com/. The tourism office is located at 120 N. Walnut Street.

FEES: None for tours. Tour guides can be picked up at various sites.

THE GRAND STAIRCASE. Just inside the main doors of Hillforest is this grand staircase leading to the second floor. The building is decked out for the holiday season.

THE VIEW FROM VERAESTAU. A panoramic view of the Ohio River with Kentucky across the river and the Indiana landscape around Aurora is showcased from Veraestau, built above Aurora. That's an afternoon shadow cast by the house in the lower left of the photo.

Hillforest and Veraestau, Aurora

AURORA—When industrialist and financier Thomas Gaff—he owned or operated more than thirty businesses—decided he wanted to build his home in Aurora along a bend in the Ohio River, he picked a site on a high, downtown hill overlooking the town and river. By 1855 the Gaffs had settled into their mansion, Hillforest, where the family lived for the next fifty years.

Slowly but surely, the Hillforest Historical Foundation has been restoring the Italianate building, nestled back into the hillside. The architecture is combined with a steamboat appearance—Gaff owned a number of them. Its round central colonnades, grand central staircase leading to the second floor, and pilothouse-like belvedere, or cupola, all resemble steamboat structures.

The mansion literally is built into the hillside, with the ground behind it rising at increasingly higher levels. As the visitor looks out the windows and rear door of the second floor, the ground is at floor level. That's equally true for the view on the back side of the belvedere.

From the front, however, it's a grand view of the town of Aurora laid out below. Of course, there's also the river stretching to the east and west.

Hillforest—Gaff originally called it Forest Hill—is symmetrical in the Italian Renaissance style of the day. The twelve-room mansion's exterior has highly ornate overhangs, brackets, balconies, and porches and, in the interior, wall coverings and furnishings.

Gaff's businesses included everything from steamboats to industry to precious metals to shipping. The senior Gaffs led a busy social life, frequenting the opera in Cincinnati along with numerous business and social trips.

Furnishings mostly are of the period and in some cases were originally part of the mansion or have been returned by Gaff family members. As funds become available, the Hillforest Foundation continues work, in recent years on the broad eaves that surround the house. Unlike some other sites, Hillforest has its own museum room where artifacts of the Gaffs' business enterprises may be seen.

For a view of the river valley, though, you have to go up Market Street to Veraestau Lane, turning left to Veraestau—Latin words combined for spring, summer, and autumn. (Jesse Holman, the builder, hoped winter would never come.)

Holman found his building site just to the east of downtown Aurora on a bluff towering 427 feet above the Ohio River. He originally built a log cabin around 1810 and later added a one-story brick addition. In

VERAESTAU. Set on a high bluff just outside Aurora, Veraestau has been added to a number of times since its first construction in 1810.

IF YOU GO

1851 his son-in-law, prominent Fort Wayne businessman Allan Hamilton, tore down a portion of the earlier house, leaving the brick wing, and built a single-story Greek Revival-style house.

The Holmans sold the house after 125 years' ownership to Lawrenceburg industrialist Cornelius O'Brien in 1933. A leading preservationist, he designed a three-room brick addition similar in scale to the older structure, reforested woodlands, established orchards, and created grazing pastures.

Today, Veraestau has been presented to Historic Landmarks Foundation of Indiana. Inside are significant appointments, including a Rembrandt Peale portrait of George Washington, federal (circa 1790–1820) furniture, and numerous other items.

But that may not be as important as the view. It's commanding—that's the word—in its majestic sweep from far to the east of Aurora, swinging around the bend in the Ohio River, across the river into the lowlands of Kentucky and then on to the west toward Vevay.

It's easy to imagine how, over the centuries, Native Americans, early settlers, and eventually Jesse Holman and his descendants savored this view in dawn's early light or as evening's shadows gathered.

GETTING THERE: Indiana 56, 148, and 350 all go into Aurora. Hillforest is at the top of Main Street in downtown Aurora. Go down Fifth Street to Market Street and turn to the left at the top of the hill to reach Veraestau.

INFORMATION: Call (812) 926–0087 for information about Hillforest. It is open Tuesday through Sunday from 1 p.m. to 5 p.m. and can be rented for weddings and meetings. Call (812) 926–0983 for information about Veraestau. Both are closed on holidays.

FEES: Admission charged at Hillforest; donation requested at Veraestau.

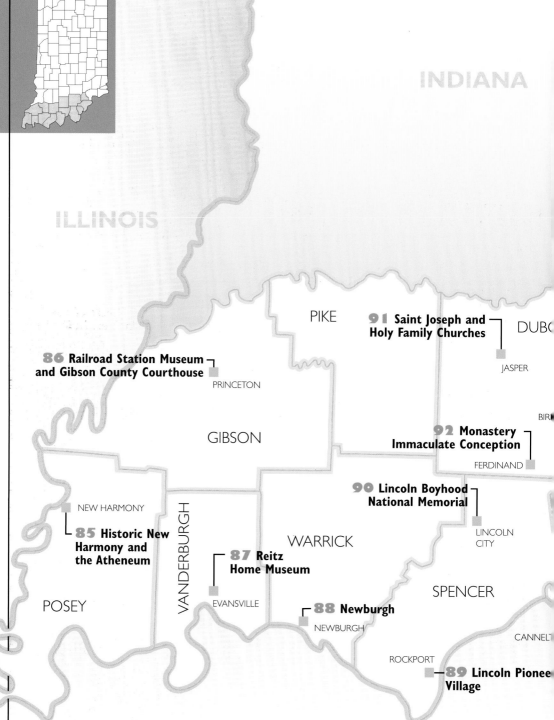

INDIANA

ILLINOIS

PIKE

91 Saint Joseph and
Holy Family Churches

DUBO

JASPER

86 Railroad Station Museum
and Gibson County Courthouse

PRINCETON

BIR

GIBSON

92 Monastery
Immaculate Conception

FERDINAND

90 Lincoln Boyhood
National Memorial

NEW HARMONY

85 Historic New
Harmony and
the Atheneum

VANDERBURGH

WARRICK

LINCOLN
CITY

87 Reitz
Home Museum

EVANSVILLE

SPENCER

POSEY

88 Newburgh

NEWBURGH

CANNELT

ROCKPORT

89 Lincoln Pionee
Village

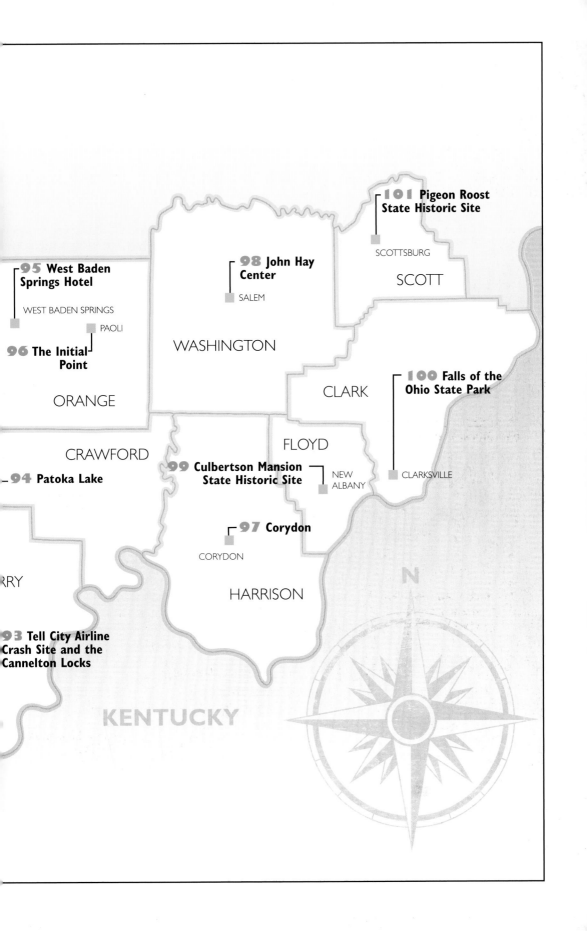

101 Pigeon Roost
State Historic Site

SCOTTSBURG

SCOTT

95 West Baden
Springs Hotel

WEST BADEN SPRINGS

PAOLI

96 The Initial
Point

ORANGE

98 John Hay
Center

SALEM

WASHINGTON

CLARK

100 Falls of the
Ohio State Park

FLOYD

94 Patoka Lake

CRAWFORD

99 Culbertson Mansion
State Historic Site

NEW
ALBANY

CLARKSVILLE

97 Corydon

CORYDON

HARRISON

N

RRY

93 Tell City Airline
Crash Site and the
Cannelton Locks

KENTUCKY

THE ATHENEUM. Tours of Historic New Harmony begin at the Atheneum. Opened in 1979, the ultramodern Atheneum houses the visitor center.

Historic New Harmony and the Atheneum

NEW HARMONY—The contrast is dramatic. You drive down a street used in the early 1800s—beside it are square, old brick buildings along with log houses—and suddenly before you is this large, ultra-modern building—angled lines of steel panels covered with gleaming porcelain.

Perhaps it's been awhile since you visited New Harmony. It had been for me, something like thirty-five years. If so, the Atheneum, the visitor center for New Harmony, provides this different-world look for one of the state's most historic sites. Opened in 1979, the Atheneum represents today's equivalent of the pioneering spirit and embracing of new ideas exhibited by the founders of New Harmony.

First, it was George Rapp and his Harmonie Society of German Pietists' effort at a perfect community in 1814 and then Robert Owen and his New Harmony program of social equality in 1825. The experiments by the two visionaries apparently failed in the short term, but in the years that followed much of what they advocated has become part of the American way of life.

"Utopia on the Wabash" is the term used today to describe Historic New Harmony, a unified program of the University of Southern Indiana and Indiana State Museum and Historic Sites. New Harmony is located on the banks of the Wabash River in Posey County, directly north of Mount Vernon deep in southwestern Indiana. It may be the state's most historically significant site.

If it did not give birth to today's broadly accepted concepts, it certainly fostered and accelerated them: planned communities; equality in all aspects of life; free education, including equal education for women and men; child labor restrictions; and women's rights.

Rapp's society purchased thirty thousand acres of woodland along the Wabash to build a community where his followers could await the millennium, which would bring forth the Second Coming of the Christ. They emigrated from Germany, first to Pennsylvania before going down the Ohio River and up the Wabash River to their new settlement.

Some eight hundred settlers quickly laid out and built ten wide streets and the buildings next to them. They produced enough food and goods on their two thousand cultivated acres that they also shipped their abundance by river to distant markets.

Despite the considerable success of the community, the Second Coming didn't happen. So, ten years later, they moved back to Pennsylvania.

EVEN BEFORE THE HARMONISTS. Looking to the east from the observation deck of the Atheneum at New Harmony, you can see to the left a double-log cabin, built in 1775. Its two cabins are connected by an open porch. To the right is the David Lenz house of typical Harmonist construction, two-story and twenty-by-thirty feet.

Robert Owen of Scotland, eager to establish a new social order, bought Harmonie and renamed it New Harmony. Here he would organize an educational center that, combined with a society of equality, he believed would create utopia. Scholars and scientists were among others who came to New Harmony, forming an intellectual center.

Utopia didn't happen either, and Owen's grand experiment lasted only two years before he left. The settlement, however, continued into the 1860s, drawing innovative thinkers and artists. During the mid-1800s New Harmony was the cultural and scientific center for the region, referred to as the "Athens of the West."

That's what remained as a historic site until 1975, when the construction of the Atheneum began. Named for Athena, the Greek goddess of wisdom and the arts, it offers special programming, a model of the town as it existed around 1824, a biographical exhibit of the community's leading personalities, and, naturally, a gift shop. Its observation deck also is an excellent spot to get a bird's-eye view of the historic town.

IF YOU GO

GETTING THERE: Interstate 64 to exit 4 at Griffin, south on Indiana 69, and west at Indiana 66 into New Harmony.

INFORMATION:
Go to the Web site at http://www.newharmony.org or call toll-free (800) 231–2168. The visitor center conducts tours between March 15 and December 30. Between January 1 and March 15 tours can be made for groups through prearrangement. The season continues through December 30.

FEES: Vary for different tours and venues.

Railroad Station Museum and Gibson County Courthouse, Princeton

ON DISPLAY AT COURTHOUSE. This popular Department 56 Original Snow Village Courthouse, displayed on a counter at the Gibson County Courthouse, is a ceramic replica of the Princeton structure.

SOME HINGE. This ornate door hinge in the Superior Courtroom is part of the original hardware of the Gibson County Courthouse, built in 1884–86.

PRINCETON—John Burris did it his way.

For more than twenty years he worked at restoring the 1875 Evansville-Terre Haute Railroad Company depot two blocks west of the Gibson County Courthouse. Quintuple heart bypass surgery slowed him down for a while, but the retired savings and loan president remained undaunted. Asked why he hadn't sought grants for his work, he paused and smiled.

"Oh," his questioner figured out, "you're avoiding bureaucracy and you want to do it your way."

Burris just smiled some more and went on to the next topic.

Since my visit, the station's interior has been completed and now houses the offices of the Gibson County Visitors and Tourism Bureau, so it's open to the public Monday through Friday, 9 a.m. to 5 p.m. Burris still is available for tours by appointment, however.

Outside the station is a 1955 caboose, obtained from the Southern Railroad and moved here from Portsmouth, Ohio. It's painted a bright caboose red.

Close at hand is the Gibson County Courthouse, completed in 1886. You may be familiar with it if you have the Department 56 Original Snow Village Courthouse. It's a ceramic replica of the Princeton building. (Incidentally, you can't find one for sale in Gibson County; they may be on their way to becoming collectors' items.)

The courthouse, now listed on the National Register of Historic Places, retains its European mosaic tile flooring, native black walnut interior woodwork, oak flooring, and pressed brick manufactured in Saint Louis—all within a Bedford limestone structure. As with similar older buildings, the detail of the nineteenth-century work is impressive. For example, in a 1984 renovation, when the stair handrails were cleaned, it was discovered they were, in fact, made not of pipes, as was believed, but of copper.

Interestingly, the original building cost $118,000 and the renovation just slightly less—$100,000—when the building was rededicated a hundred years after construction, which had started in 1884.

Not that changes haven't been made over the years. When constructed, the building had four entry doors, one from each direction. But when space became a serious problem, the east and west doors were closed, and those hallways became offices. The lack of space still is obvious, with files in some other hallways.

The second-floor Superior Courtroom was the site of the 1955 murder trial of Leslie "Mad Dog" Irvin. The trial was moved here from

PRINCETON STATION. Local resident John Burris worked at restoring this station for more than twenty years. The overhang was cut back fifteen inches because of deterioration of the roof.

Vanderburgh County because of pretrial publicity. He was found guilty, but on appeal to the U.S. Supreme Court, it was ruled Gibson County was not far enough away to avoid more publicity. Irvin was retried in Vigo County at Terre Haute and again convicted. He later died in prison.

A smaller stairway at the back of the courtroom was, and still is, used to move witnesses, defendants, and, in some cases, the jury in and out of the building to avoid crowds in the hallway and on the other stairs.

Outside the courthouse is a monument to Gibson County's Civil War soldiers. Erected in 1912, it notes that 2,200 Gibson County residents fought in that war, with 500 killed. The monument underwent renovation in the late 1900s and was rededicated in autumn 2000.

Oh, yes, as with other Indiana counties, several popular individuals have come from Gibson County. Among them was that smiling cook and race car driver who became as well known as a television ad celebrity as he was a restaurant owner—Dave Thomas, founder of Wendy's.

IF YOU GO

GETTING THERE: Princeton is on Indiana 64 and just east of U.S. 41 in southwestern Indiana.

INFORMATION: Call the Gibson County Visitors and Tourism Bureau toll-free at (888) 390–5825, go to the Web site, http://www.gibsoncountyin.org/, or write P.O. Box 1056, Princeton, Indiana 47670. The courthouse is open during regular business hours. For more information about the train depot, call either the visitors bureau or John Burris at (812) 385–4752.

FEES: None.

TIFFANY MANTEL. This Tiffany mantelpiece was moved from the Chicago Columbian Exposition when it closed to the Reitz home in Evansville. It is made of white onyx and gold. Tourists can be seen reflected in its large mirror.

FIXED STAINED GLASS? It would appear so, but actually these sitting room windows are set in brass-trimmed frames so they can be opened, more or less as shutters.

Reitz Home Museum, Evansville

EVANSVILLE—When John Augustus and Gertrude Frisse Reitz built their mansion not far from the Ohio River in downtown Evansville in 1871, people were skeptical about putting a toilet inside a house. Back then most homes had outhouses.

But put it inside John and Gertrude did, making theirs one of the first homes in Evansville with so-called indoor plumbing. To make the idea more acceptable, white tile was used throughout the bathroom to give it a hygienic look. More than 130 years later, the white tile still is there, along with the original washbasin. Their home also was among the first in Evansville to have electricity, a telephone, and city water.

The bathroom is only one of the numerous features shown during a tour of this home built by the Evansville merchant who made a fortune in the lumber milling business. By the early 1870s he wanted to build a home for his family of eight children. Actually, he and Gertrude had ten, but two had married and moved away.

Over the next twenty years, the parents and most of the children continued to live in the mansion until Reitz died in 1891; his wife passed away two years later. One son had married and moved, and two others had died, but the other five, none of whom had married, lived at the home until their deaths. Later, the mansion became a Catholic home for women and then the residence of Evansville's Catholic bishop, before it was donated to the Reitz Home Preservation Society in 1974.

Tours begin in the family's carriage house, now a visitor center and gift shop. Honestly, it's somewhat difficult to digest everything during the tour because there's so much to hold your interest.

The home's basic architecture is French Second Empire. Inside, it is a composite of Victorian styles. Our tour guide said the guiding principle was "the eye should never light on anything boring," so inside the house you will be hard pressed to find any wall, floor, or ceiling unadorned.

For example, the parquet floors used Indiana woods. To add another color in the natural woods, the builders located other woods of different colors. Throughout the mansion, among other features, are hand-painted ceilings, stained glass, damask wall coverings, and special window arrangements.

That's after you enter from First Street through a triple set of double doors. Beveled glass was placed in the first doors, which have no outside handle, so they had to be opened from the inside by a servant. The middle doors, usually folded open, are of black walnut,

REITZ MANSION. This well-maintained Victorian home near the Ohio River was built by Evansville merchant John Augustus Reitz in 1871. It has gone through several redecorations.

while the interior doors, part of a later redecoration project, have stained-glass panels.

Moorish style decorations were used throughout the hallways in wall coverings, wainscoting, friezes, and chandeliers.

The fireplace in the drawing room has a white onyx and gold mantelpiece made by Tiffany as a feature of an exhibit at the Chicago Columbian Exposition of 1893. It was shipped to Evansville and installed by Tiffany workmen. What appears to be stained-glass windows in the sitting room really are set in brass-trimmed frames so they can be opened, more or less as shutters, to allow more light; behind them are electric lights that can help illuminate the room on a dark day.

That's just some of what is to be seen on the first floor, to say nothing of the furnishings and paintings.

Upstairs on the second floor are six bedrooms. (The third floor, not open to the public, has four bedrooms for female servants and what may have been a sitting room. Male servants had quarters over the carriage house.) In the main hallway of the second floor is a portrait of one Reitz daughter, Mary, who married Herman Fendrich, manufacturer of the La Fendrich cigar. Their granddaughter was Mary Fendrich Hulman, wife of Tony Hulman of Indianapolis 500 fame. She returned much of the original furniture to the home during its restoration as a museum.

It's on the second floor that you see the white-tile bathroom.

IF YOU GO

GETTING THERE: Take Interstate 64 south into Evansville. Go north a block on Chestnut Street to First Street. The Reitz home is on the northwest corner.

INFORMATION: Call (812) 426–1871 for the Reitz home or (800) 433–3025 for the Evansville Convention and Visitors Bureau. The Web site is http://www.reitzhome.evansville.net/. Tour hours are Tuesday through Saturday, 11 a.m. to 3:30 p.m., and Sunday, 1 p.m. to 3:30 p.m. Special group tours also can be arranged.

FEES: Admission charged.

LOOKING UP RIVER. It is believed that French explorer Robert de la Salle in 1669 walked somewhere near this spot on what is now Water Street in Newburgh. He was probably the first European to see the Ohio River. He later explored the Mississippi River and claimed for France all lands drained by both rivers.

Newburgh

NEWBURGH—From across the Ohio River, would stovepipes pointed at you look like cannon?

That's what the residents of Newburgh thought they were on July 18, 1862, when Confederate Adam Johnson crossed the river from Kentucky with two boatloads of Southern militia. They captured the town—the first Northern occupation by the South during the Civil War.

Those "weapons" on the other side of the river pointed at the town were cannon, Johnson declared, so Newburgh surrendered without a shot fired. The Southerners spent a couple of hours ransacking businesses and confiscating weapons before they recrossed the river. They were hurried along when word came that Northern supporters were coming up river from Evansville, two miles away.

It's not clear how residents later learned those artillery pieces on the other shore really were stovepipes. Today, the story is an amusing part of community lore, but it was a different matter then. According to *Indiana: A New Historical Guide*, townspeople killed two residents believed to be Southern sympathizers who may have aided Johnson.

Nowadays, Newburgh and the rest of Warrick County have highlighted their past to welcome tourists. For example, it was in Warrick County where the Lincoln family crossed from Kentucky to homestead and where young Abe "learned the law." That part of the county later became the new Spencer County.

The heart of tourism in Newburgh is centered along the river on Water Street and the next street, Jennings, which also is Indiana 662. The whole Newburgh Historic District was listed on the National Register of Historic Places in 1983. Historical markers abound.

A good place to start any visit in Newburgh and the surrounding countryside is Historic Newburgh Inc., located near the intersection of Jennings and State streets.

It's next door to Rivertown Antiques which, in 1862, was the Exchange Hotel, where sick Northern soldiers were housed during the time the Confederates crossed the river and captured the town.

Among the historic structures in Newburgh is the Cumberland Presbyterian Church on State Street, built in 1851 and the first Presbyterian church to be built north of the Mason-Dixon Line. The church was used until the mid-1900s, when it was purchased by the town and converted into a town hall and community center.

Similarly, a few blocks away on Jennings Street is the Newburgh Country Store, located in what was once a Catholic church, built

WHERE UNION SOLDIERS WERE TREATED. Now it houses Rivertown Antiques, but in 1862 Union wounded and ill soldiers were treated in the old Exchange Hotel at the corner of Jennings and State streets in Newburgh.

in 1865. Directly across the street is Jennings Station Mall, currently home to businesses, retail shops, and a restaurant.

A block away is the former location of the Delaney Academy, which trained Presbyterian ministers and operated from the 1840s until 1867, when it moved to Illinois. The building is gone, but the site has a marker. At one point the academy was housed in the basement of the Cumberland Presbyterian Church.

Not far from town is the Newburgh Lock and Dam on the Ohio River. The overlook includes parking, picnic tables, and information about the dam and its use to control navigation along the river. The dam and its 1,200-foot lock were completed in 1975 at a cost of more than $100 million.

In Newburgh itself, you get the best view of the Ohio River on Water Street. Just east of the Madison Street intersection is a plaque commemorating "La Belle Riviere"—the beautiful river—and noting that Frenchman Robert de la Salle was perhaps the first European to see the river in 1669.

When you stand there, you can only imagine what the area looked like to La Salle. But you know he must have been impressed by the river.

GETTING THERE: From Interstate 64 going south, take Indiana 662 east into Newburgh.

INFORMATION: Call Historic Newburgh Inc. at (812) 853–7111 or go to the Web site at http://www.newburgh.org/.

FEES: Brochures and other information are free.

ENTRANCE BUILDING. That's a dogtrot at the left of this entrance building. It replaces an earlier structure, which was demolished after it began to sag badly.

FIRST COURTHOUSE. A replica of the Azel Dorsey house, which also served as Spencer County's first courthouse. Dorsey was briefly a teacher of Abraham Lincoln. His home was one of the few two-story cabins in the early years of the county.

LINCOLN PORTRAIT. This is one of several portraits of Abraham Lincoln in the museum at the Pioneer Village. Lincoln lived near here for fourteen years until his family moved to Illinois when he was twenty-one.

Lincoln Pioneer Village, Rockport

ROCKPORT—Although it was more than fifty years ago, Old Rockport Inc. President Lila Daniel remembers it as if it were yesterday. After all, movie stars Burt Lancaster and Walter Matthau were only a few feet away.

It was the climatic fight scene for the 1954 motion picture *The Kentuckian*. Lancaster was the hero and Matthau the villain in the battle that was filmed in the middle of Rockport's Lincoln Pioneer Village.

"Lancaster talked to all of us kids. We adored him. Matthau played to the crowd, even though he was the bad guy. I just loved him from then on and watched all of his films—good guy, bad guy, it didn't matter," remembers Daniel, a high school student at the time.

Like the ups and downs of motion picture stars' careers, Lincoln Pioneer Village has had its own sometimes troubled experiences.

The village—and Rockport, too—are tied to the life of Abraham Lincoln. It was here that the Lincoln family crossed from Kentucky to begin its fourteen-year stay in Indiana. Lincoln was seven years old. All the buildings represent those associated with Lincoln.

The village, presently made up of fourteen buildings, started as the dream of George Honig, a Rockport native. He supervised its early construction in the mid-1930s with help from the Depression-era Federal Emergency Relief Administration. Its workers constructed eleven replicas of frontier buildings, and a dedication followed on July 4, 1935. When the federal government's Works Progress Administration came along, the village received another grant. Four more buildings went up, with a rededication a year later.

That's how things stood into the 1970s with the village badly in need of repair. Three buildings had to be demolished because the expertise to restore them was not available. Four termite-damaged structures were rebuilt but with little attention to historic detail. It might have been the end.

Instead, there's a happy ending. In 1998 the village was placed on the National Register of Historic Places, and a Hometown Rehabilitation Project grant and other funding have provided for a comprehensive reconstruction of much of the village.

If you stand in the middle of the village—where Lancaster and Matthau had their movie fight—and look north toward the swimming pool in the neighboring park, here's what you will see as you turn clockwise:

Brown's Tavern—the original stood on Main Street overlooking the river and was where Lincoln appeared when he campaigned for

LINCOLN HOMESTEAD. A replica of the second Lincoln cabin built in Spencer County. It has a loft reached by a series of pegs driven into the wall. There's a lean-to adjoining the cabin at the back.

Henry Clay; the Lincoln homestead; the transportation building, constructed to be a tobacco house for the filming of the motion picture, with a hearse, buggies, and wagons; a pioneer schoolhouse; the Daniel Grass two-story dogtrot cabin (a building with a roofed space between rooms on either side); the Azel Dorsey two-story cabin, the first courthouse in the county; Little Pigeon Baptist Church; Colonel William Jones's store, originally located in Gentryville; Sarah Lincoln's cabin, where she lived after her marriage; Judge John Pitcher's law office, the first in the county; the home of James Gentry, a close friend of the Lincolns; the new main entrance, a one-story dogtrot; the Josiah Crawford home; and the back of the village's museum building.

In the museum are historical items contributed by persons from Spencer, Perry, and Warrick counties, as well as those obtained by Old Rockport Inc. Examples of war artifacts go up through World War II. Two highly prized items are a dress that belonged to Lincoln's sister, Sarah Lincoln Grigsby, and a cupboard built for Elizabeth Crawford by Lincoln's father, Thomas. The museum recently has been updated—it was painted and cleaned, and artifacts were regrouped for better display.

GETTING THERE: Where Indiana 66 turns right at the north edge of Rockport, continue south on Fifth Street to the traffic signal at Main Street. Turn right on Main Street until it dead-ends. Turn left, and the Rockport City Park entrance and Lincoln Pioneer Village are on your right.

INFORMATION: The village is open Wednesday through Friday by appointment. Call (812) 649–9147. The village is open Saturday, 10 a.m. to 5 p.m., and Sunday, 1 p.m. to 5 p.m. The Web site is http://lincolnpioneervillage.org/.

FEES: None, but contributions go toward the continued maintenance of the cabins.

SEASON OPENS IN MID-APRIL. Costumed interpreters tell about Indiana frontier life beginning in mid-April and running through September at the Lincoln Living Historical Farm, part of the Lincoln Boyhood National Memorial.

WHERE LINCOLN'S MOTHER LIES. Lincoln presenter Dean Dorrell presents the eulogy at a wreath-laying ceremony for Nancy Hanks Lincoln during the annual Lincoln Day Program.

Lincoln Boyhood National Memorial, Lincoln City

LINCOLN CITY—Indiana over the years has gotten a bad rap for doing things wrong. One author in recent years, for example, noted that Hoosiers can't even pronounce the name of their own state capital, Indianapolis.

Maybe so. We may be hicks, we may not be able to pronounce words properly, we may lag behind in this important area and that critical aspect, but Indiana has done at least one thing right: Arguably the outstanding person of the world in the nineteenth century grew to manhood in Indiana.

Referring to his Indiana years, he said, "There I grew up." Known worldwide for the last century and a half because of his deeds, his words, his beliefs, his character—all of these attributes were largely strengthened, if not developed, during his fourteen years on a southern Indiana farm.

That man, of course, was Abraham Lincoln.

For some reason, just about everyone knows that Lincoln was born in a log cabin in Kentucky. They know he practiced the law and was elected to the office of president while he lived in Illinois. What seems to somehow pass almost unrecognized is that Lincoln's boyhood-to-manhood years, from age seven to twenty-one, were spent in Indiana.

It was in 1816—the same year that Indiana achieved statehood—that the Thomas Lincoln family crossed the Ohio River from Kentucky into Indiana. What followed for the young Lincoln were hard years, tragic years, learning years, character-building years—years in which he changed from a young lad to a strong man who later led his country in perhaps its most difficult period in history.

The story of his Indiana years can best be observed by a visit to the Lincoln Boyhood National Memorial. It's here that the Lincoln farm was located and where Lincoln's mother, Nancy Hanks, died and is buried. Nearby is where his sister died in childbirth and where Lincoln walked the roads, read by the light of the fireplace, studied law, became the rail-splitter, and worked on his father's farm and for neighbors.

In other words, it was in Indiana that Lincoln became the man the world would honor as one of America's greatest presidents, the country's martyred leader in our most difficult war, and a man the world would call the Great Emancipator.

My visit to Indiana's Lincoln country was at the time of the annual Lincoln Day program. Most of it took place in the Abraham Lincoln Hall of the memorial, followed by a placing of wreaths at the Nancy Hanks grave site, just a short distance from the memorial building.

LINCOLN BOYHOOD NATIONAL MEMORIAL. This building houses exhibits, a museum, the Abraham Lincoln Hall, and the Nancy Hanks Lincoln Hall.

It was an almost-warm February Sunday afternoon. A sizable crowd gathered to sing patriotic songs, listen to an address about Lincoln, and finally to hear a "Lincoln presenter"—a Lincoln look-alike—speak about the president and Nancy Hanks after we walked to the small cemetery.

Nearby and also part of the Lincoln Boyhood National Memorial is the Lincoln Living Historical Farm, a complete, working farmstead that from mid-April through September has costumed interpreters performing their chores and talking about life on the Indiana frontier.

Inside the memorial building is a depiction of an early-nineteenth-century homestead kitchen, its centerpiece being the hearth. Outside at the cabin site of the Lincoln home is a bronze memorial, marking the cabin's location. Fireplace hearthstones from the traditional Lincoln cabin were found by the Civilian Conservation Corps during a site excavation during 1934. It was here in front of this hearth where Lincoln and his sister, Sarah, heard stories from the family Bible told by their mother and stepmother and where they practiced their reading skills.

There's more to be seen here, including nearby Lincoln State Park and its *Young Abe Lincoln* performances, an outstanding theatrical presentation of Lincoln's early years.

It's probably understandable that other states pay scant attention to Lincoln's Indiana years. What is difficult to understand, though, is why those of us in Indiana aren't more aware of them.

IF YOU GO

GETTING THERE: The Lincoln Boyhood National Memorial is located on Indiana 162 between the towns of Santa Claus and Gentryville.

INFORMATION: Call (812) 937–4541. Open daily 8 a.m. to 5 p.m.

FEES: Admission charged.

DELIVERANCE CROSS. The cross stands on the south lawn of Saint Joseph Church in Jasper, the result of a vow made by a German stone-cutter when it seemed his ship might sink during an Atlantic Ocean storm. The church's 235-foot-high bell tower is in the background.

INSIDE CHURCH. Inside Jasper's Saint Joseph Church with a view toward the main altar. Its seating capacity is 850.

JASPER'S STORY. This stained-glass window at Holy Family Church in Jasper tells the city's history. It includes a ship, a covered wagon, the "deliverance cross," a buffalo trace or trail, the Patoka River, church founders and pastors, Sisters of Providence, a mill, and the lumber industry.

Saint Joseph and Holy Family Churches, Jasper

JASPER—It took twenty-one years to complete the building and its fixtures, another sixteen years before the bell tower belfry was finished, and seven more years before the frescoes were in place. Then, forty-three years later, the entire interior was renovated at a cost of two and a half times that of the original construction.

When it was all over in 1954, however, this German Catholic parish had a church building—Saint Joseph Church—that is one of a kind.

Parishioners point out among the church's features, the German stained-glass windows, the Austrian-designed mosaics containing more than fifty million stones, and the "deliverance cross" on the lawn.

As fascinating as they are, perhaps even more remarkable is the story of the construction of the building, now listed on the National Register of Historic Places.

Father Fidelis Maute was the guiding force behind the construction of the present church building as architect, contractor, foreman, laborer, fund-raiser, and pastor. Moreover, with no training in architecture or construction, he oversaw his parishioners' construction force that supplied all the materials and labor to build the 193-foot-long and 92-foot-high church.

Construction started in 1867. Sandstone building blocks were quarried on the Patoka River and pulled on sleds by teams of oxen to the construction site. There, parishioners with chisels formed the blocks for the building. Each parishioner had his own chisel and his own method, so the blocks have a wide variety of cuts. They raised the blocks higher and higher as the building took form by winching up the blocks, again using teams of oxen.

The structure of the Romanesque building was completed in 1880 and consecrated in 1888. In its first seven years, the building did not have lighting, but, little by little, improvements were added as funds became available.

The church includes fourteen inside columns that actually are each a single virgin tulip poplar timber standing sixty-seven feet high inside veneer sandstone. The trees came from the farms of parishioners, who donated the logs. Tulip poplar was used because it is not susceptible to insects. In addition, more than one million feet of timber was used in forming the roof of the church.

The next pastor, Father Basil Heusler, completed the bell tower in 1904. It stands 235 feet high and is patterned after London's Big Ben, which Heusler saw during one of his trips. The four bells weigh twelve tons and, on occasion, can be heard ten miles away.

LIFE OF CHRIST. The "Holy Family" window of Holy Family Church in Jasper shows events in the life of Christ, beginning with an angel appearing to Mary, Elizabeth greeting Mary, Christ's birth, the flight to Egypt, and Jesus in the Temple.

IF YOU GO

It was during the 1954 renovation that the walls and columns inside the building were stripped of plaster, reinforced, and covered with sandstone veneer.

The "deliverance cross" that stands on the south lawn has an interesting story. When a group of eleven German immigrant families crossed the Atlantic in 1837, they were caught in a ferocious storm, and it appeared their ship would sink. One of the passengers, George Baumann, a stonecutter, vowed to build a stone crucifix at their New World home if they were saved. In 1848 he completed the cross. It was destroyed in a 1928 storm but replaced by the present cross in 1932.

While the visitor is in Jasper, a trip also should be made to the Holy Family Church, located south on Indiana 162. Two huge stained-glass windows, designed by Maureen McGuire of Phoenix, are part of the 1979 structure, each nearly filling a wall. The "Holy Family" window depicts events in the life of Christ, while the second, "The Jasper Story," reviews events in the development of the German American heritage of the community.

GETTING THERE: Saint Joseph Church is on U.S. 231 between Eleventh and Thirteenth streets in Jasper. Holy Family Church is southeast at 950 E. Church Avenue.

INFORMATION: Saint Joseph Church is open daily from 8 a.m. to 9 p.m. The telephone number is (812) 482–805. Holy Family Church is open daily until 8 p.m. Its telephone number is (812) 482–3076.

FEES: None to tour the churches.

SAINT FERDINAND CHURCH. You likely will go past this historic church as you drive to the monastery. It is the oldest structure in Ferdinand, built from 1845 to 1848.

Monastery Immaculate Conception, Ferdinand

FERDINAND—Its name is Monastery Immaculate Conception, but just about everybody around here calls it the "castle on the hill."

It isn't difficult to understand why. The dome of the monastery is visible for miles. As you leave Indiana 162 and turn to the east, the ground gets higher. Within a few blocks, the monastery is in sight—high on a hill and looking, indeed, much like a castle.

The heart of the monastery is the church, the dome of which rises eighty-seven feet from the floor of the building. Angels are depicted in the sixteen stained-glass windows around the dome, plus ten in the stained-glass windows behind the altar—in all, ninety-four angels are depicted throughout the church.

The church was begun in 1915, and the exterior walls were up in fourteen months. However, World War I intervened. Because of shortages and high prices, work was not resumed until 1922.

The church, today listed on the National Register of Historic Places, was completed in 1924 and features solid-oak panels and hand-carved pews made by craftsmen from Oberammergau, Germany. The church's stained-glass windows on both the lower and upper levels were designed by Father Bede Maler of Saint Meinrad, Indiana, and cast at the Frei Art Glass Studios of Munich in Saint Louis. The building is brick, faced with Indiana limestone and Italian ceramic clay trim.

The monastery church recently has undergone major restoration, both exterior—including the clay tile roof, masonry, and windows—and interior—replacement of the canvas ceiling, plaster repair, painting, and new lighting.

Other buildings on the grounds include Madonna Hall, which housed high-school girls who attended Marian Heights Academy; Benet Hall, which includes the gift shop and is also a residence for nuns; Kordes Retreat Center; Saint Joseph Hall; a gymnasium; and an art studio.

The monastery is home to the Sisters of Saint Benedict. The local community was founded in 1867 by four young Benedictine sisters who came from Covington, Kentucky, to teach the large German population living in the area. Since that time, more than a thousand women have been part of the monastery. The number most recently was 202, with 125 living at the monastery. The others were on various missions throughout Indiana, other states, and foreign countries.

The sisters are monastic women "who live the Benedictine tradition of seeking God through prayer and work." They gather three times daily in the church for prayer—morning, midday, and evening.

Until 2000 the community included three corporate ministries—the

THE CASTLE ON THE HILL. Monastery Immaculate Conception at Ferdinand sits atop a hill just east of Indiana 162. Several wings have been added since the church was completed in 1924.

monastery, Kordes Retreat Center, and Marian Heights Academy, an all-girl boarding school. However, the academy closed following the 1999–2000 school year. A 2000 summer session allowed five girls from the class of 2001 to complete their academic work and graduate.

Kordes offers a series of retreats and programs for individuals and groups. Church groups, schools, and other nonprofit organizations are also invited to rent the facility for their own programs. In one recent year, more than two thousand people took part in the center's programs.

As one might expect, the general atmosphere is one of contemplation. That's what makes the retreats so special, according to those who attend. It offers a "ten-day retreat in one day," according to one participant.

At least some of the sisters double—if not quadruple—their work assignments at the monastery. Sister Mary Lee Hillenbrand told me during my visit that she is a gardener but also presents tours, cooks, and serves as a hostess. All said, of course, with no touch of pride or of being overworked—simply a statement of fact.

While you are in Ferdinand, you also will want to stop at Saint Ferdinand Church, one block east after you turn from Indiana 162 toward the monastery. The church is the oldest building in Ferdinand, constructed during 1845–48, according to *Indiana: A New Historical Guide.* You may not be able to go in as it is not always open. Nevertheless, it is impressive in its own way.

It, too, sits on a hill.

IF YOU GO

GETTING THERE: Ferdinand is a little over a mile north of Interstate 64 on Indiana 162, about ten miles from the Ohio River.

INFORMATION: Visit the Web site at http://www.thedome.org/ for complete information, a virtual tour, and special events. On-site tours are 10 a.m. and 11 a.m. and 1 p.m., 2 p.m., and 3 p.m. Tuesday through Friday and 1 p.m., 2 p.m., and 3 p.m. Saturday and Sunday. The monastery's telephone number is (812) 367–1411, and the Kordes center is (812) 367–2777 or (800) 880–2777.

FEES: None to tour.

AT THE SITE. The visitor can only guess what this land looked like in 1960 when the large turbojet slammed into the earth with its fifty-seven passengers and six-person crew.

WHERE THE COFFINS WERE PLACED. Only two of the coffins at Greenwood Cemetery had human remains from the turbojet crash. The others were "symbolic gestures of grief."

HE KNOWS WHAT HE'S DOING. The operator of this tugboat guides barges into the Cannelton Locks, heading down the Ohio River. The hills in the background are in Kentucky.

Tell City Airline Crash Site and the Cannelton Locks, Cannelton

CANNELTON—In the hours following the crash, a number of people told of hearing it happen. A woman at a store heard an explosion, accompanied by a "terrible thud." A man heard "three popping sounds" and then saw aircraft pieces falling from the sky.

Farmer Ted Wilson, who lived about seven miles east of Cannelton, told a reporter for the *Indianapolis Star* he heard what sounded like a five hundred-pound bomb, something he knew well from his World War II experiences in the Pacific. He raced outside his house to see the plane bury itself in the ground about three hundred yards away.

Another farmer, Cyril Powers, was in his barn and heard what sounded like two sticks of dynamite. Outside he saw what appeared to be a wing falling to the north and then the "body of an airplane falling toward me." In seconds, he saw it smash into the ground, a quarter of a mile away.

It was the March 17, 1960, crash of Northwest Airlines Flight 710, bound from Minneapolis to Miami. The Lockheed Electra aircraft carried fifty-seven passengers and a crew of six. All were killed, and, at the time, it was the worst airplane crash in Indiana history.

What followed in the immediate days afterwards were efforts to determine the cause of the crash and to find bodies of the victims in the deep hole where the fuselage slammed into the ground.

As to the cause, investigators determined that the wings of the turbojet had broken off because of engine support failure. Finding bodies was another matter. According to *Indiana: A New Historical Guide*, only seventeen of the victims could be identified.

In an attempt to bring closure to the horrific event, a burial of coffins took place at the Greenwood Cemetery in neighboring Tell City. According to radio reporter Roland Brewer's account on the Perry County Web site, only two actually contained some of the remains of fifty-five of the sixty-three victims. The other coffins were empty— "symbolic gestures of grief," Brewer called them.

The crash is remembered today at two memorials.

At the crash site is a monument, dedicated a little more than a year after the crash. The nine-foot-tall Vermont granite monument lists separately the names of the passengers and crew. In addition to the names, it depicts the outline of a passenger aircraft and symbols of the four religious faiths of the persons who died—Protestant, Roman Catholic, Jewish, and Shinto. Funds for the memorial were raised by public subscription.

A second memorial stands at the Greenwood Cemetery, located on Indiana 37 at the north edge of Tell City. The obelisk lists alphabetically

THE LOCKS. The massive Cannelton Dam stretches across the Ohio River to create a 114-mile "lake" upriver toward Louisville.

IF YOU GO

the names of the victims and it, too, has symbols of their religious beliefs.

This area remembers another tragic event, too, but it has a happier ending.

In 1937 a great flood inundated lands along the Ohio River. An estimated two-thirds of Cannelton was under water.

What followed was one of the great flood prevention programs of all time, which included erection of a series of dams and locks along the river. The locks are for river navigation.

Today, experts say you should think of the Ohio River as a series of lakes, each backed up behind dams and locks. One of the longest is the 114-mile "lake" behind the Cannelton Locks, two miles east of here. That body of water stretches all the way upriver to Louisville.

The locks and dams were built over a ten-year period in the late 1960s and early 1970s and cost nearly $100 million.

There's something almost mesmerizing in watching a tug push a long line of barges over toward the Indiana side of the river and maneuver them toward one side of the locks so they will then head toward the other side of the lock, ending up by passing squarely through with what looks like inches—probably a few feet—to spare on either side.

It's something the tug operator probably does every day and doesn't give a second thought. To a landlubber, it's nothing short of amazing.

GETTING THERE: The locks are about two miles east of Cannelton on Indiana 66. To reach the air crash site, go east from the locks another five miles on Indiana 66 to Indiana 166 and follow it to the crash site.

INFORMATION: Go to the Perry County Convention and Visitors Bureau Web site at http://www.perrycountyindiana.org/, e-mail perrycountycvb@psci.net, or call toll-free (888) 343–6262. For more information about the plane crash, contact the Perry County Museum at (812) 547–3190.

FEES: None.

PATOKA DAM. This 1,550-foot dam created Patoka Lake, which holds nearly six hundred billion gallons of water spread over eighty-eight hundred acres during the summer months.

RESTFUL PATOKA. A view of Patoka Lake and surrounding hillsides. The entire Patoka Lake area includes twenty-six thousand acres.

Patoka Lake, Birdseye

BIRDSEYE—With the exception of the original thirteen states, Indiana is the third smallest in land area in the nation. Only Hawaii and West Virginia have fewer square miles than Indiana's 35,870. So you might think those of us who live in Indiana would know our state rather well.

That's not true in many cases, however. For example, those who live in northern Indiana often have not traveled all that much in southern Indiana. And vice versa, no doubt.

So, when many Hoosiers in northern Indiana hear about "the lakes," they tend to think of that area mostly north of an east-west line running through Fort Wayne. Certainly, this part of the state has many. Steuben County, for example, in the northeast corner of the state, boasts of 101 lakes.

The two biggest lakes in the state, however, are in southern Indiana—Patoka Lake and Monroe Lake. Monroe, south of Bloomington, is about two thousand acres larger than Patoka. The Patoka Reservoir area, however, is the largest property managed by the Indiana Department of Natural Resources, at twenty-six thousand acres.

Perhaps one reason why we know so little about Patoka is because of its short history. The damming of the Patoka River started in 1978, the lake filled by 1979, and the facilities were opened to the public in 1980.

While recreational use is the reason why the lake attracts attention, it wasn't the main goal of the U.S. Army Corps of Engineers project. It was to protect downriver communities from flooding and to provide water supplies for an eight-county area—some six million gallons a day.

The lake, mostly in southwestern Orange County and extending to the south into Crawford County and to the west into Dubois County, is owned by the federal government with property management leased to the state of Indiana.

Lake area highlights include:

A 1,550-foot-long, 84-foot-high, earth-and-rock-fill dam that backs up a lake twenty-five miles long—thirty miles at flood stage—with more than 160 miles of shoreline.

About six hundred billion gallons of water in the reservoir during the summer spread over eighty-eight hundred acres. (Monroe's lake acreage is 10,750.) The lake's average depth is twenty feet.

Drainage area above the dam is 168 square miles.

Availability of 455 class A campsites, forty-five class C primitive sites, and a fisherman's primitive campsite. All class A sites can be reserved by calling a central reservation system (866) 622–6746 during the reservation season.

VISITOR CENTER. Solar paneling is no longer used at the Patoka Lake Visitor Center—too costly to repair. Inside are exhibits and information about the lake, animals, birds, and fish.

There is a beach for swimming, although when I visited, it was mostly under water because of heavy rains.

Other lake facilities include boat ramps, hunting in season, hiking and bike trails, interpretive naturalist service, picnic areas, shelters, a visitor center, and, of course, fishing. The stocked lake has bass, bluegill, redear, crappie, catfish, and pike.

Of the hiking trails, the loop to Totem Rock is best known. It reaches a rock shelter used years ago as a hunting camp by Native Americans and early settlers. The full trail, termed "rugged," has a shortcut back to the visitor center.

At the south edge of the lake in the Newton-Stewart State Recreation Area is the privately managed Patoka Lake Marina and Lodging. In addition to on-ground lodging, grocery, and gas station, the marina offers watercraft, including houseboats, pontoons, ski boats, wave surfers, fishing boats, and, the latest, floating cabins. The two-bedroom cabins have air-conditioning, bathrooms, television, and a kitchen—in other words, a home away from home. They are thought to be the first in the state.

As big as the lake is, the land area is twice as large—seventeen thousand acres of forests, hills, and sandstone outcroppings. Plus, you may see a bald eagle. The visitor center offers presentations about eagles, red-tail hawks, and barred owls.

IF YOU GO

GETTING THERE: Turn north off Indiana 164 at the Wickcliffe United Methodist Church. (Sign at the turn reads "Newton-Stewart SRA.")

INFORMATION: To reach the Patoka Lake Visitor Center, call (812) 685–2447 or fax (812) 685–2448. The reservoir's headquarters telephone is (812) 685–2464. The toll-free marina telephone is (888) 819–6916. Its Web site is http://www.patokal akemarina.com/.

FEES: Various venues have different fees. It's best to call for information.

APOLLO SPRING. This mineral spring on the grounds of the West Baden Springs Hotel—the Apollo—was filled in and eventually cemented by the Jesuits during the order's thirty-year occupation of the hotel.

COMPLETELY REBUILT. This wall of the West Baden Springs Hotel collapsed from ice and water during the winter of 1991. It was rebuilt as part of the restoration of the hotel and grounds.

NO QUESTIONS ASKED. The upper glass windows of these doors leading into the lobby of the hotel were found by the FBI in Louisville. With the promise that no questions would be asked about how they were obtained, the windows were returned and restored.

West Baden Springs Hotel, West Baden

WEST BADEN SPRINGS—The story of West Baden Springs Hotel reads like a sprawling epic saga covering three centuries with a plot involving sex, religion, bad guys, good guys, ups and downs, a nation in turmoil, depression and wars, millions of dollars—you name it.

And it all takes place in Indiana. Here's the basic story line:

A Revolutionary War hero in the late 1700s discovers mineral springs in the rolling hills of present-day southern Indiana, what was then the western frontier.

In the early 1800s an entrepreneur builds a hotel there and, when the railroad comes through, it begins to attract guests from throughout the Midwest. Another aggressive entrepreneur acquires control, but as the twentieth century arrives, the hotel burns to the ground.

The owner, rather than being dismayed, seizes the chance to rebuild. His plans are considered outrageous. He wants a circular building with the world's largest dome and decorated like the grandest spas in Europe. And he wants it done in a year.

The job gets done—in eleven months—and it is an enormous success. The hotel's atrium is two hundred feet across—two-thirds the length of a football field—and more than one hundred feet high. It is declared "the eighth wonder of the world." Guests arrive from all over the country—among them the rich and famous—to take the waters, gamble, and enjoy life.

Along the way, the owner dies, and his daughter and her husband take over. During World War I the hotel is converted into an army hospital, where the daughter falls in love with a recuperating officer. She divorces her husband and marries the officer, but eventually has to sell the hotel in the early 1920s to another southern Indiana operator. He has made a fortune managing casinos.

The stock market crash ends it all. The hotel closes in the early 1930s, but the next thing anyone knows, the hotel reopens—as a religious seminary! The religious order (Jesuits) tears out much of the hotel's ostentatious decorations and uses it for thirty years.

Finally, the expenses become too much, and the seminarians accept a one dollar donation from a private college for the hotel and grounds. These investors, too, are forced to give up. The 250 acres fall into disrepair; an outside wall of the hotel collapses. Vandals ransack the hotel, and heaps of debris cover the floor of the atrium.

By the 1980s states have the fever for legalized gambling. One group wants to use the hotel as a gambling site but can't convince state government to allow a gambling boat to be put in a man-made

INSIDE THE ATRIUM. It's two hundred feet across and more than one hundred feet high, with six floors of hotel rooms encircling what was the largest freestanding dome in the world before the Astrodome in Houston was built. Circuses performed here, and later Larry Bird held basketball camps in the atrium.

lake they would build—the infamous "boat in a moat." After a few years, they also throw in the towel. Ownership of the hotel ends up in the courts, and the legal tangles drag on for years.

To the rescue come the preservationists. They buy the hotel for $250,000, but they need millions. Then from nearby Bloomington comes a financial savior. He invests more than $28 million in a partial restoration.

Finally, the casino folks win, and an Indiana license is transferred to Orange County to be used between the West Baden Springs and French Lick hotels.

The earlier restoration process had first focused on emergency repairs and otherwise stabilizing the structure, in addition to bringing the atrium, lobby, and sunken gardens back to their 1920s splendor. Now the rush is on for a new owner to rapidly move ahead with restoration to coincide with the opening of a casino, possibly in 2006.

Don't bet against them. Truth really is stranger than fiction.

THE INITIAL POINT. These wooden railings frame the state's "initial point," used for land surveys since Ebenezer Buckingham Jr. first marked the spot in 1805. It is located seven miles south of Paoli.

THAT'S WHERE THE POST WAS. This limestone rock marks where Ebenezer Buckingham Jr. drove a post in the ground to mark Indiana's "initial point" for surveying, seven miles south of Paoli. The limestone replaced the post late in the nineteenth century.

PROMINENT NAMES. This photograph shows the center of the historical marker that was removed from "the initial point" site in the early 1970s because of vandalism and placed on the lawn of the Orange County Courthouse square at Paoli. Some prominent "landowners" were included around the initial or pivot point.

The Initial Point, Paoli

PAOLI—On September 1, 1805, U.S. Deputy Surveyor Ebenezer Buckingham Jr. drove a post into the ground south of Paoli that determined boundary lines for land in the Indiana Territory. It formed the basis of all Indiana land surveys, and we still use his measurements today.

It's called "the initial point," locally referred to as the "pivot point."

According to a nearby historical marker, the post Buckingham used was replaced by a limestone rock, probably between 1879 and 1886, placed at the same site to commemorate the event. The marker is located at an automobile turnaround, a short distance away from where the surveyor intersected his lines.

From that post in the ground, six-mile-square townships, acres, and sections of Indiana followed systematically. It doesn't take too much imagination to grasp the significance of Buckingham's work.

How in the world did he do this, tramping through forests, over rivers, up and down hills in largely uninhabited country except for a few struggling towns and tribes of Native Americans?

Well, he started his line, according to the historical marker, "at or near the westerly corner of the Vincennes tract as surveyed by Thomas Freeman." He intersected this line "12 miles east of the southerly corner of Mr. Freeman's survey of the Vincennes tract." (Maybe even a better question would be how did Freeman do it first?)

This Buckingham intersection became "the initial point" and was intended to be the geographical center of what would be the new state of Indiana. The historical marker explains in detail the point's exact location, based on measurements relative to Greenwich, England, and the equator. Quite frankly, it's beyond me to fully understand it.

If you're interested in seeing this "initial point," here's what you do.

About seven miles south of Paoli on Indiana 37 is Young's Creek Road. Just beyond it is a road marker, headed "Pivot Point." You turn off to the west about six hundred yards beyond the sign. That road ends in a turnaround.

You will see the historical marker when you reach the turnaround. One side of the marker has been removed. (More about that later.) Face away from the marker where information about the initial point and Historic Landmarks Foundation of Indiana Inc. is displayed. You will observe a path running down the side of a hill directly in front of you. It's only a path, but, at least when I followed it, it was distinct. Follow it, including going down some wooden steps at one place. At the bottom, to the left, you will see wooden railings. They frame the limestone rock that marks the initial point.

COURTHOUSE SQUARE. The Orange County Courthouse, built between 1848 and 1850, sits in the middle of the town square in Paoli. The initial point historical marker was placed on the lawn of the courthouse.

What about the other side of the historical marker at the turn-around?

That was removed in the early 1970s and placed on the lawn of the Orange County courthouse square in Paoli.

The names surrounding the initial point on this courthouse marker, supposedly landowners, reads like a who's who of early Americana—George Washington, Thomas Jefferson, Chief Little Turtle, Tecumseh, the Prophet, George Rogers Clark, William Henry Harrison, Rufus Putnam, Rufus King, and the Wea, Potawatomi, Delaware, Ottawa, Wynadot, Shawnee, Piankashaw, Kaskaskia, and Kickapoo tribes.

The number one section of land, however, went to Albert Gallatin, who served as secretary of the treasury at the time the surveying was done. Apparently these surveyors knew their politics, too.

GETTING THERE: At Paoli, follow Indiana 37 south and then follow the specific directions included in the article to the state's "initial point."

INFORMATION: The Orange County Historical Society's telephone number is (812) 723–6916. The toll-free number for the Orange County Convention and Visitors Bureau is (877) 422–9925. Visit the Web site history page at http://www.historicsouthernindiana.com/.

FEES: None.

THE SEAT OF GOVERNMENT. When Indiana became a state in late 1816, its first general assembly met in this Corydon building—along with the state supreme court.

WHAT'S LEFT. All that remains of the "Constitution Elm," under whose shade delegates gathered in Corydon during their drafting of the Indiana constitution.

GOVERNOR'S HEADQUARTERS. Home of William Hendricks in Corydon while he was governor, 1822–25. The front room was his headquarters. Hendricks also served as secretary of the constitutional convention.

Corydon

CORYDON—Those forty-three delegates from thirteen counties in the Indiana Territory had a big job on their hands when they met at Corydon on June 10, 1816. They were to draft a constitution that would guide the new state of Indiana.

And it was hot.

Their meeting place was an unfinished log house, being used at the time for the territorial capitol. Because of the size of the small building and the heat, many of their deliberations took place under the spreading branches of a nearby elm tree—or at least so Indiana folklore has it.

Not that it was just any elm tree. The trunk was five feet across, its branches spread out over 132 feet, and the tree stood fifty feet high. If any shade could be found, it was under this tree. Also, nearby was a spring with cool water.

Not surprisingly, the tree became known as the "Constitution Elm." You probably know what happens to elm trees in Indiana. The so-called Dutch elm disease nearly destroyed the tree in 1925, so that today only part of its trunk remains, enclosed in a sandstone memorial.

What's left of the elm is about two blocks from the historic state capitol building. You might remember from your Indiana history lessons that Corydon was the state capital from 1816 to 1825, before the capital was moved to Indianapolis.

The two-story Federal-style structure—originally planned to be the Harrison County Courthouse—was under construction when the delegates met in 1816. Up to that time, space had been rented for the territorial government in that log house near the elm tree—"the courthouse on the hill."

Somewhere along the line, the decision was made instead to use the new limestone building under construction as the seat of Indiana government. Getting their money's worth, county and district courts used the building when the legislature was not in session.

It still stands today, much as it did then. The well-kept building and its grounds are maintained by the Indiana State Museum and Historic Sites. You can tour the building on your own, or you might luck into a guided tour along with schoolchildren, as I did when I visited.

You're going to have a hard time believing that the Indiana House of Representatives met on the first floor, while the Indiana Senate and the Indiana Supreme Court occupied the upstairs, but they did. Among the legislature's laws for the new state was the death penalty for four crimes—treason, murder, arson, and horse stealing.

BRANHAM TAVERN. This two-story log building was constructed in 1800 by William Henry Harrison. It became a tavern operated by William Branham in 1821.

One block away is Governor William Hendricks's headquarters and home that he used when he served as Indiana governor from 1822 to 1825. It was during his administration that the decision was made to move the state capital from Corydon to Indianapolis. It's another two-story, Federal-style building with a small garden at the rear. Indiana acquired the property in 1979 to be used as another of its Corydon historic sites.

One block west of the capitol building is the Posey House, built in 1817. It had been maintained by the Daughters of the American Revolution until it became part of the historic sites property. The brick building was constructed by Colonel Thomas L. Posey, the son of Indiana's last territorial governor. Colonel Posey never married but raised fourteen orphan children.

Another historic site—the first state office building—also now is owned by the state. In those early years, it was rented by the state and, so the story goes, the treasury of the state of Indiana—silver stored in strongboxes—was kept in a cellar under the house.

Aiding you in your tour is a map, titled "Corydon Historic Downtown Walking Tour." It contains brief descriptions of each site, indicating which are open to the public, plus an easy-to-understand street map.

If it's early Indiana history you want, Corydon is the place.

IF YOU GO

GETTING THERE: Leave Interstate 64 and go south on Indiana 135, business route, into Corydon.

INFORMATION:
Go to the Harrison County Convention and Visitors Bureau Web site at http://www.tourindiana .com/, e-mail info@tourindiana .com, or call toll-free (888) 738–2137. When you arrive in Corydon, a good place to start is the Harrison County Convention and Visitors Bureau at the corner of Elm and Walnut streets, just behind the state capitol building.

FEES: None to visit these state historic sites, but donations are accepted.

EARLY ORGAN. This 1873 organ came to the Washington County Historical Society from the Ruby Reister estate. It's on the second floor of the Stevens Memorial Museum at the John Hay Center.

STEVENS MEMORIAL MUSEUM. It houses galleries, displays, artifacts, a genealogy and historical library, a banquet room, and offices for the Washington County Historical Society in Salem.

HOUSEWIFE'S DREAM. Well, perhaps only in the early 1800s, when this hand-operated scrubbing device served as an early washing machine.

John Hay Center, Salem

SALEM—There's a certain amount of pride in Willie Harlen's voice when he talks about the finances of the John Hay Center near downtown Salem. The center is a complex that includes historic—mainly log cabin—buildings; the brick-home birthplace of American statesman John Hay; the depot, a replica of Salem's third railroad station; and the Stevens Memorial Museum.

"We only get $7,000 from the county toward annual expenses of around $80,000. The rest comes from memberships, publishing, and events," states Harlen, the president of the Washington County Historical Society.

Harlen also points out that all the improvements in the nine-building village, along with the Stevens Memorial Museum, were paid for up front. "We never built anything we couldn't pay for," he says with understandable pride—no small accomplishment for any museum.

Sometimes, the historical society got lucky.

When the 1866 H. H. McClellan General Store from New Philadelphia was moved to Salem, "they also gave us everything that was in it," Harlen says. That included the "New Philadelphia post office," a series of open-ended letter boxes, as well as items still on the shelves of the general store.

The significant breakthrough in Salem's history came in 1847 when businessmen coupled with those in New Albany to build a railroad joining the two towns—a line later extended far north to Lake Michigan.

Today's depot, a replica of the Salem railroad station, is the pride of Cecil J. Smith, stationmaster. It is the third on the site of what was first the New Albany and Salem Railroad; later the Louisville, New Albany and Chicago when the line was extended all the way to Lake Michigan; and, finally, the Monon before the station closed in 1971.

Much of this history has been captured in the Stevens Memorial Museum along with the Pioneer Village. The museum could be considered the center's outstanding structure.

Built in 1970, the two-and-a-half-story brick building was constructed using native brick from other local historic buildings. Additions came in 1984 and 1995.

One of the museum's most used resources is its genealogy and historical library. On typical days, researchers from across the United States can be found there.

Some museums only have the resources to offer a few shelves dedicated toward genealogy and other historical documents. Not so here. This library is housed in the handsome 1984 addition to the museum

HISTORICAL MARKER. Located at the John Hay Center in Salem. The complex includes the house where American diplomat John Hay was born in 1838.

and includes, on row upon row of shelving, family histories; church, cemetery, census, and marriage records; obituaries; newspapers; state and county histories; and antique photographs—all carefully cataloged and maintained. Records from states other than Indiana also are part of the collection.

A small staff is on hand to assist researchers.

Galleries and displays of historic artifacts are featured throughout the rest of the museum in addition to a large banquet room, used for large-scale community events.

An interesting side note to the museum and its village is that the idea for collecting the old buildings and putting them together as a village came from a basketball coach! Not any basketball coach, mind you, but Everett Dean, a Washington County native and later the fabled coach of Stanford University, where his team won the NCAA title in 1942—and a person obviously interested in local history.

His presence and memorabilia are much in evidence in the museum.

IF YOU GO

GETTING THERE: In Salem, turn onto High Street and follow signs.

INFORMATION: Call (812) 883–6495. The Stevens Museum is open, and library tours are held Tuesday through Saturday, 9 a.m. to 5 p.m. Closed Sunday, Monday, and holidays. The depot is open Saturday afternoons during winter months. Beginning in April, it is open Tuesday through Saturday afternoons, 1 p.m. to 4 p.m. The Web site is http://www.salemdepot.com/.

FEES: Admission charged.

SIDE ENTRANCE. This east door, which opens into the library of the Culbertson Mansion, is illustrative of the decorative work found in Second Empire homes built in the mid-1800s.

Culbertson Mansion State Historic Site, New Albany

NEW ALBANY—The idea in the 1960s was to tear down the old Culbertson Mansion and put up a gasoline station. That's when Historic New Albany stepped in and purchased the property with plans to restore the Victorian home to its 1869 glory.

However, the group had underestimated what the costs would be. The work moved slowly until 1976, when the state of Indiana came to the group's aid. It accepted the house as a state historic site. For a number of years after that, most of the efforts went into the exterior of the home in an effort to recapture more of its nineteenth-century look.

Now, well past its twenty-fifth anniversary as a state historic site, it's a work still in progress.

William S. Culbertson, another of those enterprising Hoosier entrepreneurs of the nineteenth century, had come to the state at age twenty-one from his boyhood home at New Market, Pennsylvania. He started as a clerk in a dry-goods store before ultimately becoming a successful, independent businessman.

He retired from the dry-goods business in 1868 and went on to found the major utilities of New Albany, including lighting the streets. He went into the banking business, too, and was a major investor in the Kentucky-Indiana railway bridge. Eventually, he was considered Indiana's wealthiest resident, with a fortune estimated at $3.5 million at his death in 1892 at age seventy-eight.

He started building his mansion in 1867, soon after he married his second wife, Cornelia. He had been left with the care of six children following his first wife's death. He spent about $120,000 to build what was one of the state's finest homes when it was completed in 1869.

Transportation to and from the house certainly was never a problem for Culbertson. The streetcar ran along the road in front of his home, and he sold land to the railroad, which built a track running only a few feet behind the mansion.

The twenty thousand-square-foot house has gone through several modifications over the years.

Another New Albany resident, John McDonald, bought the house at auction in 1899 for $7,100. When McDonald died, his daughter sold it to the American Legion. The Legion made some structural changes to meet its needs for a meeting place for its members and for hosting community events. Some years later, the gasoline company planned to tear it down to build a service station.

What's so special about this house?

CULBERTSON MANSION. Listed on the National Register of Historic Places in 1974, the Culbertson Mansion in New Albany was accepted two years later as a state historic site by the state of Indiana.

"Everything," says my tour guide the day I visited the mansion. "It really is. After you're really in it for a while, it just grows on you." An example would be the breakfast room. My guide says that Culbertson's daughter, Ann, had desserts served there at the end of her outdoor parties.

"I'm anxious to see what's under this paint. Why would they come in here? It had to be pretty fancy," she believes.

She especially likes to point to the artistic details of the three-story, Second Empire mansion with its twenty-five rooms. Included are a carved rosewood and mahogany staircase, marble fireplaces, crystal chandeliers—and don't forget the hand-painted ceilings.

"It's so interesting to see what the artists do today with these ceilings, starting with cotton swabs to remove the paint. Then they use cotton balls and sponges. It takes hours and hours," she says.

The work progresses as funds become available. The second floor, with its bedrooms, and the third floor's additional bedrooms and ballroom are open to the public but are unfinished.

When I visited, the first floor was ready to be painted. The mansion will remain open during the process, termed a replication since no adequate description or photos of the home's former interior exist today. As the work progresses, however, artists uncover original designs, colors, and finishes to produce some documentation.

IF YOU GO

GETTING THERE: The Culbertson Mansion is at 914 E. Main Street in downtown New Albany.

INFORMATION: The telephone number is (812) 944–9600. The fax is (812) 949–6134. Open Sunday 1 p.m. to 5 p.m., Tuesday through Saturday 9 a.m. to 5 p.m. Closed Monday and mid-December through April 1.

FEES: Free admission, but donations are encouraged.

WAS HE FIRST? A depiction of what Welsh Prince Madoc may have looked like, lower right, is part of one of the exhibits at the park's Interpretive Center. Some believe he led an expedition into the Gulf of Mexico that went as far north as the Falls of the Ohio in present-day southern Indiana, three hundred years before Columbus's journey.

FOUR HUNDRED MILLION YEARS AGO. Explorers, lower center, look at fossils and other forms of ancient life at the Falls of the Ohio State Park. By starting out as far from the cliff as possible, you can work your way back through four hundred million years of fossils and time.

Falls of the Ohio State Park, Clarksville

CLARKSVILLE—Would you go off your route one mile while traveling south on Interstate 65 to see a geological panorama of time spread over millions of years?

That's the Falls of the Ohio State Park, one mile to the west of exit 0 at Clarksville, just before you cross into Kentucky. Brown state park signs direct you.

What you can walk through is a span of time measuring back almost four hundred million years when the area was an inland, tropical sea.

As coral sand fish and other sea inhabitants died, they were buried in layers of sediment that fossilized them. When Ice-Age glaciers melted many millenniums later, waters carved out the Ohio River basin, exposing these fossil beds on the seafloor, preserved in stone.

State park officials say the best time to view this fossilized world is between August and November, when the Ohio River is at its lowest level. The recommendation is to go down the concrete steps as far out toward the river channel as you can, then start back to the cliffs and the steps. Here's what you will see, as described by a booklet you can buy there, *Probing the Wonders of the Falls*:

First is the coral zone, the lowest level. You are standing on a petrified floor of a former tropical sea that existed about 386 million years ago. It's frequently mud covered and is flat—smooth and polished through water erosion. If you splash water on the gray limestone, fossils will almost magically appear.

Continuing toward the cliffs, you come to the upper coral zone. You can see shallow caves, formed less than a million years ago. Some trees try to take hold here.

In the Paraspirifer zone above the cliff are more fossils, along with white morning glory and bindweed vines, wild grapevines, and prairie mimosa.

In the floodplain and glacial deposit zone are multicolored glaciated pebbles and rocks deposited by many glaciers—the most recent being the Wisconsin glacier only fifteen thousand years ago!

Finally, next to the steps is quarried limestone rock, put there to prevent river erosion of the bank.

All of this in a half-mile walk, with an elevation change of about forty-five feet. You also can make arrangements for a guided tour. Remember, don't take anything from the park.

There's also a woodland trail walk where numerous species of flowering plants have been identified.

INTERPRETIVE CENTER. The $5 million Interpretive Center that opened in 1994 at the Falls of the Ohio State Park in Clarksville, across the river from Louisville.

The Interpretive Center charges a small fee, but it's worth it. The structure opened in June 1994. An interesting fourteen-minute movie about the Falls is shown every half hour, while the exhibits describe the Falls area.

The park has its own library to encourage study of the locale. Books, periodicals, files, photographs, and videos are included. A special part of the library is the Leonard Brecher Ornithology Collection. It includes hundreds of books and periodicals from 1678 to 1975, including works by John James Audubon and Alexander Wilson. The library requires advance notice for visitor use.

It's called the Falls of the Ohio because in the days before dams and locks, the Ohio River churned its way through rapids that dropped the riverbed twenty-six feet in two miles. Old-timers had to "shoot the falls." The state park is 145 acres, while the National Wildlife Conservation Area, managed by the U.S. Army Corps of Engineers, is 1,404 acres.

The park is only a mile off your course. Plus, it's been a special Indiana site for the two hundredth anniversary of the Lewis and Clark expedition, which started "when they shook hands" in meeting at brother George Rogers Clark's nearby cabin. The cabin at Clark's Point also is part of the state park.

IF YOU GO

GETTING THERE: South on Interstate 65, take exit 0 and follow the brown state park signs to Riverside Drive. Only a mile off the highway.

INFORMATION: Call (812) 280–9970. The park is open 6 a.m. to 11 p.m. The Interpretive Center is open Monday through Saturday 9 a.m. to 5 p.m. and Sunday 1 p.m. to 5 p.m. It is closed Thanksgiving Day and Christmas Day.

FEES: No fees to enter the park. The Interpretive Center has a charge.

MEMORIAL OBELISK. A fence surrounds the forty-four-foot-tall stone obelisk that commemorates the Pigeon Roost Massacre and supposedly marks the common grave of the settlers who were killed.

Pigeon Roost Massacre State Historic Site, Scottsburg

SCOTTSBURG—While you are en route south on Interstate 65, you'll need thirty minutes, an interest in history, and a good sense of imagination to relive an unfortunate time in Indiana's past.

Just slightly to the south and east of Scottsburg—up against U.S. 31—is the site where a small settlement was attacked by a Shawnee war party on September 3, 1812. When the so-called Pigeon Roost massacre was over, somewhere between twenty-two and twenty-four of the pioneers were dead. They are believed to have been buried in a common grave at the site.

There's not much to see—that's where your imagination is important. What is known is recounted on a marker and also on the forty-four-foot obelisk that marks the site of the massacre. Interestingly, the two disagree about the number killed.

The marker states, "A community established here in 1809 was attacked by Indians on September 3, 1812; 15 children and 9 adults were massacred; only one family escaped to spread the alarm."

The engraving on the stone obelisk reads, "In memory of the pioneer heroes, twenty-two in number. Massacred at Pigeon Roost defeat by the Shawnee Indians. Sept. 3, 1812."

(*Indiana: A New Historical Guide* agrees with the marker in reporting "24 men, women and children dead." Local Scott County writers Marilyn Chamberlin and Bob Hollis, however, call the number twenty-two, "mainly women and children.")

Whether twenty-two or twenty-four were killed, the exact cause of the massacre also is not clear. The *Guide* says the raiders were a Shawnee war party, and the attack "has been linked to the emotions triggered by the War of 1812 and to thievery and fraud perpetrated by the whites against the Indians."

Remember, 1812 was four years before Indiana became a state. Scott County had not even been organized yet. This was the West, and the British and Indians had not yet given up hope of wresting these lands away from the new American nation.

The site was commemorated in 1903 when the Indiana General Assembly appropriated two thousand dollars for the erection of the monument. It was dedicated in 1904 and became a state historic site in 1929.

Why the name "Pigeon Roost"?

Chamberlin and Hollis say it was so named because of thousands of now-extinct passenger pigeons "which gathered in flocks so dense

TWENTY-FOUR KILLED? This marker of the Indiana Historical Bureau, posted in 1949, reports twenty-four killed in the massacre. The obelisk's stone engraving refers to the "pioneer heroes, twenty-two in number" who died.

they eclipsed the sun and by sheer weight of their roosting bodies broke large limbs from trees."

Today, it is a quiet spot. Down a hillside from the obelisk is a picnic shelter, but no restrooms. A few yards away is a separate cemetery. Some headstones are unreadable, but others show dates ranging from 1869 through 1991.

Close to the obelisk are two headstones of the Collins family. William E. Collings—note the difference in spelling—was supposed to have founded the community in 1809. Chamberlin and Hollis say the settlement was a scattered collection of farms stretching from present-day Vienna, about two miles to the north, down to the banks of Silver Creek to the south.

So, that's it. An obelisk, a marker, two graves, a nearby small cemetery, and a picnic shelter.

But the woods still are nearby, and the area seems removed from any nearby civilization. With just a little imagination, you can sense the Shawnee war party creeping closer to the rough cabins and then, with a battle cry, attacking.

IF YOU GO

GETTING THERE: At Scottsburg, take exit 29A and go east less than a mile on Indiana 56. Turn south on U.S. 31 to the sign indicating a left turn to the historical site. After your visit, go south on U.S. 31 to Henryville and back west on Indiana 160 to Interstate 65 to continue your journey, or do the opposite if you're coming from the south.

INFORMATION: Call the Lanier Mansion State Historic Site at (812) 265–3526. The historic site closes at dusk.

FEES: None.

Notes

Notes

Notes

Notes

Notes